Cambridge
IGCSE®
and International Certificate

German
Foreign Language

SHREWSBURY SCHOOL

GERMAN FACULTY

Date	Name	House
	CRISTINA PUYOL F.	EDH
	Antonia Kimpton-Smith	M

Any book lost will incur a charge for replacement

Marian Jones
Helen Kent
Birgit Linton
Janet Searle (original edition)

Series Editor:
Mike Thacker

HODDER
EDUCATION
AN HACHETTE UK COMPANY

Hodder Education, an Hachette UK company, Carmelite House, 50 Victoria Embankment, London EC4Y 0DZ

Orders

Bookpoint Ltd, 130 Milton Park, Abingdon, Oxfordshire, OX14 4SB

tel: 01235 827827

fax: 01235 400401

e-mail: education@bookpoint.co.uk

Lines are open 9.00 a.m.–5.00 p.m., Monday to Saturday, with a 24-hour message answering service. You can also order through the Hodder Education website: www.hoddereducation.co.uk

ISBN 978-1-4718-3302-1

First printed 2015
Impression number   5   4   3   2
Year   2019   2018   2017   2016   2015

® IGCSE is the registered trademark of Cambridge International Examinations.

Exam-style questions and sample answers have been written by the authors.

All efforts have been made to trace copyright on items used.

Illustrations by Emily Hunter-Higgins and Jim Watson

Cover photo is reproduced by permission of Fotolia.

Other photos are reproduced by permission of: **p. 9** © WENN Ltd/Alamy; **pp. 16–17** Ingram Publishing; **p. 26** Fotolia; **pp. 34–35, 38** Birgit Linton; **p. 45** Corel; **p. 48** Birgit Linton; **p. 52** Corel; **p. 56** P. PLAILLY/E. DAYNES/SCIENCE PHOTO LIBRARY; **p. 57** Fotolia; **pp. 65, 67** Birgit Linton; **p. 69** *tl* TopFoto (Cologne cathedral), *others* Birgit Linton; **p. 70** Fotolia; **p. 73** TopFoto; **p. 74** Birgit Linton; **p. 79** Fotolia; **p. 88** *t* Corel, *c* Alamy, *b* TopFoto; **p. 101** Birgit Linton; **p. 102** *l* Fotolia, *r* © INTERFOTO/Alamy; **p. 105** Ingram Publishing; **pp. 112–13** Fotolia; **p. 114** Birgit Linton; **p. 116** Oxfordian Kissuth/Wikipedia; **pp. 118–19** Fotolia; **p. 122** Fotolia; **p. 132** Birgit Linton; **p. 133** Ingram Publishing; **pp. 134–35** Fotolia; **p. 138** Ingram Publishing; **pp. 139, 141, 142** Fotolia.

Typeset by Aptara, Inc.

Printed in Italy

Inhalt

Karte der deutschsprachigen Länder

How to make the most of this book

About Exam Corner

Erster Teil 1

Thema 1 Ich persönlich

1 Ich stelle mich vor.....................2
- Say who you are
- Say where you come from and where you live
- Give your age and date of birth
- Ask others for this information
- Use regular and irregular verbs in the present tense
- Use conjunctions: *und, aber*

2 Familie.....................4
- Talk about your close family
- Ask others about their family
- Learn to form the plural of nouns
- Learn about gender, case, definite articles and indefinite articles

3 ...und wer gehört noch dazu?.....................6
- Understand family relationships
- Talk about your relatives and your pets
- Learn how to use possessive adjectives

4 Und wie siehst du aus?.....................8
- Describe your appearance
- Describe your character
- Use quantifiers: e.g. *sehr, ziemlich*

Thema 2 Mein Zuhause

1 ...ist das dein Traumhaus?.....................10
- Say where you live
- Say what type of house you have
- Learn how to use adjectives in different ways

2 Wo ist...meine Lampe?.....................12
- Describe the rooms in your house
- Describe where things are
- Use prepositions with the dative case

3 Was an meinem Tag so läuft.....................14
- Talk about your daily routine
- Use reflexive verbs

4 Im Haushalt helfen.....................16
- Talk about helping at home
- Use separable verbs

Thema 3 Freizeit

1 Hobbys.....................18
- Talk about your hobbies and interests
- Ask how others spend their spare time
- Discuss what you do: when, where and how often
- Express opinions on leisure activities

2 Geld.....................20
- Talk about pocket money
- Talk about part-time jobs
- Talk about spending and saving
- Use subordinating conjunctions (*dass, weil, wenn*)

3 Ich bin fit.....................22
- Talk about sport
- Express preferences
- Use adjectives

4 Und am Samstag?.....................24
- Say what else you do in your free time
- Talk about an outing
- Use correct word order in longer sentences

Zeitschrift 1.....................26

Prüfungsecke 1.....................28

Vokabular 1.....................32

Zweiter Teil 2

Thema 4 Die Schule

1 Ich besuche.....................34
- Talk about the kind of school you go to
- Describe your school
- Talk about your uniform
- Understand how to use *kein*

2 ...und das ist mein Stundenplan.....................36
- Talk about your school day
- Revise subordinating conjunctions (*weil, obwohl*)

3 Was ich heute gemacht habe........................38
- Talk about events in the past
- Use the perfect tense of verbs with *haben*

4 Ich bin zu spät gekommen........................40
- Continue talking about the past
- Learn how to use verbs of movement in the perfect tense
- Learn how to use separable verbs in the perfect tense

Thema 5 Berufe, Berufe...

1 Was soll ich werden?.....................42
- Learn how to describe different jobs
- Learn about masculine and feminine job titles
- Learn how to use sentences with *um...zu*

2 Mein Arbeitspraktikum.....................44
- Talk about your forthcoming work experience week
- Use expressions of time to talk about future intent

3 Nach dem Praktikum.....................46
- Talk about your work experience in the past

Thema 6 ...und in Zukunft?

1 Wie geht es weiter?......................................48
- Discuss your plans for after your exams
- Learn to use the future tense

2 ...und nach dem Abitur?...........................50
- Talk more about your future plans
- Use adverbs to express probability

3 Ich suche einen Job...................................52
- Apply for a job
- Understand *Sie* form of address

4 Im Büro 54
- Send and receive messages at work
- Form questions

Zeitschrift 2..56

Prüfungsecke 2..58

Vokabular 2...62

Dritter Teil 3

Thema 7 Unterwegs

1 Am Bahnhof...64
- Understand signs at the train station
- Get information about train travel
- Buy train tickets

2 Wie komme ich zum Bahnhof? 66
- Ask for and give directions
- Use the imperative

3 Was kann man in Köln machen? 68
- Learn how to ask about tourist activities
- Learn to understand instructions
- Use modal verbs

4 Wie reisen wir weiter?..............................70
- Learn about public transport in German-speaking countries
- Understand and use the genitive case

Thema 8 Ferien

1 Haben Sie Zimmer frei? 72
- Learn to ask about accommodation
- Revise asking questions
- Use prepositions that always take the accusative case

2 Wohin fährst du...und mit wem? 74
- Say where you spend your holiday and how you get there
- Say who you travel with
- Use prepositions that always take the dative case
- Use prepositions that can take the accusative or dative case

3 Wo warst du und was hast du gemacht? 76
- Talk about what you did on holiday
- Learn more about the imperfect tense

4 Ich möchte mich beschweren... 78
- Make a complaint

Thema 9 Gesundheit

1 Wie bleibe ich gesund? 80
- Talk about healthy eating and drinking
- Say how you keep fit and healthy

2 ...und was ist nicht so gesund? 82
- Talk about and give advice on unhealthy lifestyles
- Use the modal verbs *müssen* and *dürfen*

3 Gute Besserung! 84
- Say that you are unwell and what is wrong with you
- Understand questions and instructions from the doctor
- Use the dative case

4 Was ist denn passiert?...................................86
- Find out about accidents and injuries
- Learn about the passive voice

Zeitschrift 3..88

Prüfungsecke 3...90

Vokabular 3...94

Vierter Teil 4

Thema 10 Meine Stadt und meine Gegend

1 Was kann man in deiner Stadt machen?......96
- Describe your town
- Say what you can do in your town

2 ...und wie findest du deine Stadt?.................98
- Give more detail about your home town and talk about your local area
- Use the verb *gefallen* to express likes and dislikes
- Revise other ways of expressing positive and negative opinions

3 Großstadt, Kleinstadt?...................................100
- Discuss and understand the advantages and disadvantages of living in a big or a small town

4 Meine Kindheit in Berlin............................102
- Talk about childhood
- Revise talking about the past
- Revise personal pronouns

Thema 11 Einkaufen und so weiter

1 Klamotten kaufen...104
- Shop for clothes
- Describe items of clothing
- Use *dieser*, *welcher* and the question words *was für*

2 Das sind die Skier, die €200 kosten............106
- Talk about buying things for your hobbies
- Use relative pronouns

3 Auf der Post, in der Bank und im Fundbüro 108
- Talk about buying stamps and sending items
- Talk about changing money
- Report a loss

Thema 12 Essen und Trinken

1 ...und was soll ich einkaufen? 110
- Revise food items
- Revise how to form plurals

2 Ich hätte gern ein langes Brot... 112
- Practise shopping transactions
- Revise definite and indefinite articles in the nominative and accusative cases
- Revise adjective endings in the nominative and accusative cases

3 ...und wo gehen wir essen? 114
- Order meals in a restaurant and learn how to make a complaint
- Express preferences in your choice of meals
- Revise the present tense of *geben*, *essen* and *nehmen*
- Use the dative to express your likes and dislikes

4 Gesund essen.................................... 116
- Talk about healthy eating
- Understand a recipe
- Use subordinating conjunctions

Zeitschrift 4 118

Prüfungsecke 4 120

Vokabular 4 124

Fünfter Teil 5

Thema 13 Medien

1 Gehen wir lieber ins Kino?.......................... 126
- Talk about television programmes
- Make arrangements to go out
- Talk about films

2 Was liest du so?.............. 128
- Talk about what you like to read
- Learn more about the imperfect tense
- Learn more about the pluperfect tense

3 Ich brauche meinen Computer und mein Handy... 130
- Talk about the internet, e-mails and mobile phones
- Revise the future tense

4 ...und wer ist ein Superstar?.......... 132
- Learn about famous musicians

5 Die virtuelle Welt 134
- Talk about technology and social media
- Use indefinite pronouns with adjectival nouns

Thema 14 Die Umwelt

1 Und wie ist das Wetter?.............. 136
- Talk about the weather
- Understand weather reports

2 Luft, Wasser, Müll.............. 138
- Discuss major environmental problems
- Use the conditional

3 Und was können wir tun?.......... 140
- Talk about protecting the environment

4 Das geht uns alle an.................. 142
- Learn about global problems
- Use the comparative and the superlative

Prüfungsecke 5 144

Vokabular 5 148

Grammatik 150

Wortschatz 166

Karte der deutschsprachigen Länder

How to make the most of this book

This book provides all you need to prepare for your **Cambridge IGCSE® in German** or **Level 1/Level 2 International Certificate in German** qualification. It also teaches you about the way of life of the people in the German-speaking world and about the language they speak.

Each of the five *Teile* contains a sequence of texts and activities that enable you to discover the language and use it effectively. Each section includes the following features:

At the beginning of each section, a list of the topic content and the main **grammar** items covered

Lots of **listening** activities to practise this skill

Tasks to ensure effective **writing** in German

Up-to-date **reading** passages based on life in German-speaking countries

Varied activities to practise **speaking**

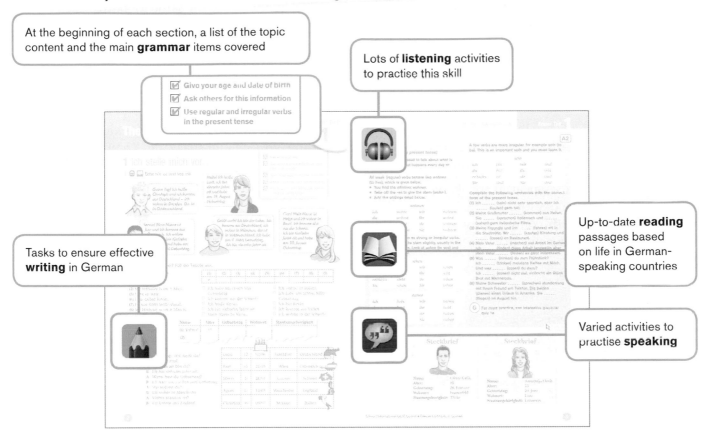

Watch out for these special features throughout the book too:

Grammatik These sections explain the key grammar points you need to know to communicate successfully in German.

A1 Follow these links to the end grammar section for further explanation.

1/1 Practise the grammar points in interactive quizzes from the accompanying Teacher Resource.

Top-Tipp Under this heading, important language points (e.g. how to use certain phrases) are highlighted.

At the end of each *Teil* you will find:

Zeitschrift Additional reading practice that focuses on German-speaking cultures, current affairs and social issues.

Exam Corner Specific preparation for the kind of tasks that you have to complete in the exams.

Vokabular Lists of key vocabulary relating to the main topic areas covered in the *Teil*.

Towards the end of the book are:

Grammatik A summary of all the grammar that you need to know with handy verb tables for quick reference.

Wortschatz A combined list of all the key vocabulary used in this book, in alphabetical order.

About Exam Corner

The examinations

The **Cambridge IGCSE® German** and **Cambridge International Level 1/Level 2 Certificate German (UK schools)** qualifications are made up of four compulsory papers that test the four language skills. Each paper is taken at the end of the course. The content and questions are the same for both qualifications.

Exam Corners

At the end of each *Teil* are Exam Corner pages that give specific advice and practice for the exam papers. Each Exam Corner covers all four skills: listening, reading, writing and speaking. The Exam Corners progress in difficulty throughout the book.

The following features appear in the Exam Corners:
- sample exam-style questions
- sample answers with commentary
- questions for further practice
- Tips for success
- Points to remember

Topics

You need to cover the topics listed below.

- **Area A**   Everyday activities
- **Area B**   Personal and social life
- **Area C**   The world around us
- **Area D**   The world of work
- **Area E**   The international world

Paper	Skill	Marks	Timing	Proportion of qualification
1	Listening	45 marks	Approx. 45 min	25%
2	Reading	45 marks	1 hour	25%
3	Speaking	100 marks	Approx. 15 min	25%
4	Writing	50 marks	1 hour	25%

🎧 Paper 1: listening

Paper 1 is divided into three sections, each worth 15 marks. The extracts get longer as you work through the paper. **Section 1** recordings are mainly factual, **Section 2** requires listening for main points and identifying details and **Section 3** involves more detailed, longer recordings. You hear each recording twice. The instructions are written in German. You must attempt to answer all three sections.

📖 Paper 2: reading

Paper 2 is divided into three sections, each worth 15 marks. All instructions and questions are written in German. **Section 1** has three questions, requiring you to read short pieces of text and answer the short questions. **Section 2** consists of questions on two texts, one short and the other longer. The longer text requires short answers in German. **Section 3** includes two longer, more detailed texts with two questions that test general and specific comprehension. You must attempt to answer all three sections.

💬 Paper 3: speaking

The speaking test is divided into three tests during a single interview.

Test 1 is a role play worth 30 marks that lasts approximately 5 minutes. You are given two role plays on a card in German and have 15 minutes to prepare. Your teacher plays the part of the other person. You can keep the role-play card with you, but you must not make notes. The first role play is more straightforward than the second. Each role play consists of five tasks.

Test 2 is a presentation/conversation worth 30 marks and lasts approximately 5 minutes. You start by giving a 1–2-minute presentation on a topic of your choice, which you have prepared in advance. You are not allowed any notes. After your presentation, the teacher asks you spontaneous questions on the topic for a further 3 minutes.

Test 3 is a general conversation worth 30 marks and lasts approximately 5 minutes. This conversation takes place straight after your presentation conversation, but it is more general in nature. Your teacher tells you when this test is going to start. You may be asked some general questions about your everyday life and are expected to have a conversation about at least two of the topic areas A–E. To be awarded the highest marks you must use past and future tenses accurately.

The final 10 marks are awarded by the teacher for your overall performance, including pronunciation, intonation and fluency.

✏️ Paper 4: writing

Paper 4 is divided into two sections. All instructions and questions are written in German.

Section 1 is worth 20 marks and has two questions. Question 1 is worth 5 marks and requires you to write single-word answers on a topic. Question 2 is a directed writing task worth 15 marks, of which 10 marks are available for communication and 5 marks for language.

Section 2 is worth 30 marks and offers a choice of three tasks from which you must select one to complete. For this longer writing task, 10 marks are available for communication, 8 marks for verbs and 12 marks for other linguistic features.

Thema 1 Ich persönlich

1 Ich stelle mich vor...

1  Bitte hör zu und lies mit.

☑ Say who you are
☑ Say where you come from and where you live
☑ Give your age and date of birth
☑ Ask others for this information
☑ Use regular and irregular verbs in the present tense
☑ Use conjunctions: *und, aber*

Guten Tag! Ich heiße Christoph und ich komme aus Deutschland — ich wohne in Dresden. Das ist in Ostdeutschland.

Hallo! Ich heiße Lara. Ich bin vierzehn Jahre alt und habe am 19. August Geburtstag.

Servus! Mein Name ist Jens und ich komme aus Österreich. Ich wohne in Linz. Ich bin fünfzehn Jahre alt und habe am 24. Juni Geburtstag.

Grüßt euch! Ich bin der Lukas. Ich komme aus Deutschland, ich wohne in München, das ist in Süddeutschland. Ich habe am 4. März Geburtstag. Ich bin vierzehn Jahre alt.

Ciao! Mein Name ist Helga und ich wohne in Basel. Ich komme also aus der Schweiz. Ich bin fünfzehn Jahre alt und habe am 30. Januar Geburtstag.

2 Was passt zusammen? Füll die Tabelle aus.

(1) My name is Kevin.
(2) I come from Italy.
(3) I am 17.
(4) My birthday is on 1 May.
(5) I live in Italy.
(6) I am called Kevin.
(7) I come from Switzerland.
(8) My birthday is on 8 March.
(9) I'm Kevin.

(1)	(2)	(3)	(4)	(5)	(6)	(7)	(8)	(9)
e								

a Ich habe am ersten Mai Geburtstag.
b Ich komme aus der Schweiz.
c Ich heiße Kevin.
d Ich bin siebzehn Jahre alt.
e Mein Name ist Kevin.
f Ich wohne in Italien.
g Ich habe am achten März Geburtstag.
h Ich bin Kevin.
i Ich komme aus Italien.
j Ich wohne in der Schweiz.

3 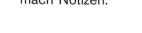 Bitte hör zu und mach Notizen.

Name	Alter	Geburtstag	Wohnort	Staatsangehörigkeit
(1) Roland	18	22. Oktober	Bristol	Engländer
(2)				

4 Macht Dialoge.

Beispiel A Guten Tag! Wie heißt du?
B *Ich heiße Peter.*
A Und wie alt bist du?
B *Ich bin siebzehn Jahre alt.*
A Wann hast du Geburtstag?
B *Ich habe am zweiten Juni Geburtstag.*
A Wo wohnst du?
B *Ich wohne in Vaduz.*
A Woher kommst du?
B *Ich komme aus Liechtenstein.*

Lucia	12	02/06	Frankfurt	Deutschland
Paul	15	31/10	Wien	Österreich
Mario	21	25/01	Luzern	Schweiz
Agnes	17	13/03	Manchester	England
Christina	30	09/07	Meran	Italien

Grammatik F1

Das Präsens (*the present tense*)

The present tense is used to talk about what is happening now or what happens every day or regularly.

All weak (regular) verbs behave like *wohnen* (to live), which is given below.

- You find the infinitive: *wohnen*.
- Take off the *-en* to give the stem (*wohn-*).
- Add the endings listed below.

wohnen			
ich	*wohne*	*wir*	*wohnen*
du	*wohnst*	*ihr*	*wohnt*
er/sie/es/ man	*wohnt*	*Sie/sie*	*wohnen*

Some verbs are known as strong or irregular verbs. These verbs change the stem slightly, usually in the *du* and *er/sie/es* forms. Look at *sehen* (to see) and *haben* (to have) below.

sehen			
ich	*sehe*	*wir*	*sehen*
du	*siehst*	*ihr*	*seht*
er/sie/es/ man	*sieht*	*Sie/sie*	*sehen*

haben			
ich	*habe*	*wir*	*haben*
du	*hast*	*ihr*	*habt*
er/sie/es/ man	*hat*	*Sie/sie*	*haben*

A few verbs are more irregular, for example *sein* (to be). This is an important verb and you must learn it.

sein			
ich	*bin*	*wir*	*sind*
du	*bist*	*ihr*	*seid*
er/sie/es/ man	*ist*	*Sie/sie*	*sind*

1/1

Grammatik H3

Konjunktionen (*coordinating conjunctions*)

Conjunctions link two parts of a sentence. The coordinating conjunctions *und* (and), *aber* (but) and *oder* (or) do not require a change in the word order.

> *Ich heiße Maria **und** ich wohne in Köln.*
> *Ich möchte einen Hund **oder** eine Katze.*
> *Ich wohne in Köln, **aber** ich gehe in Leverkusen zur Schule.*

Other coordinating conjunctions are:
entweder...oder (either...or), *denn* (because, as), *sondern* (but, used after a negative)
*Ich wohne nicht in München **sondern** in Düsseldorf.*

3/1

5 Beschreibe Günay und Anastasija.

Steckbrief

Name:	Günay Celik
Alter:	16
Geburtstag:	26. Februar
Wohnort:	Frauenfeld
Staatsangehörigkeit:	Türke

Steckbrief

Name:	Anastasija Ozols
Alter:	15
Geburtstag:	24. Juni
Wohnort:	Linz
Staatsangehörigkeit:	Litauerin

2 Familie

- ☑ Talk about your close family
- ☑ Ask others about their family
- ☑ Learn to form the plural of nouns
- ☑ Learn about gender, case, definite articles and indefinite articles

1 📖 Was passt zusammen?

(1) *Also ich bin der Marius, ich habe einen Zwillingsbruder, er heißt Steffen. Ich habe keine Schwestern. In meiner Familie sind noch meine Eltern. Ich habe einen Vater. Er ist 43 und arbeitet in London und eine Mutter, die halbtags als Sekretärin arbeitet. Mein Bruder und ich sind 15 Jahre alt.*

(2) *Ich heiße Lisa und bin 14 Jahre alt. Ich habe einen Vater, eine Mutter, einen älteren Bruder und eine kleine Schwester. Sie heißt Lena und ist sehr lieb. Meine Mutter arbeitet im Moment nicht, aber mein Vater ist Lehrer. Mein Bruder ist in der Oberstufe und macht nächstes Jahr Abitur. Er heißt Peter.*

(3) *Annika ist mein Name. Meine Eltern sind geschieden und meine Schwester und ich wohnen bei meinem Vater. Wir sehen unsere Mutter am Wochenende. Sigrid ist meine Stiefmutter. Ich mag sie sehr gern. Sie hat auch Kinder. Ich habe eine Stiefschwester, sie ist auch 15 wie ich und zwei Stiefbrüder, sie sind 8 und 10 Jahre alt. Sie sind sehr laut und wild. Ich habe auch einen Halbbruder, er ist 9 Monate alt. Sigrid ist seine Mutter und mein Vater ist auch sein Vater.*

(4) *Mein Vater ist vor zwei Jahren gestorben. Das war sehr traurig. Ich habe einen kleinen Bruder, Sven heißt er. Wir wohnen mit unserer Mutter zusammen; sie arbeitet als Kindergärtnerin. Ich heiße Sophie und bin 14 und Sven ist 9.*

2 🏛 Ein Bild hat keinen Text. Bitte schreib einen kurzen Text wie in Übung 1.

3 📖 Brauchst du eine Endung und was ist die richtige Endung? Versuch es doch mal!

A Hallo, hast du ein____ Bruder?

B *Ja, ich habe ein____ Bruder und ein____ Schwester. Und du?*

A Ich habe ein____ Stiefschwester und ein____ Stiefvater und ein____ Halbbruder. Meine Eltern sind geschieden.

B *Möchtest du ein____ Bruder?*

A Nein, mein____ Stiefschwester ist schon verheiratet. Sie hat ein____ Mann und ein____ Kind. Das Kind ist ein Junge.

Grammatik

[A2]

Der Plural (the plural)

In English we simply add an -s to most nouns to indicate plural (more than one). In German there are different endings, depending on the gender (masculine, feminine, neuter) of the noun.

Singular	Plural
der Bruder	die Brüder
die Schwester	die Schwestern
das Kind	die Kinder

4 💬 Macht Dialoge.

Beispiel

A Wie heißt du?
B *Ich heiße* _____
A Wie alt bist du?
B *Ich bin* _____
A Hast du Geschwister?
B *Ja, ich habe einen/eine/ein* _____
A Wie heißt dein Bruder/Halbbruder/
   Stiefbruder/Zwillingsbruder?
B *Er heißt* _____
A Wie heißt deine Schwester/Halbschwester/
   Stiefschwester/Zwillingsschwester?
B *Sie heißt* _____
A Wie alt ist sie/ist er?
B *Sie ist/er ist* _____
A Wie heißt deine Mutter/dein Vater?
B *Sie heißt/er heißt* _____
A Wie alt ist sie/ist er?
B *Sie ist/er ist* _____

Stiefvater, Michael, 48 — Mutter, Franziska, 39 — **Lisa**, 15 — Stiefbruder, Jörg, 16 — Halbschwester, Terese, 4

Mutter, Inge, 40 — Vater, Werner, 44 — Jana, 10 — **Thomas**, 13 — Timo, 13 — Lena, 8

Grammatik

Genus, Fall, bestimmte und unbestimmte Artikel *(gender, case, definite and indefinite articles)*

All German nouns have a **gender**. They can be masculine, feminine, or neuter.

The article (definite article = the, indefinite article = a, an) changes depending on the gender, e.g.:

   der *Vater* = the father (masculine)
   die *Mutter* = the mother (feminine)
   das *Auto* = the car (neuter)

All German nouns also have a **case**. This can be nominative, accusative, genitive or dative. If the noun is the **subject** of the sentence, it is in the nominative case. If it is the **object** of the sentence, as in the examples of the indefinite article (a, an) below, it is in the accusative case.

   Ich habe **einen** *Bruder*. I have a brother.
   Ich habe **eine** *Schwester*. I have a sister.
   Ich habe **ein** *Auto*. I have a car.

More information about cases is given in the grammar reference section A6.

A1, A3, A4, A6

Du bist:
(1) Lisa
(2) Thomas
(3) Du bist du selbst! Sprich über deine Familie!

5a 🎧 Bitte hör zu.
Vier Jugendliche sprechen über ihre Familien. Was ist richtig und was musst du korrigieren?

(1) Florians Mutter ist jetzt mit Michael verheiratet.
(2) In Florians Familie sind drei Jungen und zwei Mädchen.
(3) Jens ist Einzelkind.
(4) Sonjas Eltern sind geschieden.
(5) Sonja hat zwei Stiefschwestern.
(6) Kerstins Mutter ist Hausfrau.
(7) Kerstins Geschwister sind älter als sie.
(8) Alle Kinder in Kerstins Familie sind Teenager.

b Bitte mach einen Stammbaum von Kerstins Familie.

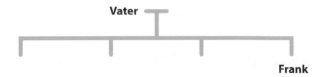

Vater ⊤

Frank

6 📝 Schreib einige Sätze über deine Familie. Schau dir noch einmal die Partnerübung an!

🖱 1/3

3 ...und wer gehört noch dazu?
Verwandte und Tiere

☑ **Understand family relationships**

☑ **Talk about your relatives and your pets**

☑ **Learn how to use possessive adjectives**

Mein Stammbaum

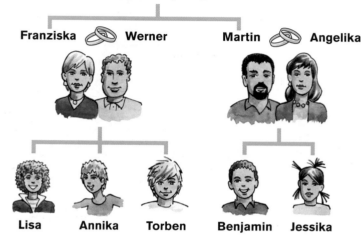

Maria ⚭ Anton

Franziska ⚭ Werner   Martin ⚭ Angelika

Lisa   Annika   Torben   Benjamin   Jessika

1  Bitte sieh dir den Stammbaum an und mach Dialoge.

(1) Du bist Jessika.
(2) Du bist Torben.

A Ich bin Jessika.
B *Wer ist Angelika?*
A Sie/Angelika ist meine Mutter.
B *Wer ist Werner?*
A Er/Werner ist mein Onkel.
B *Wer ist* _____
A Er/sie ist _____

2 Bitte schreib jetzt fünf von deinen Sätzen auf.

Beispiel   *Angelika ist meine Mutter.*
               Werner ist mein Onkel.

3 Schau dir die Grammatik und den Stammbaum an und mach andere Sätze.

Beispiel   *Das ist Franziska. Maria ist **ihre** Mutter.*
               *Das ist Torben. Benjamin ist **sein** Cousin.*
               *Das ist Werner. Torben ist **sein** Sohn.*

Grammatik
Possessivpronomen
(possessive adjectives)

B5

When you want to indicate who something or somebody belongs to, you need to use possessive adjectives.

m	f	n	
mein	meine	mein	my
dein	deine	dein	your (familiar form)
sein	seine	sein	his
ihr	ihre	ihr	her
sein	seine	sein	its
unser	unsere	unser	our
euer	eure	euer	your (plural familiar)
ihr	ihre	ihr	their
Ihr	Ihre	Ihr	your (polite form, singular and plural)

Note: if you use the polite form in writing, you need to spell it with a capital letter.

If the possessive adjective is placed in front of a masculine (*der*) or neuter (*das*) noun, you do not add the *-e* at the end. For feminine (*die*) nouns and for the plural you need to add the *-e*.

Das ist mein Vater.
Das ist mein Auto.
*Das ist mein**e** Mutter.*
*Das **sind** meine Eltern.*

There are different endings for the possessive adjectives, depending on the case of the noun.

*Ich mag mein**en** Vater.*
*Ich besuche mein**en** Opa.*

1/4

Ich habe Haustiere

der Hund

das Kaninchen

der Fisch

die Schildkröte

die Katze

das Pferd

das Meer-
schweinchen

der Goldhamster

die Schlange

der
Wellensittich

4 Arbeite mit einem Partner und schreib dann die Sätze auf.

a Was sagt Oliver (a–g)?

Beispiel   *Das ist mein Hund.*

b Was fragt Oliver (h, i)?

a

b

c

d

Oliver   **Oliver**

5a Bitte lies den Text und such die richtigen Endungen für die Possessivpronomen.

Das ist unser___ Familie. Mein___ Mutter, Maria, mein___ Stiefvater, Michael, und mein___ Geschwister. Mein___ Name ist Stefan. Ich mag mein___ Stiefvater, er spielt elektrische Gitarre und mag Rock wie ich. Mein___ Schwester heißt Tina und ist älter als ich. Sie ist 16.

Dann ist da noch Nicole, das ist Michaels Tochter, also er ist ihr___ Vater und sie ist mein___ Stiefschwester und auch Tinas Stiefschwester, unser___ Stiefschwester. Sie ist 2 Jahre jünger als Tina.

Unser___ Großeltern wohnen auch bei uns. Wir haben ein großes Haus am Stadtrand. Mein___ Großvater ist super nett und sein___ Bruder, unser___ Onkel besucht uns oft. Er ist nicht verheiratet und hat keine Kinder und mag unser___ Haus.

i

e

h

g

f

b Was ist richtig und was ist falsch?

(1) Stefan hat keinen Bruder.
(2) Stefans Schwester heißt Nicole.
(3) Nicole ist 16.
(4) Stefan und seine Großmutter wohnen in einem Haus.
(5) Sein Onkel wohnt auch da.
(6) Der Onkel ist ledig.

6 Bitte hör die vier Jugendlichen an. Was sagen die vier Personen?

Person	Geschwister?	Cousins, Kusinen?	Andere Verwandte?	Haustiere?
Lisa	eine Schwester	_____	_____	✗
Bettina				

7 Bitte schreib ein paar Sätze über deine Familie und deine Tiere.

4 Und wie siehst du aus?

☑ **Describe your appearance**
☑ **Describe your character**
☑ **Use quantifiers:** e.g. *sehr, ziemlich*

1 📖 Bitte lies diese Beschreibungen.

a *Ich bin groß und ziemlich schlank. Ich habe kurze, glatte, braune Haare und graue Augen.*

b *Ich habe lange, lockige, schwarze Haare und braune Augen. Ich trage eine Brille. Ich bin nicht sehr groß.*

c *Ich trage eine Brille und habe grüne Augen. Ich habe lockige, braune Haare. Ich bin ganz klein. Ich trage einen Ohrring.*

d *Ich bin ganz groß und relativ dick. Ich trage eine Brille und habe blaue Augen und lange, blonde Haare.*

e *Ich habe lange, lockige, rote Haare und blaue Augen. Ich bin mittelgroß und schlank. Ich trage Ohrringe.*

f *Ich bin ganz groß und sehr schlank. Ich habe lange, lockige, blonde Haare und blaue Augen.*

Wer ist das?

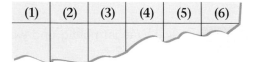

(1)	(2)	(3)	(4)	(5)	(6)

(1) Athina   **(2) Hanni**   **(3) Martin**

(4) Roland   **(5) Martyna**   **(6) Oliver**

2 📖 Wer bin ich?

A beschreibt eine Person und *B* rät, wer das ist.

Angelika   **Magdalena**   **Max**   **Evangelos**

3 Bitte schreib eine kurze Beschreibung von einer der Personen in Übung 2.

Beispiel *Angelika ist ziemlich groß und schlank. Sie hat...*

4a Wie bist du?

Ordne zehn dieser Eigenschaften in zwei Gruppen (jeweils fünf in jeder Gruppe).

lustig
schlecht gelaunt
frech
ruhig
glücklich
sympathisch
schüchtern
gut gelaunt
traurig
ärgerlich
freundlich
geduldig
launisch
sportlich
unordentlich
pünktlich
fleißig
ehrlich
höflich
hilfsbereit
böse
faul

Fünf positive Eigenschaften ☺	Fünf negative Eigenschaften ☹
lustig	faul

b Suche Gegenteile.

Beispiel *höflich* → *frech*

ordentlich → *unordentlich*

fleißig → _____

traurig → _____

Top-Tipp
Describing someone's appearance

Wie siehst du aus?   Wie sieht er/sie aus?

● **Build**

	ziemlich	groß
Ich bin	nicht sehr	klein
Du bist	ganz	schlank
Er/sie ist	relativ	dick
	sehr	
		mittelgroß

● **Hair and eyes**

Ich habe	kurze/lange/	} Haare
Du hast	lockige/glatte/schulterlange	
Er/sie hat	grüne/blaue/	} Augen
	braune/schwarze	

● **Extras**

Ich trage	eine Brille
Du trägst	einen Ohrring
Er/sie trägt	Ohrringe

5 Bitte hör zu und mach Notizen über Natalia, Fabian, Stefan, Julia und Oma.

Natalia   Meine Freundin
Aussehen   mittelgroß
Charakter   _____
             _____

6a Bitte lies den Text über Yvonne Catterfeld.

Ich heiße Yvonne Catterfeld und ich bin Schauspielerin und Sängerin. Ich bin 27 Jahre alt. Ich habe keine Geschwister. Ich habe lange, blonde Haare und blaue Augen. Ich bin schlank. Ich bin meistens gut gelaunt, immer ruhig und sehr ehrgeizig. Ich komme aus Erfurt aber ich wohne jetzt in Berlin.

b Füll die Tabelle *auf Deutsch* aus.

Familienname:	Wohnort:
Vorname:	Beruf:
Alter:	Aussehen:
Staatsangehörigkeit:	Charaktereigenschaften:

Grammatik **B10**
Modaladverbien (*quantifiers*)

Use quantifiers with adjectives to give a more precise idea of amount or extent. Here are some examples:

Er ist groß. He is tall
Er ist sehr groß. He is very tall.
Er ist relativ groß. He is quite tall.

Find other examples of quantifiers on pages 8–9.

 1/5

7 Suche dir eine berühmte Person aus und schreib einen kurzen Text über sie.

Thema 2 Mein Zuhause

1 ...ist das dein Traumhaus?

☑ Say where you live

☑ Say what type of house you have

☑ Learn how to use adjectives in different ways

Ich habe ein schönes Haus. Ich wohne in einem Einfamilienhaus mit Schwimmbad und Tennisplatz. Wir haben eine große Garage. Mein Vater liebt schnelle Autos. Mein Zimmer hat einen Balkon. Das Haus liegt an einem See und wir haben ein neues Motorboot.

1a 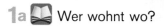 Wer wohnt wo?

(1) *Ich wohne in einem schönen Einfamilienhaus am Stadtrand von Hamburg. Das Haus ist gekauft.*

(2) *Ich wohne in einem kleinen Doppelhaus in einer Neubausiedlung in Essen.*

(3) *Ich wohne in einem modernen Reihenhaus am Meer in der Nähe von Büsum.*

(4) *Ich wohne in einem romantischen Bauernhaus auf dem Land im Schwarzwald.*

(5) *Ich wohne in einer hübschen Wohnung in einem Wohnblock im Stadtzentrum von München. Die Wohnung ist gemietet.*

(6) *Ich wohne in einem neuen Bungalow in den Bergen bei Oberstdorf.*

(7) *Ich wohne in einem riesigen Hochhaus an einem Fluss. Unsere Wohnung ist in Frankfurt und ist gemietet.*

b 💬 Und du, wo wohnst du?

2 💬 Bitte mach Sätze. Arbeite mit einem Partner. Sieh dir noch einmal die Bilder in Übung 1 an.

Beispiel   *Ich wohne in einem Bauernhaus am Meer.*

3 Verstehst du alles?
Bitte kombiniere!

(1) der Stadtrand
(2) der Gemüsegarten
(3) der Keller
(4) die Himbeere
(5) gemütlich
(6) die Küche
(7) das Badezimmer
(8) das Wohnzimmer
(9) der Blick
(10) das Schlafzimmer
(11) lecker
(12) das Büro

a view
b cosy
c bedroom
d living room
e tasty
f bathroom
g office
h kitchen
i raspberry
j edge of the town
k vegetable garden
l cellar

4 Du hast ein Traumhaus mit Schwimmbad…Tennisplatz, du hast zehn Schlafzimmer…!
Wie sieht dein Traumhaus aus?
Bitte macht Dialoge mit den Adjektiven im Kasten.

groß
mittelgroß hässlich
klein interessant billig unmodern
modern lustig neu hell dunkel alt
schön lecker gemütlich teuer

Beispiel

A Hast du ein Haus?
B *Ja, wir haben ein großes Einfamilienhaus.*
A Wo liegt das Haus?
B *Es liegt am Stadtrand an einem See.*
A Bitte beschreib dein Haus.
B *Wir haben eine moderne Küche, zehn große Schlafzimmer, drei kleine Badezimmer und einen schönen Keller. Da ist unsere Tischtennisplatte.*
A Super, hast du auch ein eigenes Zimmer?
B *Ja, ich habe auch ein gemütliches Zimmer. Wir haben auch einen neuen Tennisplatz.*

B

Grammatik
Verschiedene Stellungen des Adjektivs im Satz (*different ways to place adjectives*)

Adjectives are words that describe things or people, e.g. *groß*, *klein*, *alt*, *neu*, *schön* etc. If you place an adjective after the noun, there is no change in spelling:

> *Das Haus ist **groß**. Mein Garten ist **schön**.*

If you place an adjective before a noun, you have to make sure that it agrees in gender, in case and in number (singular or plural). Here are some nominative examples with 'the' (*der, die, das*):

	Masculine	*Feminine*	*Neuter*
Das ist…	*der kleine Garten*	*die große Küche*	*das alte Auto*

In the accusative, when the adjective describes the object of a sentence, the feminine and neuter endings stay the same, but you need to watch out for masculine (*der*) nouns.

Here are some examples with the indefinite article, 'a' (*einen, eine, ein*):

	Masculine	*Feminine*	*Neuter*
Ich habe/möchte/ kaufe…	*einen kleinen Garten*	*eine große Küche*	*ein altes Auto*

Note that in German the indefinite article does not include the word for 'some'. The nominative and accusative plural adjective endings all end in -e.

Masculine	*Feminine*	*Neuter*
kleine Gärten	*große Küchen*	*alte Autos*

Das ist Stefans Haus. Was sind die richtigen Endungen? Du brauchst nicht immer eine Endung!

Also, meine Eltern haben ein alt___ Haus am Stadtrand. Unsere Garage ist groß___ und wir haben einen schön___ Garten. Ich mag unseren interessant___ Gemüsegarten, im Sommer haben wir lecker___ Karotten, süß___ Himbeeren und viel Salat.
   Im Haus ist eine gemütlich___ Küche, ein modern___ Badezimmer, ein hell___ Wohnzimmer mit einem großen Fernseher. Wir haben auch eine klein___ Gästetoilette. Oben im Haus sind vier Schlafzimmer. Ich habe ein mittelgroß___ Zimmer mit Blick auf die Stadt.

2/1

5 Wo wohnen Florian, Sergej, Elke und Marius?
Mach Notizen.

Name	Haus?/ Wohnung?	Wo?	Wie viele Zimmer?	Andere Informationen?

2 Wo ist… meine Lampe?

☑ Describe the rooms in your house
☑ Describe where things are
☑ Use prepositions with the dative case

Die Lampe ist auf dem Tisch.

Die Lampe ist an der Wand.

Die Lampe ist neben dem Bett.

1 Was schreibst du für Bilder (1)–(6)?

(1) (2) (3) (4) (5) (6)

Hier sind die Namen für die Möbel für deine Sätze:

die Kommode	der Kleiderschrank	der Schreibtisch	der Papierkorb	der Fernseher	der Stuhl

das Klavier	der Tisch	das Sofa	das Regal	der Sessel

Hier sind die Präpositionen für deine Sätze:

unter	under	gegenüber	opposite
hinter	behind	neben	next to
vor	in front of	zwischen	between

2 📖✏️ Hier ist eine Liste mit Wörtern für Möbel und andere Sachen in Timos Zimmer. Bitte füll die Lücken mit dem richtigen Dativartikel aus.

das Fenster window
das Bett
die Lampe
der Schreibtisch
der Kleiderschrank
die Wand wall
das Regal
der CD-Spieler
der Computer
die Bücher

Das ist Timos Zimmer. Sein Schreibtisch steht vor ___ Fenster. An ___ Schreibtisch ist der Stuhl und auf ___ Schreibtisch ist eine rote Lampe. Der Computer steht neben ___ Regal. Vor ___ Fenster hängen die Vorhänge. Die Maus ist natürlich neben ___ Computer. Timo hat auch einen Fernseher neben ___ Bett. Er sieht abends gern fern. Seine Bücher stehen in ___ Regal, auf ___ Kleiderschrank und neben ___ CD-Spieler. Vor ___ Büchern liegen viele CDs. Timo liest nicht so gern. CDs sind auch unter ___ Bett und hinter ___ Lampe. Timo ist nicht sehr ordentlich. An ___ Wand hängt ein Poster von Australien. Timo möchte unheimlich gern mal Australien besuchen.

Grammatik

E2, E3

Präpositionen mit dem Dativ
(*prepositions with the dative case*)

an auf hinter in neben über unter vor zwischen

These prepositions are followed by the **dative** when they are used to describe the position of something. You might ask a question such as '*Wo ist die Lampe?*' and the answer could be:

auf **dem** Tisch	an **der** Wand	neben **dem** Bett
(masculine: *der*)	(feminine: *die*)	(neuter: *das*)

The masculine and neuter forms are identical. The feminine form turns into '*der*'. Note that '*an dem*' and '*in dem*' are often pulled together to form '*am*' and '*im*'.

In the plural you use the same article regardless of which gender the noun is:

*Die Lampen sind auf **den** Tischen.*
*Die Lampen sind an **den** Wänden.*
*Die Lampen sind neben **den** Betten.*

In the dative you add -*n* to plural nouns unless the plural ends with an -*s*:

*auf den Tische**n***   *neben den Radio**s***

🖱 2/2–2/4

3 🎧 Sieh dir das Bild an, hör gut zu und mach Notizen.
Was sagt Annika zu Marius? Was stimmt nicht?

4 Bilder beschreiben.

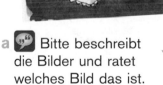

a 💬 Bitte beschreibt die Bilder und ratet welches Bild das ist.

b ✏️ Bitte schreib die Beschreibung von einem Zimmer.

5 💬 Macht Dialoge.

Mein Zimmer

A Bitte beschreib dein Zimmer.
B *Ich habe ein Bett, einen großen Kleiderschrank… Und du?*
A Ich habe einen Schreibtisch und einen Fernseher.
B *Wo ist dein Fernseher?*
A Mein Fernseher ist auf dem Schreibtisch.
B *Und wo ist dein Bett?*
A Mein Bett ist vor dem Fenster.

6 📖 Annika hat ein neues Haus und schreibt eine E-mail an ihre Freundin.
Bitte lies die E-mail.

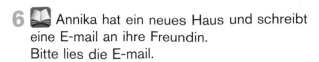

Hallo Sophie,

Wir haben ein neues Haus!

Jetzt wohnen wir in Wiesbaden in einem Einfamilienhaus. Das Wohnzimmer ist groß.

Im Wohnzimmer sind zwei Sofas und drei Sessel, ein Tisch ist zwischen den Sofas. Der Fernseher ist in dem modernen Regal und viele Bilder sind an der Wand. Mein Zimmer ist auch schön. Mein Kleiderschrank ist hinter der Tür und mein Bett neben dem Fenster. Vor dem Schreibtisch steht ein roter Stuhl. An der Tür habe ich ein Poster von Afrika. Nächstes Jahr gehen wir auf Safari, super, nicht?

Das Gästezimmer ist zwischen dem Elternschlafzimmer und meinem Zimmer. Da kannst du dann schlafen, wenn du im Oktober kommst. Dein Bett ist gegenüber der Tür und du hast eine Kommode neben dem Bett.

In der Küche haben wir einen neuen amerikanischen Kühlschrank mit viel Cola, ich weiß, das ist nicht gesund!

Im Keller haben wir eine Tischtennisplatte.

Spielst du auch gern Tischtennis? Ich hoffe ja?

Tschüs

Annika

a ✏️ Bitte suche alle Ausdrücke mit Dativpräpositionen und schreib sie auf.

Beispiel   neben dem Bett

b ✏️ Sophie hat die E-mail zu schnell gelesen und erzählt ihrer Mutter davon. Korrigiere Sophies Sätze und schreib sie auf.

Beispiel   Annika wohnt jetzt in einem Reihenhaus in Wiesbaden.
    *Annika wohnt jetzt in einem **Einfamilienhaus in Wiesbaden**.*

(1) Der Fernseher ist an der Wand.
(2) Annika hat ein Poster von Afrika an der Wand.
(3) Das Gästezimmer ist direkt neben dem Bad.
(4) Im Gästezimmer ist der Kleiderschrank neben dem Bett.
(5) Annika fliegt dieses Jahr nach Afrika.
(6) Sie haben eine neue Spülmaschine.
(7) Bald kauft Annika eine Tischtennisplatte.

3 Was an meinem Tag so läuft

1 🎧📖 Welcher Satz passt zu welchem Bild?
Hör gut zu und ordne die Sätze in die richtige Reihenfolge.

Beispiel   *a* 10, *b* ___

(1) Ich frühstücke um halb acht.
(2) Ich dusche mich.
(3) Ich gehe um halb elf ins Bett.
(4) Ich esse zu Abend mit meiner Familie.
(5) Ich esse zu Mittag in der Kantine.
(6) Ich ziehe mich an.
(7) Ich stehe um 7 Uhr auf.
(8) Ich ziehe mich aus.
(9) Ich schlafe ein.
(10) Ich wache um Viertel vor sieben auf.
(11) Ich wasche mich.

2 🎧 Hör bitte zu. Wer spricht? Lara, Lukas,
Angelika, Helga, Christoph oder Jens?

Lara

Lukas

Jens

Angelika

Christoph

Helga

Nummer (1), das ist _____
Nummer (2), das ist _____

Grammatik   **D3**

Reflexivverben (*reflexive verbs*)

Reflexive verbs are very common in German.
A reflexive verb is used when the person
doing the action does it to himself/herself:

I wash **myself**	*Ich wasche **mich***
I get (**myself**) dressed	*Ich ziehe **mich** an*

Reflexive verbs always have reflexive pronouns, as
follows:

ich wasche **mich**	**wir** waschen **uns**
du wäschst **dich**	**ihr** wascht **euch**
er/sie wäscht **sich**	**sie** waschen **sich**
Sie waschen **sich**	**Sie** waschen **sich**

Other examples of reflexive verbs are:

sich amüsieren	to enjoy oneself
sich anziehen	to get dressed
sich beeilen	to hurry up
sich duschen	to shower
sich entspannen	to relax
sich fragen	to wonder
sich interessieren für	to be interested in
sich rasieren	to have a shave
sich treffen	to meet

Setze die richtigen Reflexivpronomen ein.

(1) Interessierst du _____ für Musik?
(2) Jeden Morgen rasiert _____ mein Vater.
(3) Meine Eltern interessieren _____ für alte
Bücher.
(4) Meine Schwester amüsiert _____ gut beim
Einkaufen.
(5) Ich frage _____ , wo mein Freund ist.
(6) Amüsiert ihr _____ auf der Party?
(7) Wo treffen wir _____ heute Abend?
(8) Setzen Sie _____ hier bitte.

3 Schreib jetzt drei Sätze über die Person, die in Übung 2 nicht spricht.

4 Bitte lies diese E-mail von Angelika.

a Was ist hier richtig? Und was ist falsch?

(1) Angelika wacht um 6 Uhr auf.
(2) Angelika steht um 7 Uhr auf.
(3) Angelika duscht sich am Morgen.
(4) Angelika isst kein Frühstück.
(5) Angelika isst zu Mittag zu Hause.
(6) Angelika macht am Nachmittag Schularbeiten.
(7) Angelika relaxt vor dem Abendessen.
(8) Angelika geht um 10 Uhr ins Bett.

b Korrigiere jetzt die falschen Sätze.

Hi Maggi!

Du wolltest wissen, was an einem typischen Tag so läuft. Also, los...

Meine Eltern stehen schon um 6 Uhr auf und verlassen das Haus gegen 7 Uhr. Ich wache so um Viertel vor sieben auf und stehe alleine um 7 Uhr auf, ich wasche mich und ziehe mich an. Dann frühstücke ich ganz schnell, so ein Marmeladenbrot und ein Glas Orangensaft zum Beispiel. Um 7.35 Uhr fahre ich mit dem Rad in die Stadt und meine erste Stunde beginnt um 7.50 Uhr.

Ich habe sechs Stunden und die sechste Stunde endet um 13.10. Meistens esse ich zu Mittag in der Schule oder ich nehme ein Brötchen mit von zu Hause. Am Nachmittag bin ich mit Freunden zusammen und wir machen Hausaufgaben. Abends bin ich gegen 5 Uhr zurück und ich entspanne mich ein bisschen: Ich sehe vielleicht fern oder ich helfe beim Kochen.

Wir essen alle zusammen am Abend, das finde ich eigentlich toll. Nach dem Abendessen sehe ich fern oder ich surfe im Internet. Ich dusche mich gegen 10 Uhr und ich gehe ins Bett. Normalerweise lese ich eine kurze Zeit lang und dann schlafe ich ein.

Der Tag ist leider zu kurz!

Schreib mir bald! Deine Angelika

5 Macht Dialoge. *A* beschreibt die Routine. *B* rät, wer das ist. Benutze viele Adjektive (seht euch Thema 2.1 noch einmal an).

Sabine	Evangelos	Magdalena	Kevin	Katja

6 Schreib jetzt ein paar Sätze über Evangelos, Magdalena oder Kevin. Benutze auch Adjektive, wenn du schreibst.

Beispiel   *Angelika steht um halb sieben auf.*
Sie frühstückt und dann geht sie in die Schule...

4 Im Haushalt helfen

☑ Talk about helping at home
☑ Use separable verbs

1 📖 Bitte lies diesen Brief von Magdalena.

Liebe Tante Emma!

Hast du Liebeskummer? Ärger mit den Eltern? Streit mit den Freunden? Schwierigkeiten in der Schule?

Schreib an Tante Emma! Sie hilft dir bei diesen Problemen!

Hilfe! Bitte!

Ich bin 16 Jahre alt und ich glaube, ich muss zuviel im Haus helfen!

Ich mache jeden Tag mein Bett und am Wochenende mache ich mein Zimmer sauber. Ich räume abends den Tisch ab und den Geschirrspüler räume ich morgens aus. Ich bringe den Müll einmal pro Tag nach draußen. Ich sauge jede Woche im ganzen

Haus Staub. Meine Schwester ist 12 Jahre alt und sie räumt ihr Zimmer nie auf. Sie deckt jeden Abend den Tisch und manchmal putzt sie die Toilette. Aber das ist alles!

Es ist schon sehr unfair, nicht wahr?

Ich bin eine Sklavin!

Deine Magdalena

a Was muss Magdalena machen? Trage die richtigen Buchstaben ein.

Beispiel   j

b Wie oft macht sie das?

Beispiel   j : jeden Tag

c Findet Magdalena diese Situation gut oder nicht gut?
Woher weißt du das? Was schreibt sie?

2  Hör bitte zu.
Sieh dir die Bilder in Übung 1 nochmals an. Was machen diese Jugendlichen (Angelika, Evangelos, Magdalena und Kevin)? Wie oft und was meinen sie dazu? Mach Notizen.

	Was?	Wie oft?	Meinung?
Beispiel Angelika Evangelos	*a*	jeden Tag	schrecklich ☹

Grammatik

Trennbare Verben (*separable verbs*)

Separable verbs come in two parts: the prefix and the verb. In the present tense you separate the prefix from the verb and put it at the end of the sentence:

saubermachen: *Am Wochenende mache ich mein Zimmer **sauber**.*

anziehen: *Angelika zieht sich schnell **an**.*

aufstehen: *Kevin steht immer um 7 Uhr **auf**.*

fernsehen: *Jeden Abend sehen wir 2 Stunden **fern**.*

(1) Now look at Magdalena's letter in Übung 1 and see how many examples of separable verbs you can find.

(2) Bilde zehn Sätze mit diesen trennbaren Verben:

- **a** einkaufen
- **b** abfahren
- **c** einschlafen
- **d** ankommen
- **e** umsteigen
- **f** aufmachen
- **g** abwaschen
- **h** vorbereiten
- **i** anrufen
- **j** aufräumen

 2/5

3a 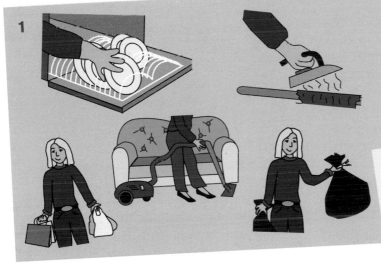 Macht Dialoge.

A Was machst du, um im Haushalt zu helfen?
B *Ich sauge im Wohnzimmer Staub.*
A Und wie oft/wann machst du das?
B *Einmal pro Woche.*
A Und wie findest du das?
B *Ich finde es stinklangweilig.*

2
morgen
nächsten Dienstag
nächste Woche
in drei Tagen
einmal pro Woche
jeden Tag
abends
manchmal
jeden Freitag

3
stinklangweilig ☹
ekelhaft ☹
toll ☺
ermüdend ☹
O.K. ☺

b 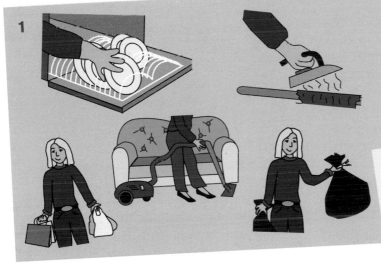 Alles zusammen? Bilde jetzt Sätze!

Beispiel Ich sauge einmal pro Woche im Wohnzimmer Staub und das finde ich stinklangweilig! Nächste Woche muss ich einkaufen und das finde ich OK.

4 Schreib einen kurzen Brief an Magdalena. Erzähl ihr, was du im Haushalt machen musst, um deinen Eltern zu helfen!

Liebe Magdalena,

Thema 3 Freizeit

1 Hobbys

1 Was passt zusammen?

(1) Am Wochenende gehe ich gern ins Kino. Im Moment ist „Herr der Ringe" mein Lieblingsfilm.

(2) Ich bin Computerfan. Man kann mit Freunden überall in der Welt chatten.

(3) Ich gehe gern mit Freunden einkaufen. Es gibt gute Kleidungsgeschäfte in der Stadt. Die neue Mode finde ich super.

(4) Ich mag lesen, am liebsten Krimis oder Comichefte.

(5) Ich spiele Blockflöte. Ich muss jeden Tag üben.

(6) Ich bin Fernsehfan. Ich sehe jeden Abend 2 Stunden fern. Das entspannt richtig.

(7) Ich bastele gern. Im Sommer fliege ich jeden Samstag mein Modellflugzeug.

(8) Ich esse gern im Restaurant. Besonders mag ich chinesisches Essen. Wir essen einmal im Monat im China Restaurant.

(9) Ich treffe mich oft mit Freunden. Wir sitzen abends in meinem Zimmer und quatschen.

(10) Ich gehe am Freitag in einen Klub. Es gibt einen super Nachtklub in der Stadt.

(11) Ich interessiere mich für Musik. Meine Lieblingsband ist „Revolverheld". Die sehe ich nächsten Sommer live.

2 Bitte hör zu und lies mit.

Ingo Ich gehe mit Freunden ins Kino. Filme sind interessant. Wir gehen oft am Dienstag, weil die Karten für Schüler dann billiger sind. Nächste Woche sehen wir den neuen James Bond Film.

Katja Meine ältere Schwester Lena und ich kaufen einmal pro Monat in Mainz ein. Ich kaufe gern modische Kleidung, wenn ich Geld habe. Ich fahre sehr gern mit Lena in die Stadt, weil es Spaß macht.

Aline Blockflöte spielen macht mir keinen Spaß. Ich habe jede Woche Unterricht, das ist am Mittwoch eine halbe Stunde nach der Schule. Ich übe jeden Tag 20 Minuten in meinem Zimmer, weil meine Eltern Musik wichtig finden.

Lukas Ich habe viele Freunde. Wir treffen uns am Wochenende in der Stadt und essen ein Eis im italienischen Eiscafé. Manchmal treffen wir uns auch bei mir zu Hause. Dann sitzen wir oft auf dem Boden und hören Musik und unterhalten uns. Das finde ich super.

Sara Popmusik finde ich toll. Ich habe mindestens 100 CDs. Popkonzerte sind teuer und ich war erst einmal in Hamburg in einem Konzert, weil ich Geburtstag hatte.

Timo Lesen finde ich blöd. Zu Weihnachten bekomme ich immer viele Bücher, aber ich arbeite lieber am Computer.

a Bitte füll die Lücken aus.

> um 13 Uhr
> einmal pro Woche   am Computer
> in einem Konzert   jede Woche   mit Freunden
> am Dienstag   ins Kino   mit Lena   in die Stadt
> in Mainz   in Hamburg   am Wochenende
> einmal   im Eiscafé

(1) Ingo und seine Freunde gehen ____ ins Kino.
(2) Katja und Lena fahren gern ____ .
(3) Sie kaufen ____ modische Kleidung.
(4) Aline hat ____ nach der Schule Blockflötenunterricht.
(5) Lukas isst am Wochenende ____ in der Stadt ein Eis.
(6) Sara war ____ in einem Konzert.
(7) Timo arbeitet gern ____ .

b Wie finden sie das? Bitte hör noch einmal zu.

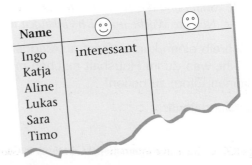

Name	🙂	🙁
Ingo	interessant	
Katja		
Aline		
Lukas		
Sara		
Timo		

3 🎧 Bitte hör gut zu und füll die Tabelle aus.

Name	Hobby	Wann?	Wie oft?	Mit wem?	Wo?	😊 😞
Elke	Einkaufen	samstags	1 × pro Woche	Freundin Terese	in München	macht Spaß 😊
Florian	_____					

4 💬 Jetzt bist du dran! Bitte frag deinen Partner und wechselt euch ab! Bitte macht Dialoge.

Beispiel

nachmittags

Schule   entspannend

A Was machst du in deiner Freizeit?
B *Ich spiele Gitarre.*
A Wann spielst du Gitarre?
B *Ich spiele nachmittags Gitarre.*

A Mit wem spielst du Gitarre?
B *Ich spiele mit Freunden Gitarre.*
A Wo spielst du Gitarre?
B *Ich spiele in der Schule Gitarre.*
A Wie findest du das?
B *Ich finde das entspannend.*

Grammatik

Wann, wie, wo (*time, manner, place*)

When talking about your hobbies you often mention:
- the time (**when** you do something)
- the manner (**how** or **with whom** you do something)
- the place (**where** you do something)

*Lukas isst **am Wochenende** mit Freunden in der Stadt ein Eis.*
(**time**)

*Lukas isst am Wochenende **mit Freunden** in der Stadt ein Eis.*
(**manner**)

*Lukas isst am Wochenende mit Freunden **in der Stadt** ein Eis.*
(**place**)

German speakers like to keep this information in the order time, manner, place, as shown in the example.

🖱 3/1

H2

5 📝 Was machst du am Montag, am Dienstag, am Mittwoch…? Bitte schreib sieben Sätze.

2 Geld

1 Bitte hör zu und lies mit.

- ☑ Talk about pocket money
- ☑ Talk about part-time jobs
- ☑ Talk about spending and saving
- ☑ Use subordinating conjunctions (*dass, weil, wenn*)

Ich bekomme monatlich €30 von meiner Mutter und €10 von meinen Großeltern, weil ich viel im Haushalt helfe. Ich bin ganz zufrieden.

Christoph

Ich bekomme gar kein Taschengeld. Ich gehe viermal die Woche mit dem Hund von unseren Nachbarn spazieren. Ich verdiene €45 im Monat. Ich habe leider wenig Freizeit, weil ich arbeiten muss.

Lukas

Ich arbeite, weil ich kein Taschengeld kriege. Nach der Schule trage ich Zeitungen aus, und am Wochenende gehe ich babysitten. Ich finde es unfair.

Lara

Ich kriege €20 Taschengeld im Monat. Das ist genau richtig. Ich verdiene ein bisschen Geld dazu: Samstags kaufe ich für eine alte Frau ein und sie gibt mir €5 die Woche.

Helga

Jens

Ich bekomme €80 Taschengeld, wenn ich in der Schule fleißig arbeite und gute Noten im Zeugnis habe. Ich finde es klasse so!

Mach Notizen.

Name	Taschengeld? ✔✗	Arbeit? ✔ ✗	Was? Wie viel?	Glücklich? ✔✗
(1) Christoph	✔ €40, hilft im Haushalt	✗		✔ zufrieden
(2) Lara				

Grammatik

H4

Dass, weil, wenn (*subordinating conjunctions*)

You can use the subordinating conjunctions **dass**, **weil** and **wenn** to join two shorter sentences together to make a longer sentence. Unlike coordinating conjunctions (*und, aber*), which do not affect the sentence order, these subordinating conjunctions send the verb to the end of the sentence. If it is a complicated sentence, they send the verb to the end of the clause.

Ich finde es gut,	*dass ich Taschengeld*	*bekomme.*
Es ist unfair,	*dass du kein Taschengeld*	*bekommst.*
Ich bekomme Taschengeld,	*wenn ich im Haushalt*	*helfe.*
Meine Oma gibt mir Geld,	*wenn ich Geburtstag*	*habe.*
Ich habe einen Nebenjob,	*weil ich kein Taschengeld*	*bekomme.*
Ich habe viel Geld,	*weil ich einen Nebenjob*	*habe.*

Join these sentences using *dass*, *weil* or *wenn* (there may be more than one possibility).

(1) *Mein Bruder hat viel Geld.* — *Er arbeitet samstags im Supermarkt.*
(2) *Ich finde es toll.* — *Ich darf am Wochenende einen Nebenjob finden.*
(3) *Meine Freundin spart €25 jeden Monat.* — *Sie will ein neues Handy kaufen.*
(4) *Meine Oma gibt mir ein wenig Geld.* — *Ich besuche sie.*
(5) *Ich bin sehr ärgerlich.* — *Ich muss mein Geld für Kleidung ausgeben.*
(6) *Es ist schrecklich.* — *Frank bekommt kein Taschengeld.*
(7) *Sofie verdient €7 die Stunde.* — *Sie arbeitet im Restaurant.*
(8) *Es stimmt.* — *Ich kaufe zu viele Bonbons.*

3/2

2  Bitte lies die Texte unten. Wofür gibst du dein Geld aus?

> *Ich bekomme €40 im Monat. Ich spende €10 an eine Organisation – ähnlich wie Unicef. Ich gebe mein Geld für Zeitschriften, CDs und Süßigkeiten aus. Und meine Handykosten muss ich selber zahlen: Die sind manchmal richtig hoch! Klamotten und Schuhe bezahlen meine Eltern. Schulsachen muss ich auch nicht selber zahlen. Ich spare aber nicht, weil ich leider kein Geld übrig habe. Im Grunde reicht mir mein Geld.*

Christoph

> *Ich habe €40 im Monat und das reicht mir völlig aus. Ich lege immer €20 auf mein Sparkonto zurück, weil ich noch keinen MP3-Player habe und mir einen kaufen möchte. Die andere Hälfte meines Geldes gebe ich für meine Hobbys aus. Ich kaufe Schmucksachen oder gehe Schlittschuhlaufen. Alle 2 Monate gebe ich €11 für Schildkrötenfutter aus, was noch geht. Ich gebe eigentlich nicht so viel Geld aus, außer vielleicht für Geburtstagsgeschenke für Freunde oder Familie.*

Helga

a   b   c   d   e   f

g   h   i   j Sparbüchse   k   l   m

Wofür geben Christoph und Helga ihr Geld aus?
Füll die Tabelle aus.

Christoph	Helga

3 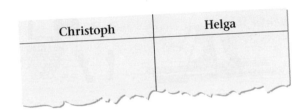 Bitte hör zu.

a Richtig oder falsch? Christoph und Lara sprechen über Geld.

Beispiel Lara bekommt kein Taschengeld.   *richtig*

(1) Lara macht nichts im Haushalt.
(2) Lara verdient €15 pro Woche, wenn sie Zeitungen austrägt.
(3) Lara geht nicht gern babysitten.
(4) Lara interessiert sich nicht für Sport.

(5) Lara gibt das Geld für Schminken aus.
(6) Lara bekommt Kleidung als Geschenke.
(7) Lara spart viel Geld.
(8) Christoph hat schon einen Nebenjob.
(9) Christoph will ein neues Handy kaufen.

b Korrigiere jetzt die falschen Sätze.

4  Macht Dialoge.

Beispiel

A Bekommst du Taschengeld?
B *Ja, ich bekomme €35 im Monat.*
A Was musst du für das Geld machen?
B *Ich muss mein Zimmer aufräumen.*
A Hast du auch einen Nebenjob?
B *Ja, ich arbeite samstags in einem Supermarkt.*
A Wofür gibst du dein Geld aus?
B *Ich gebe mein Geld für CDs aus.*
A Sparst du auch?
B *Ja, ich spare für eine neue Xbox.*

€35
€25
€10
€17
€0
pro Woche
im Monat

Sparbüchse

3 Ich bin fit

1 📖

Ich spiele gern Tennis.

Ich gehe ins Fitnessstudio.

Joggen macht Spaß.

Reiten ist fantastisch.

Turnen mache ich sehr gern.

Leichtathletik finde ich klasse.

Machst du auch Karate?

Am allerliebsten schwimme ich.

Tauchen mag ich sehr gern.

Schlittschuhlaufen ist super.

Fußball sehe ich unheimlich gern.

Wie findest du Snowboarding?

Am allerliebsten fahre ich Rad.

Ich laufe im Winter Ski.

Ich spiele oft Basketball.

Mein Hobby ist Tischtennis.

2 🎧 Bitte hör zu und füll die Tabelle aus. Die Information für Timo hast du schon.

Name	Sportart	Wie oft?	Wo?	☺ ☹
Timo	Schwimmen	2 × pro Woche	Klub	☺

Grammatik

C2

Vorlieben ausdrücken (expressing preferences)

There are various ways of expressing your likes and dislikes.

If you like doing something, you can put *gern* after the verb:

> Ich spiele **gern** Fußball.
> Ich schwimme **gern**. ☺

If you prefer something, you can use *lieber*:

> Ich tauche **lieber**. ☺ ☺

You can also compare it with another activity:

> Ich spiele **lieber** Tennis **als** Fußball. ☺ ☺

Use *am liebsten* to talk about your favourite sport:

> Ich laufe **am liebsten** Ski. ☺ ☺ ☺

To talk about the best sport ever, use am *allerliebsten*:

> Ich spiele **am allerliebsten** Basketball. ☺ ☺ ☺ ☺

And if you don't like something:

> *Wassersport mache ich nicht gern.* ☹
> *Leichtathletik mache ich noch weniger gern.* ☹ ☹
> *Ich gehe nie/absolut nicht/überhaupt nicht ins Fitnessstudio.* ☹ ☹ ☹

You could also say:

> Ich mag (I like)…
> *Basketball mag ich.* ☺
> *Leichtathletik mag ich nicht.* ☹

Or use some adjectives:

> *Fußball ist…*
> *Fußball finde ich…*
> ☺klasse, interessant, faszinierend, aufregend, super, einmalig
> ☹stressig, stinklangweilig, anstrengend, gefährlich, zu teuer

🖱 3/3

Wann?

in den Ferien   jede Woche

um 17 Uhr

einmal/zweimal im Jahr   am Donnerstag

am Wochenende

3 🗨 Bitte sprich mit deinem Partner.

Wo?

im Fitnessstudio   im Schwimmbad

im Park   im Klub

in der Schule   in Österreich

Beispiel

A   Hallo Anya, treibst du Sport?
B   *Ja, ich spiele gern Tischtennis.*
A   Wann spielst du Tischtennis.
B   *Am Montag und am Mittwoch um 15 Uhr.*
A   Wo machst du das?
B   *In der Schule.*
A   Warum spielst du gern Tischtennis?
B   *Ich spiele gern Tischtennis, weil es Spaß macht.*

Warum?

…weil ☺   …weil ❄ ☺   …weil

weil ich da
Freunde treffe   …weil

4a ✏ Bitte schreib einen kurzen Brief.

Ich 〰⚽ ☺ *. Ich trainiere am Mittwoch und am*

Samstag, also _____ pro _____ .

Ich trainiere am Mittwoch

und am Samstag

Ich mag 〰⚽ *, weil ich es* ☺ *finde.*

b ✏ Und zum Schluss: Was machst du?
Bitte schreib ein paar Sätze über dich.

Das hat Timo geschrieben:

Ich bin der Timo. Ich mache lieber
Wassersport als Leichtathletik.
Ich bin Mitglied in einem Klub.
Wir trainieren zweimal pro Woche,
abends von 19 bis 21 Uhr.
Am allerliebsten mache ich
Brustschwimmen. Ich finde
Schwimmen toll. Ich spiele auch
Wasserball. Ich glaube, ich bin fit.

Was schreibst du?

4 Und am Samstag?

1 📖 Welches Bild ist das?

(1) Ich spiele am Computer.	(2) Ich besuche ein Rockkonzert.
(3) Ich schaue (mir) ein Fußballspiel an.	(4) Ich gehe einkaufen.
(5) Ich mache eine Radtour.	(6) Ich gehe auf eine Party.
(7) Ich schreibe E-mails an Freunde.	(8) Ich schreibe SMS/Ich simse.
(9) Ich spiele mit meiner Playstation.	(10) Ich bin Hobbykoch.

2 📖 Bitte lies diese E-mail von Angelika.

Hi Maggi!

Wie geht es dir? Ich freue mich schon aufs Wochenende. Es ist immer viel los hier!

Für mich fängt das Wochenende schon am Freitagabend an. Manchmal treffe ich mich mit Freunden und wir gehen kegeln, oder wir chillen ganz einfach. Manchmal bleibe ich zu Hause und chatte im Internet, schicke E-mails an Freunde in Chile und Namibia oder spiele einfach Videospiele.

Jeden Samstagvormittag spiele ich Geige in einem Orchester. Das macht mir enorm viel Spaß, weil wir nicht nur klassische Musik sondern auch moderne Stücke spielen. Manchmal geben wir sogar Konzerte.

Am Nachmittag treffe ich mich normalerweise mit meinem Freund und wir fahren mit der U-Bahn in die Stadtmitte. Oft gehen wir zum Markt, weil man dort günstige alte Musikplatten kaufen kann (ich interessiere mich wahnsinnig für Musik!). Samstagabend gehen wir dann ins Theater oder ins Kino, wenn etwas Gutes läuft, sonst gehen wir auf eine Party.

Sonntags mache ich 3 Stunden lang meine Hausaufgaben. Danach muss ich meine Großeltern besuchen. Meine Oma backt immer einen Kuchen und wir trinken zusammen Kaffee und essen Kuchen. Nach dem Abendessen lese ich oder ich sehe fern, um mich zu entspannen. Manchmal komponiere ich auch Lieder.

Das Wochenende ist mir leider zu kurz!

Schreib mir bald! Deine Angelika

Mach Notizen. Verstehst du, was Angelika in ihrer Freizeit macht?

Tag	Aktivitäten	Mit wem?/ Wo?	Wann?
(1) Freitag	(a) kegeln (b) (c) (d) (e)	mit Freunden zu Hause	abends
(2)			

Grammatik 【H1】

Wortstellung (word order: inversion)

In German the verb must always be the second idea in a sentence. This means that you might need to invert (swap over) the position of the pronoun and the verb.

So: ***Wir fahren** nächsten Samstag mit dem Zug nach Westerland.*

can become: *Nächsten Samstag **fahren wir** mit dem Zug nach Westerland.*

and: ***Wir hören** unterwegs Musik.*

becomes: *Unterwegs **hören wir** Musik.*

Look again at Angelika's e-mail in Übung 2 and see how many examples of inversion you can find.

3 Bitte hör zu. Ein Tagesausflug nach Sylt. Wie läuft der Tag ab? Was ist die richtige Reihenfolge?

Beispiel (1)f

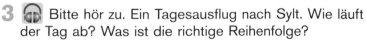

Jetzt füll die Tabelle aus.

4 Erzähl deinem Partner von einem Ausflug, den du machen willst.

Was?	Wann?	Andere Informationen?
(1) f Bahnfahrt nach Sylt	nächsten Samstag	
(2)		
(3)		

a

b

5 Schreib eine E-mail an Angelika (150 Wörter). Erzähl ihr von deinen Plänen für einen Tagesausflug.
- Wohin fährst du und wie kommst du dorthin?
- Mit wem bist du unterwegs und was macht ihr?

Top-Tipp
Writing longer sentences: five easy steps

(1) Use linking words to join shorter sentences:
   und   oder   aber

(2) Use subordinating conjunctions to join two shorter sentences together:
   dass   weil   wenn

(3) Use expressions of time to say when:
   *Um 10 Uhr   am Abend
   danach   dann   manchmal*

(4) Use inversion. Begin your sentences with an expression of time, manner or place:
   Am Wochenende besuche ich immer meine Großeltern.

(5) Use adjectives to describe things:
   günstige Musikplatten

Stefan ist 17 Jahre alt und wohnt in St. Anton in Österreich. Er beschreibt einen typischen Tag seines Lebens.

Ein typischer Tag in St. Anton

Morgens stehe ich früh auf, weil mein Bus zur Hotelfachschule um 7 Uhr abfährt. Ich helfe meinen Eltern, wenn ich noch etwas Zeit habe. Sie haben das *Hotel zur Sonne* (dort wohnen wir auch), und vor dem Frühstück ist immer viel zu tun.

Die Touristen bleiben eine Woche in St. Anton, genießen den Schnee im Winter und die grünen Wiesen in den Bergen im Sommer.

Um 8 Uhr komme ich in der Hotelfachschule in Innsbruck an. Ich habe dort viele Freunde. Mein Freund Michael hilft auch viel im Hotel bei sich zu Hause. In der Schulpause planen wir, was wir am Nachmittag machen. Ich laufe sehr gern Ski und möchte bei den Olympischen Winterjugendspielen eine Medaille gewinnen.

Gegen 14 Uhr bin ich wieder in St. Anton. Im Winter fahren Michael und ich dann mit dem Skilift auf unseren Hausberg und machen Abfahrtslauf. Das macht uns unheimlich viel Spaß. Manchmal kommt mein Bruder auch mit. Der Lift ist direkt hinter dem Hotel. Später helfe ich wieder meinen Eltern, wenn sie das Abendessen vorbereiten. Die Hotelgäste sind immer sehr nett und meine Eltern bezahlen mich für die Arbeit. Ich spare das Geld für ein Auto.

Abends treffe ich mich mit Freunden. Wir trinken eine Cola oder quatschen nur etwas. Von sonntags bis donnerstags gehe ich um 10 Uhr ins Bett, denn ich stehe ja schon um 6 Uhr auf.

1a 📖 Lies den Text. Was ist richtig (R) und was ist falsch (F)? **Vier** Sätze sind falsch. Korrigiere die falschen Sätze.

(1) Stefan hilft seinen Eltern regelmäßig mit dem Frühstück.
(2) Die Hotelfachschule ist in St. Anton.
(3) Nach der Schule hat er keine Zeit und kann nicht Ski laufen.
(4) Er läuft machmal mit seinem Bruder Ski.
(5) Er wohnt nicht in der Nähe von dem Skilift.
(6) Er bekommt kein Geld für die Arbeit im Hotel.

b 📖 Beantworte die Fragen.

(1) Warum steht Stefan früh auf? Gib zwei Gründe an.
(2) Wo arbeiten Stefans Eltern?
(3) Welchen Sport treibt Stefan nachmittags im Winter?
(4) Mit wem macht Stefan das?
(5) Was möchte er kaufen, wenn er genug Geld hat?

PROBLEMPUNKT   Feste

Frage von Anja42:

Mein Vater ist seit fünf Jahren wieder verheiratet und das ist okay. Meine Stiefmutter ist ganz sympathisch, aber seit drei Monaten wohnt meine Stiefschwester auch bei uns im Haus. Sie ist 27 und hat früher in Hamburg gearbeitet, aber jetzt ist sie arbeitslos und kann ihre Wohnung dort nicht mehr bezahlen. Sie ist sehr deprimiert und es ist schwer, mit ihr zusammen zu leben. Das Problem – wir müssen uns mein Zimmer teilen! Sie ist sehr unordentlich, ihre Musik ist viel zu laut and gefällt mir gar nicht. Ich muss jeden Tag in meinem Zimmer meine Hausaufgaben machen, aber ich habe keine Ruhe. Was kann ich tun?

Antwort von Hausmaus:

Habt ihr ein separates Esszimmer in eurem Haus? Vielleicht könnt ihr dort ein Zimmer für sie einrichten und vorübergehend in der Küche oder im Wohnzimmer essen? Sie findet hoffentlich bald eine neue Arbeitsstelle and zieht dann wieder aus!

Antwort von Kleine Katze:

Du kannst Kopfhörer für deine Stiefschwester kaufen!

Antwort von Lizel:

Du musst dieses Problem mit deiner Stiefmutter, deiner Stiefschwester und mit deinem Vater besprechen und ihr müsst gemeinsam eine Lösung finden. Es ist wichtig, dass du auch zufrieden bist, und dass deine Familie versteht, wie du dich fühlst. Das kannst du nicht allein machen.

2 📖 Finde die deutschen Wörter oder Ausdrücke.

> stepsister
> out-of-work
> depressed
> peace
> headphones
> discuss
> solution

3 ✏️ Bist du einer Meinung mit Hausmaus, Kleine Katze oder Lizel? Wenn ja – warum? Oder hast du eine ganz neue Idee für Anja42? Schreib deine Gedanken für das Forum auf. Schreib ungefähr 50 Wörter.

4 📖 Lies den Text über Weihnachten. Mach eine Liste mit Wörtern über die Weihnachtszeit. Kannst du insgesamt acht Wörter finden?

> **Weihnachtsmärkte**
> **Glühwein**

Weihnachten

Weihnachten ist ein christliches Fest, das Ende Dezember gefeiert wird.

Im Dezember gibt es überall Weihnachtsmärkte, wo man Weihnachtsgeschenke, Weihnachtsschmuck, Weihnachtsplätzchen und viele andere schöne Dinge kaufen kann.

Oft ist das Wetter sehr kalt und es schneit und die Menschen treffen sich auf dem Weihnachtsmarkt, um Glühwein zu trinken und vielleicht ein Würstchen zu essen.

Die Weihnachtsmärkte schließen am 24. Dezember. Das ist Heiligabend. Die Familien schmücken den Weihnachtsbaum, gehen vielleicht in die Kirche und danach essen sie ein gutes Abendessen. Typisch ist Karpfen, ein Fisch, aber viele Familien essen ein anderes Gericht.

Danach ist die Bescherung. Die Kerzen brennen am Weihnachtsbaum und man packt die Geschenke aus. Das ist besonders aufregend für die Kinder, weil sie lange aufbleiben dürfen. Am 1. und 2. Weihnachtstag besucht man Verwandte und Freunde und isst weiter besonders gutes Essen.

5 📖 Welches Wort passt in den Satz? Finde die Wörter im Kasten.

Abendessen	Geschenke
Bescherung	Plätzchen
besuchen	Verwandte
bleiben	Weihnachtsmarkt
feiern	Weihnachtsschmuck
Fest	Wetter
Freunde	

(1) Auf dem .... gibt es viele schöne Sachen.
(2) Für den Baum kann man .... kaufen.
(3) Am Heiligabend freuen sich die Kinder über ihre ....
(4) Die Kinder .... lange auf.
(5) Am 1. Weihnachtstag .... viele Familien Verwandte.
(6) Die Zeit nach dem Abendessen am Heiligabend heißt die ....

🎧 Paper 1: listening

These questions test your understanding of individual words and short statements.

> In the exam all instructions will be in the *Sie* form, as it is a formal situation, e.g. *Hören Sie ein Gespräch* (Listen to a conversation). To find out more about when to use *du* (informal) and when to use *Sie* (formal) see Grammar section D2.

In dieser Aufgabe hören Sie ein Gespräch. Sie hören jede Bemerkung zweimal. Suchen Sie die Antwort heraus, die am besten passt, und kreuzen Sie das richtige Kästchen an.

Stefan aus Deutschland telefoniert mit seiner Brieffreundin Julia in der Schweiz.

1 Julia fragt, was Stefan am Abend macht. Er antwortet.
Was macht Stefan am Abend?

A	
B	
C	
D	

[1]

2 Stefan will wissen, wie Julia aussieht. Sie antwortet.
Wie sieht Julia aus?

A	
B	
C	
D	

[1]

3 Julia fragt Stefan über seine Familie. Er antwortet.
Wie viele Geschwister hat er?

A	
B	
C	
D	

[1]

4 Julia beschreibt ihr Schlafzimmer. Sie sagt, wo ihre Katze schläft.
Wo schläft die Katze?

A	
B	
C	
D	

[1]

[Total: 4]

Paper 2: reading

The question below tests your understanding of short statements using familiar language.

Was macht Ulrike am Samstag? Sehen Sie sich die Bilder an.

Tragen Sie die richtigen Buchstaben (A, B, C, D, E oder F) in die richtigen Kästchen ein.

1 Sie isst zu Mittag. ☐

2 Sie duscht sich. ☐

3 Sie zieht sich aus. ☐

4 Sie wacht auf. ☐

5 Sie räumt ihr Zimmer auf. ☐

[Total: 5]

🗨️ Paper 3: speaking

Part 1 of the speaking exam consists of two role plays. You will be given a card containing the two role-play situations and you will have 15 minutes to prepare your answers. This task shows a sample role play A.

A

Kandidat(in): Sie selbst bei Ihrer deutschen Austauschfamilie

Lehrer: Der Vater von Ihrem/Ihrer Austauschpartner(in)

Der Vater von Ihrem/Ihrer Austauschpartner(in) will über Ihre Hobbys wissen.

1 **(i)** Begrüßen Sie den Vater **und**
   (ii) Nennen Sie eine Aktivität, die Sie gern in Ihrer Freizeit machen.

2 Sagen Sie, wie oft Sie das machen.

3 Beschreiben Sie **zwei** positive Gründe, warum Sie dieses Hobby machen.

4 Sagen Sie, welche Sportarten Sie nicht mögen.

5 Fragen Sie den Vater nach seinen Hobbys.

Points to remember

- Read through the instructions carefully.
- Make sure you cover all the points 1–5.
- Note that in point 3 you need to include more than one detail.

🎧 Look at and listen to the sample dialogue below. The candidate has not given complete answers. How could you change it for yourself and improve on it?

1 Lehrerin	Hallo. Was machst du gern in deiner Freizeit?	
Kandidatin	*Hallo. Ich spiele gern Gitarre.*	
2 Lehrerin	Wie oft musst du Gitarre üben?	
Kandidatin	*Jeden Abend.*	
3 Lehrerin	Und warum hast du dieses Hobby gern?	
Kandidatin	*Ich finde es toll.*	
4 Lehrerin	Aber du bist nicht sehr sportlich? Welche Sportarten machst du nicht sehr gern?	
Kandidatin	*Ich spiele nicht gern Tennis oder Fußball.*	
5 Lehrerin	Möchtest du mir vielleicht eine Frage stellen?	
Kandidatin	*Ja, was machen Sie gerne in Ihrer Freizeit?*	

Tips for success

- The student could have said more about how long she spends practising the guitar.
- In statement 3 the candidate should have given *two* positive reasons.
- Answer 4 could have been extended by giving a reason.

Paper 4: writing

In the first task you have to write a list of eight items in German.

---

1 Sie ziehen in ein neues Haus um. Was nehmen Sie mit? Machen Sie eine Liste von
8 Dingen **auf Deutsch**.

Beispiel: Sessel

[Total: 5]

Points to remember

- You do not need to include the words *der, die, das*.
- Aim to be as accurate as possible with spellings.
- The pictures are just a guide. You can use your own ideas.

In the second task you have to write sentences about yourself.

---

2 Sie schreiben ein Blog über sich selbst.
Sagen Sie…

(a) wie Sie aussehen.

(b) wer in Ihrer Familie ist.

(c) was Sie im Haushalt machen, um Ihren Eltern zu helfen.

(d) wie viel Taschengeld Sie bekommen und wofür Sie das Geld ausgeben.
Schreiben Sie 80–90 Wörter **auf Deutsch**.

[Total: 15]

Points to remember

- To produce a good blog, you need to cover all the bullet points.
- You can make up details about yourself. They don't have to be true.
- Use a range of vocabulary and grammatical structures.

Erster Teil Vokabular 1

Family

der **Bruder** (¨)   brother
der **Cousin** (-s)/die **Cousine** (-n)   cousin
das **Einzelkind** (-er)   only child
die **Eltern**   parents
die **Familie** (-n)   family
die **Frau** (-en)   woman, wife
die **Großmutter** (¨)   grandmother
der **Großvater** (¨)   grandfather
der **Halbbruder** (¨)   half-brother
die **Halbschwester** (-n)   half-sister
die **Hausfrau** (-en)   housewife
der **Junge** (-n)   boy
das **Kind** (-er)   child
das **Mädchen** (-)   girl
der **Mann** (¨-er)   man, husband
die **Mutter** (¨)/**Mutti** (-s)   mother/mum
der **Nachbar** (-n)   neighbour
der **Name** (-n)   name
der **Neffe** (-n)   nephew
die **Nichte** (-n)   niece
die **Oma** (-s)   grandma
der **Onkel** (-)   uncle
der **Opa** (-s)   granddad
der **Partner** (-)/die **Partnerin** (-nen)   partner
die **Schwester** (-n)   sister
der **Sohn** (¨-e)   son
der **Stiefbruder** (¨)   step-brother
die **Stiefschwester** (-n)   step-sister
die **Tante** (-n)   aunt
die **Tochter** (¨)   daughter
der **Vater** (¨)/**Vati** (-s)   father/dad
die **Verwandten**   relatives
der **Zwilling** (-e)   twin

Personal descriptions

alt (**älter**)   old (older)
angenehm   pleasant, nice, kind
die **Augen**   eyes
der **Bart** (¨-e)   beard
die **Brille** (-n)   glasses, spectacles
dick   fat
dumm   stupid
ehrlich   honest, decent, fair
ernst   serious
faul   lazy
freundlich   friendly, kind, nice
glücklich   happy, pleased, glad
groß   tall, big
großzügig   generous
das **Haar** (-e)   hair
hässlich   ugly
höflich   polite
hübsch   pretty
jung (**jünger**)   young (younger)
klein   small, short (*person*)
klug   clever
lang   long
ledig   single, unmarried

lockig   curly
müde   tired
die **Ohrringe**   ear-rings
schlank   slim
schön   beautiful, lovely
schüchtern   shy
selbstsicher   self-confident
selbstsüchtig   selfish
sportlich   sporty
stark   strong
süß   sweet
sympathisch   nice
toll   great, super
tot   dead
unhöflich   rude, impolite
verwöhnt   spoilt

Pets

der **Goldfisch** (-e)   goldfish
das **Haustier** (-e)   pet
der **Hund** (¨-e)   dog
das **Kaninchen** (-)   rabbit
die **Katze** (-n)   cat
die **Maus** (¨-e)   mouse
das **Meerschweinchen** (-)   guinea pig
die **Schildkröte** (-n)   tortoise

Identity and relationships

der **Familienname** (-n)   surname
der **Freund** (-e)/die **Freundin** (-nen)   friend
geboren   born
geschieden   divorced
heiraten   to marry
kennen   to know (a person)
kennen lernen   to get to know
lachen   to laugh
lieben   to love
der **Nachname** (-n)   surname
verheiratet   married
der **Vorname** (-n)   first name

House and home

das **Badezimmer** (-)   bathroom
der **Bauernhof** (¨-e)   farm
das **Büro** (-s)   office, study
das **Doppelhaus** (¨-er)   semidetached house
das **Einfamilienhaus** (¨-er)   detached house
das **Erdgeschoss** (-e)   ground floor
das **Esszimmer** (-)   dining room
der **Garten** (¨)   garden
das **Haus** (¨-er)   house
im ersten Stock   on the first floor
der **Keller** (-)   cellar
das **Klo** (-s)   toilet (*informal*)
die **Küche** (-n)   kitchen
der **Rasen** (-)   lawn
das **Schlafzimmer** (-)   bedroom
der **Stock** (¨-e)   floor, storey
die **Terrasse** (-n)   patio, terrace
die **Toilette** (-n)   toilet

die **Treppe**   stairs
die **Wohnung** (-en)   flat
das **Wohnzimmer** (-)   sitting room
das **Zimmer** (-)   room

Around the home

der **Abfall** (¨-e)   rubbish
abspülen   to wash up
abwaschen   to wash up
angenehm   pleasant
das **Bad** (¨-er)   bath
bequem   comfortable
das **Bett** (-en)   bed
der **Boden** (¨)   floor
der **Dosenöffner** (-)   tin opener
duschen   to shower
das **Fenster** (-)   window
der **Flaschenöffner** (-)   bottle opener
der **Fußboden** (¨)   floor
die **Gabel** (-n)   fork
der **Gefrierschrank** (¨-e)   freezer
die **Geschirrspülmaschine** (-n)   dishwasher
das **Glas** (¨-er)   glass
der **Herd** (-e)   cooker
die **Kaffeemaschine** (-n)   coffee maker
der **Kühlschrank** (¨-e)   fridge
das **Licht** (-er)   light
der **Löffel** (-)   spoon
die **Mauer** (-n)   wall (outside, external)
das **Messer** (-)   knife
die **Mikrowelle** (-n)   microwave
die **Möbel** (-)   furniture
das **Möbelstück** (-e)   piece of furniture
der **Müll**   rubbish, refuse
der **Mülleimer** (-)   dustbin
der **Schrank** (¨-e)   cupboard
der **Sessel** (-)   armchair, easy chair
das **Sofa** (-s)   sofa, settee
die **Spülmaschine** (-n)   dishwasher
der **Stuhl** (¨-e)   chair
der **Teppich** (-e)   carpet
der **Teppichboden** (¨)   fitted carpet
die **Tür** (-en)   door
die **Wand** (¨-e)   wall (inside, internal)
die **Waschmaschine** (-n)   washing machine
wohnen   to live

Daily routine

arbeiten   to work
aufräumen   to tidy up
aufstehen   to get up
aufwachen   to wake up
ausgehen   to go out
ausmachen   to switch off, turn off
die **Bettdecke** (-n)   blanket, duvet
das **Bett machen**   to make the bed
bügeln   to iron
decken   to set/lay (the table), to cover
duschen (**sich**)   to shower
einkaufen gehen   to go shopping

früh   early
frühstücken   to have breakfast
helfen   to help
ins Bett gehen   to go to bed
kochen   to cook
manchmal   sometimes
morgens   in the mornings
nach Hause gehen   to go home
oft   often
putzen   to clean (teeth etc.)
das **Regal (-e)**   shelf, shelving
sauber machen   to clean
selten   rare(ly)
Spaß machen   to be fun
Spaß haben   to have fun
spät   late
waschen (sich)   to wash
die **Zähne putzen (sich)**   to clean one's teeth
zu Hause   at home

Prepositions

an   on
auf   on
gegenüber   opposite
hinter   behind
in   in
neben   next to, beside, near to
vor   in front of, before
zwischen   between

Adjectives

allein   alone
besser   better
böse   angry, bad
eigen   own
ekelhaft   disgusting
ermüdend   tiring
erschöpft   exhausted
falsch   incorrect, false
gefährlich   dangerous
gleich   same
gut   good
gut gelaunt   in a good mood
hart   hard
hoch   high, tall
kaputt   broken
komisch   funny
kompliziert   complicated
kurz   short, brief
laut   loud, noisy
letzt   last
Lieblings-   favourite
nächst   next
neu   new
nötig   necessary
notwendig   necessary
nützlich   useful
prima   great
richtig   correct, true
ruhig   quiet, peaceful

sauber   clean
schlecht   bad
schlecht gelaunt   in a bad mood
schlimm   bad
schmutzig   dirty
schrecklich   terrible, dreadful
schwer   heavy, hard (difficult)
wahr   true

Conjunctions

aber   but
also   so, therefore, well
auch   also, too
dann   then
dass   that
oder   or
und   and
weil   because
wenn   if, when

Colours

blau   blue
braun   brown
dunkel   dark
gelb   yellow
grau   grey
grün   green
hell   bright, light
rot   red
schwarz   black
weiß   white

Musical instruments

die **Blockflöte (-n)**   recorder
die **Flöte (-n)**   flute
die **Geige (-n)**   violin
das **Klavier (-e)**   piano
das **Schlagzeug**   drums
die **Trompete (-n)**   trumpet

Sports and hobbies

angeln   to fish
ausgehen   to go out
ausruhen (sich)   to rest, relax
das **Brettspiel (-e)**   board game
die **Eisbahn (-en)**   skating rink
die **Freizeit**   free time, spare time
der **Fußball ("-e)**   football
gehören   to belong to
genießen   to enjoy
das **Hobby (-s)**   hobby, pastime
hören   to hear, listen to
jobben   to do casual jobs
joggen   to jog
der **Jugendklub (-s)**   youth club
die **Kegelbahn (-en)**   bowling alley
laufen   to run
lesen   to read
malen   to paint
die **Mannschaft (-en)**   team

musizieren   to play a musical instrument
der **Nachtklub (-s)**   nightclub
Rad fahren   to ride a bike, go cycling
reiten   to ride (a horse)
relaxen   to rest, relax
der **Roman (-e)**   novel
das **Schach**   chess
der **Schläger (-)**   racket
schwimmen   to swim
segeln   to sail
Ski laufen   to ski
spazieren gehen   to go for a walk
das **Spiel (-e)**   game, match
spielen   to play
der **Spieler (-)**/die **Spielerin (-nen)**   player
das **Spielzeug**   toy
Sport treiben   to do/play sport
das **Sportzentrum (-zentren)**   sports centre
springen   to jump
das **Stadion (Stadien)**   stadium
tanzen   to dance
das **Turnen**   gymnastics
wandern   to hike, go rambling
Wasserski fahren   to waterski
windsurfen   to windsurf
zeichnen   to draw

Time expressions

der **Abend (-e)**   evening
am nächsten Tag   on the following day
bald   soon, shortly
bis morgen   see you tomorrow
halb   half
heute   today
heute Abend   this evening
heute Morgen   this morning
im Frühling   in the spring
im Herbst   in the autumn
immer   always
im Sommer   in the summer
im Winter   in the winter
das **Jahr (-e)**   year
jeden Tag   every day
jetzt   now
der **Mittag**   midday
die **Mitternacht**   midnight
der **Monat (-e)**   month
der **Morgen (-)**   morning
morgen   tomorrow
morgen früh   tomorrow morning
der **Nachmittag (-e)**   afternoon
die **Nacht ("-e)**   night
pünktlich   punctual(ly), on time
der **Tag (-e)**   day
täglich   daily, every day
übermorgen   the day after tomorrow
der **Vormittag (-e)**   morning
die **Woche (-n)**   week
die **Zeit**   time

Thema 4 Die Schule

1 Ich besuche…

1 Bitte lies diese zwei Texte.

a Suche dir die fünf richtigen Sätze aus.

(1) Kevin besucht eine Schule für Jungen.
(2) Alle Schüler wohnen in der Schule.
(3) Kevin wohnt in der Schule.
(4) Kevins Schule ist in Afrika.
(5) Die Bibliothek ist sehr altmodisch.
(6) Zu Mittag isst Kevin in der Schule.
(7) Kevin kann jederzeit in der Schule einen Snack kaufen.
(8) Man kann am Nachmittag in der Schule schwimmen.
(9) Diese Schule besucht Kevin gern.
(10) Kevin trägt keine Schuluniform.

- ☑ Talk about the kind of school you go to
- ☑ Describe your school
- ☑ Talk about your uniform
- ☑ Understand how to use *kein*

Ich besuche eine kleine, gemischte Internatsschule. Es gibt nur 250 Schüler: 150 leben im Internat, und 100 sind Tagesschüler aus der Nähe. Ich bin Internatsschüler, weil meine Eltern in Afrika arbeiten.

Die Schule ist alt aber schön. Die Bibliothek hat man total modernisiert. Hier gibt es die modernste Kommunikationstechnologie, also nicht nur Bücher sondern auch PCs mit Internetzugang.

Wir nehmen alle Mahlzeiten in dem großen Speisesaal ein.

Da isst man gut, finde ich. Leider haben wir noch keinen Kiosk, und das ist eigentlich schade.

Die Sportnachmittage finde ich toll, weil wir eine moderne Turnhalle und ein neues Hallenbad haben. Abends findet oft ein Schauspiel in unserem Theater statt. Hier ist immer viel los!

Schuluniform gibt es nicht bei uns aber wir tragen keine Jeans. Die meisten Schüler tragen eine Hose, ein T-Shirt oder ein Hemd und einen Pulli oder so.

Kevin

Grammatik

A5, G4

Verneinung und Negationswörter
(negation and negative forms)

If you want to make a sentence negative, you usually place *nicht* after the verb.

    *Ich kann **nicht** schwimmen.*

In a longer sentence, *nicht* is sometimes placed at the end.

    *Ich kenne deinen Freund **nicht**.*

If you never do something, place *nie* after the verb.

    *Ich esse **nie** Fleisch.*

Kein means 'not a' or 'not any'. It is used instead of ***nicht ein***. It behaves just like ***ein***, but it also has a plural form:

	m	f	n	pl
Nominative	*kein*	*keine*	*kein*	*keine*
Accusative	*keinen*	*keine*	*kein*	*keine*
Dative	*keinem*	*keiner*	*keinem*	*keinen*

m *Es gibt **keinen** Kiosk.*
    There is**n't a** tuck shop.

f *Wir tragen **keine** Schuluniform.*
    We do **not** wear a school uniform.

n *Unsere Schule hat **kein** Sprachlabor.*
    Our school does **not** have a language lab.

pl *Meine Schule ist eine Mädchenschule, es gibt* **keine** *Jungen.*
    My school is for girls; there aren't **any** boys.

4/1

b Beantworte diese Fragen auf Deutsch.

(1) Was für eine Schule besucht Angelika?

(2) Wie ist die Schule?

(3) Was hat die Schule?

(4) Was machen die Schüler zu Mittag?

(5) Wie groß ist die Schule?

(6) Was trägt Angelika in der Schule?

Ich besuche eine sehr moderne, relativ große Gesamtschule. Die Gebäude sind alle nagelneu! Für den Unterricht gibt es viele Fachräume: Wir haben zum Beispiel ein Sprachlabor für Fremdsprachen. Für den Nachmittag haben wir eine große Sporthalle und vier Tennisplätze. Im Moment haben wir kein Schwimmbad.

Weil die Schule ganztags ist, gibt es eine Mensa. Hier essen Schüler und Lehrer zu Mittag. Für den kleinen Hunger haben wir auch ein Café.

Meine Schule ist gemischt und wir haben 750 Schüler. Es gibt etwa 40 Lehrer.

Bei uns gibt es keine Schuluniform. Normalerweise trage ich Jeans aber manchmal trage ich einen Rock, ein T-Shirt und eine Jacke.

Ich gehe sehr gern in meine Schule.

Angelika

2 💬 Macht Dialoge.

A Was für eine Schule besuchst du?

B *Ich besuche eine Realschule.*

A Wie groß ist deine Schule?

B *Es gibt 1000 Schüler und Schülerinnen und 80 Lehrer und Lehrerinnen.*

A Und wie ist deine Schule?

B *Sie ist gemischt und modern. Wir haben eine neue Bibliothek aber leider kein Schwimmbad.*

A Trägst du eine Schuluniform?

B *Ja, wir tragen eine Schuluniform. Ich trage einen schwarzen Rock, ein weißes Hemd und einen schwarzen Pulli. Die Uniform finde ich schrecklich!*

3 🎧 Was finden Christoph, Lara und Lukas positiv an der Schule? Und was finden sie negativ?

Mach Notizen.

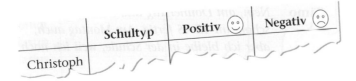

	Schultyp	Positiv 😊	Negativ 😞
Christoph			

Wie heißt es auf Englisch? Schlage im Wörterbuch nach.

A

die Gesamtschule

die Privatschule   das Gymnasium

das Internat   die Hauptschule

die Grundschule   die Realschule

B

der Schulhof

die Bibliothek   der Speisesaal

die Aula   die Mensa   der Kiosk

4 🏔 Beschreibe deine Schule. Schreib ein paar Sätze über die Schulgebäude, die Lehrer und Schüler und die Uniform usw.

Schule

3 Was ich heute gemacht habe...

1 📖 Bitte sieh dir Timos Stundenplan auf der Seite 36 an.

Jetzt lies diese E-mail von Timo.

Hallo Lara!

Hoffentlich geht's dir gut!

Heute ist Montag. Nach dem schönen Wochenende hat die Schule wieder begonnen.

Heute Morgen habe ich zuerst eine Doppelstunde Mathe gehabt. Ich bin nicht so begabt in Mathe aber ich habe mir große Mühe gegeben, alles richtig zu machen. In der Pause habe ich am Kiosk einen Snack gekauft: Ich habe ein Brötchen gegessen und einen Orangensaft getrunken. Ich habe auch auf dem Schulhof mit meinen Freunden geplaudert. Nach der Pause habe ich eine Stunde Sport gehabt: Wir haben in der Turnhalle Fußball gespielt, weil es draußen geregnet hat. Es hat enorm viel Spaß gemacht. Danach habe ich in der Französischstunde fleißig gearbeitet und wirklich viel gelernt. In der Religionsstunde habe ich auch viel geleistet.

Wir schreiben nächste Woche nämlich Klassenarbeiten und ich möchte gute Noten im Zeugnis bekommen, damit ich nicht sitzen bleiben muss. Meine Schwester hat letztes Jahr gar nicht gelernt und hat keine guten Noten im Zeugnis bekommen. So bleibt sie dieses Jahr sitzen, das heißt sie ist zum zweiten Mal im Jahrgang 10 und muss den gleichen Stoff wiederholen.

Zu Mittag habe ich noch ein Brötchen gegessen und am Nachmittag habe ich die Foto-AG gehabt. Da habe ich mich gut amüsiert und ganz viele Fotos gemacht. Mein Schultag hat um halb drei geendet. Zu Hause habe ich meine Hausaufgaben gemacht und nochmals für die Klassenarbeiten gelernt. So ein Stress!

Und du? Was hast du heute alles gemacht?

Dein Timo

Grammatik
Das Perfekt mit *haben* (1)
(perfect tense with haben*)*

F3

To talk about events in the past you need to:
- use expressions of time
  e.g. *heute Morgen*   this morning
      letztes Jahr   last year
      gestern   yesterday

- use the perfect tense

You need two parts to make the perfect tense:
- the correct form of *haben*
- the **past participle**

ich	habe	*wir*	haben
du	hast	*ihr*	habt
er/sie/es/man	hat	*Sie/sie*	haben

To form the past participle of regular verbs:
- take the infinitive, e.g. *kaufen*
- remove the *-en* at the end and add *-t*
- add *ge-* to the beginning of the word

So the past participle of *kaufen* is *gekauft*: *gekaufen*. The past participle *always* stays the same when *haben* is used to make the perfect tense.

(1) Look at Timo's description of his day in the e-mail. Find all the regular past participles.

(2) What happens to the verbs *arbeiten*, *enden* and *leisten*? Why do you think this happens?

(3) Have you noticed where the past participle stands in the sentence?

🖱 4/2

Grammatik

Das Perfekt mit *haben* (2) *(the perfect tense with* haben *continued)*

Some verbs have irregular past participles: they still have *ge-* at the beginning but they have *-en* at the end rather than *-t*:

e.g. infinitive = *geben*
past participle = *gegeben*

Sometimes the vowel changes as well:

e.g. infinitive = *trinken*
past participle = *getrunken*

There is a full list of all these irregular past participles on pages 164–165.

(1) Look at Timo's e-mail again. Can you spot any of these irregular past participles?

Verbs that begin with *be-*, *emp-*, *ver-* or that end in *-ieren* do not add *ge-* at the beginning to form the past participle. They end in *-t* or *-en* depending on whether they are regular.

(2) Can you find the two examples of such verbs in Timo's e-mail?

(3) Make a list of all examples of the perfect tense in Timo's e-mail.

⟲ 4/3

F3

3 🎧 Hör bitte zu. Was hat Elizabeth heute gemacht?

Setz diese Bilder in die richtige Reihenfolge.

2 🏔 Bitte bilde Sätze im Perfekt.

Beispiel
Ich – kaufen – gestern – Schokolade.
Ich habe gestern Schokolade gekauft.

(1) Er – spielen – in der Sportstunde – Fußball.
(2) Wir – surfen – in der Pause – im Internet.
(3) Ich – essen – zu Mittag – in der Kantine.
(4) Du – lernen – heute – Physik?
(5) Ich – lesen – gestern – Zeitschriften.
(6) Sie – telefonieren – in der zweiten Pause – mit ihrem Freund.
(7) Ihr – bekommen – im Zeugnis – gute Noten?
(8) Meine Eltern – sprechen – am Elternabend – mit den Lehrern.
(9) Wir – sehen – in Erdkunde – einen Dokumentarfilm.
(10) Die erste Stunde – beginnen – am Dienstag – um zwanzig nach acht.

4 💬 Beschreib deinen Schultag von gestern.

Beispiel

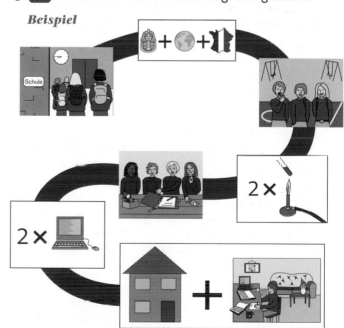

5 🏔 Schreib jetzt eine E-mail an Timo über deinen Schultag von heute oder gestern.

4 Ich bin zu spät gekommen…

Ich bin zu spät aufgestanden.

Mein Zug ist schon abgefahren.

Ich bin mit dem Bus gefahren.

Ich bin zum Chemieraum gegangen.

Ich bin zur Turnhalle gerannt.

Ich bin zu spät gekommen.

Ich bin im Musikraum gewesen.

1 Bitte sieh dir die Sätze oben und das Partizip Perfekt an. Kannst du die Infinitive finden?

Beispiel   *abgefahren – abfahren*

F3

Grammatik

Das Perfekt mit *sein* (the perfect tense with *sein*)

Most verbs form the perfect tense with *haben*. However, some verbs need *sein* to form the perfect tense:

- verbs of movement (e.g. *gehen, fliegen, fahren*)
- verbs that indicate a 'change of state' (e.g. *aufwachen*/to wake up, *einschlafen*/to go to sleep)
- *bleiben* (to stay)

Below is a reminder of the verb *sein* in full:

ich	bin	wir	sind
du	bist	ihr	seid
er/sie/es/man	ist	Sie/sie	sind

Most of the participles of verbs of movement are not regular as you saw in Übung 1, so you have to learn them. For the full list see pages 164–165.

Look at these example sentences:

> *Ich **bin** nach Hamburg **geflogen**.*
> I have flown to Hamburg.

> *Wir **sind** ins Theater **gegangen**.*
> We have gone to the theatre.

> *Er **ist** mit dem Auto **gefahren**.*
> He has gone by car.

> *Du **bist** zu Hause **geblieben**.*
> You have stayed at home.

Did you spot that the extra information in the sentence is placed between the form of *sein* and the participle? This is the same as with the verbs that use *haben*.

2 💬 🏰 Bitte macht sinnvolle Sätze und wählt die richtige Form von *sein*.

ich	**(sein)**	zur Schule	gerannt
du		nach Berlin	gekommen
er/sie/es		zur Turnhalle	gefahren
Sie		zum Bahnhof	gegangen
wir		zu spät	geschwommen
ihr		mit dem Bus	geflogen
sie		im Schwimmbad	geklettert
Sie		zu Fuß	geblieben
		zum Lehrerzimmer	

3 🎧 Bitte hör zu. Bei wem ist was passiert?

Beispiel

A	ist zu spät zur Schule gekommen	
B	Lehrer war böse	
C	ist mit dem Bus gefahren	
D	ist zur Schule gelaufen	1
E	ist in der Schule schwimmen gegangen	
F	ist zum Chemielabor gerannt	
G	ist fast eingeschlafen	

4 📖 Bitte setz die Sätze in die richtige Reihenfolge.

(1) *Der Bus ist schon um 7.48 abgefahren.*
(2) *Frau Müller, seine Französischlehrerin, ist sehr ärgerlich gewesen.*
(3) *Steffen ist heute zu spät aufgestanden.*
(4) *Er hat schnell gefrühstückt und nur eine Scheibe Toast ohne Butter gegessen.*
(5) *Sein Wecker ist kaputt.*
(6) *Er ist aus dem Haus gerannt.*
(7) *Steffen ist zu Fuß zur Schule gegangen.*
(8) *Steffen ist um 7.50 an der Bushaltestelle angekommen.*
(9) *Er ist zu spät zur Französischstunde gekommen.*

F3

Grammatik
Trennbare Verben im Perfekt
(*separable verbs in the perfect tense*)

Separable verbs take either *haben* or *sein* to make the perfect tense, depending on their meaning:

- *einschlafen, aufwachen, ankommen, abfahren* etc. all depict a change of state or a movement and take *sein*.
- *einkaufen, anrufen, anschauen, aufhören* etc. take *haben* to form the perfect tense.

The usual perfect prefix *ge-* is put in the middle of the separable verb and not at the beginning:
    aufwachen – **aufgewacht**
    einkaufen – **eingekauft**

The handy thing is that any irregular verbs stay equally irregular as part of a separable verb.
    kommen – **gekommen**
    ankommen – **angekommen**
    schlafen – **geschlafen**
    einschlafen – **eingeschlafen**

Haben **or** ***sein*****? Choose the correct verb form.**

(1) Timo _____ erst um 8 Uhr aufgewacht.
(2) Meine Mutter _____ in der Schule angerufen.
(3) In Biologie _____ wir einen Film angeschaut.
(4) Der Schulbus _____ zu spät abgefahren.
(5) Ich _____ in Deutsch fast eingeschlafen, weil es so langweilig war.
(6) Nach der Schule _____ Kerstin und ich eingekauft.
(7) Auf der Klassenfahrt _____ wir spät in der Jugendherberge angekommen.
(8) Die Kunststunde _____ schon um 12 Uhr aufgehört.

🖱 4/4

5 🏰 Wann bist du zu spät gekommen? Bitte schreib deine Geschichte auf.

- Wann war das?
- Wie bist du zur Schule gekommen?
- Warum bist du zu spät gekommen?
- Wie hat die Lehrerin/der Lehrer reagiert?

Thema 5 Berufe, Berufe...

2

1 Was soll ich werden?

1 📖 ✏️ Welcher Beruf ist das? Was passt zusammen? Schreib Sätze.

Tierarzt Verkäufer
Bankkauffrau Automechanikerin
Architekt Polizistin

☑ Learn how to describe different jobs

☑ Learn about masculine and feminine job titles

☑ Learn how to use sentences with *um...zu*

Beispiel *Frau Möller ist Polizistin.*

Ich mache Designs für ganz moderne Wohnhäuser mit viel Glas. Die Häuser sind auf dem Land oder auch im Zentrum der Stadt. Ich habe ein Büro in meinem Haus. Ich arbeite mit dem Computer, denn es gibt sehr gute Programme.

Gino Corelli

Tiere habe ich schon immer gern gehabt. Zu Hause hatten wir drei Hunde und viele Katzen. In den Ferien habe ich in einem Tierheim gearbeitet, um Erfahrung zu sammeln und später bessere Chancen an der Universität zu haben. Jetzt habe ich schon seit 5 Jahren meine eigene Praxis. Es gibt so viele verschiedene Probleme und es wird nie langweilig.

Dr. Stelios Zavos

Ich habe mich schon immer für Technik interessiert und meine Freunde haben mich ausgelacht. Das ist mir egal. Der Porsche ist mein Lieblingsauto. Wenn ich viel Geld habe, werde ich mir einen kaufen. Mein Beruf ist auch mein Hobby, super nicht? Man muss viel Geduld haben, um Autos zu reparieren.

Maria Platt

In meinem Beruf gibt es viel Stress und viel Schichtarbeit. Ich arbeite entweder in der Frühschicht von 6 Uhr bis 14 Uhr oder in der Spätschicht, dann komme ich erst um 22 Uhr nach Hause. Einmal pro Monat muss ich drei Nächte Nachtschicht machen. Wir müssen 24 Stunden erreichbar sein, um den Menschen zu helfen.

Marta Bosak

Ich arbeite in einem großen Elektrogeschäft. Ich berate die Kunden, um für sie den besten Computer, die beste Digitalkamera oder den besten DVD-Spieler auszuwählen. Manche Kunden möchten viel Geld ausgeben und andere weniger, aber bei uns gibt es viel Auswahl.

Jens Fink

Wir haben viele Kunden. Sie möchten Information über ihr Konto, brauchen Geld, um ein Haus zu kaufen oder nur eine neue Scheckkarte. Ich arbeite von 9.30 bis 12.30 an meinem Schalter, nachmittags arbeite ich in einem Büro der Bank oder habe Termine mit Kunden.

Frau Hansen

A9

Grammatik
Berufsbezeichnungen (*job titles*)

In German every job title has a feminine form.

* Usually you just add *-in* to the masculine form.
  der Designer – die Designerin
  der Musiker – die Musikerin

* When there is *-mann* at the end of the word for the masculine job title, it turns into *-frau* for a woman.
  der Geschäftsmann – die Geschäftsfrau

* Sometimes when there is an 'a' or an 'o' in the word for the masculine job title, the 'a'/'o' nearest the end is turned into 'ä'/'ö' in the feminine form, as it is easier to pronounce the word that way.
  der Arzt – die Ärztin
  der Rechtsanwalt – die Rechtsanwältin (solicitor)

Note: You do not need an article to give your or someone else's job title.
  Ich bin Polizistin. I am a policewoman.
  Er ist Architekt. He is an architect.

 5/1

2 📖 🔺 Bitte suche die Maskulin-/Femininformen für die Berufe in Übung 1 und für die folgenden Berufe:

> die Journalistin
> die Dolmetscherin der Programmierer
> der Zahnarzt die Köchin der Lehrer der Kassierer
> die Politikerin die Ingenieurin der Pilot
> der Informatiker

Schau die Wörter, die du nicht kennst, im Wörterbuch nach und schreib eine Liste.

Beispiel *der Tierarzt/die Tierärztin = vet*

3 📖 🔺 Bitte lies die Texte von Übung 1 noch einmal. Welches Wort passt?

> Schichtarbeit Programme Auswahl
> Erfahrung Praxis beraten Geduld
> Termine Schalter Kunden Computer

(1) Frau Hansen hat viele ____ mit ihren ____ .
(2) Dr. Zavos hat in den Ferien ____ gesammelt und hat jetzt seine eigene ____ .
(3) Für seine Designs hat Gino gute ____ .
(4) Maria muss viel ____ haben.
(5) Marta Bosak hat nur ____ .
(6) Jens Fink muss seine Kunden ____ .
(7) In dem Elektrogeschäft gibt es viel ____ .

4 💬 Bitte macht passende Sätze. Arbeite mit einem Partner.

> Briefträger
> Informatiker Physiotherapeut
> Sänger Krankenschwester
> Köchin Kassierer Journalist
> Frisör Sekretärin

Beispiel Ich möchte *Stewardess* werden, ____ .

> um Artikel für die Zeitung zu schreiben
> um in einem berühmten Salon zu arbeiten
> um viel mit Computern zu machen
> um kranke Sportler zu behandeln
> um viele Menschen zu treffen
> um gutes Essen zu kochen
> um an der frischen Luft zu sein
> um Opern zu singen

Grammatik G2

Nebensätze mit „um…zu"
(*subordinate clauses with 'um…zu'*)

If you want to say that you are doing something in order to achieve something, you use a construction with *um…zu* followed by the infinitive.

> *Ich möchte Dolmetscher werden,* **um** *im Ausland* **zu** *arbeiten.*
> I want to be an interpreter, in order to work abroad.

Note: If you are using a separable verb, the *zu* is put between the prefix and the main verb.

> *Ich fahre nach London, um Kleidung ein***zu***kaufen.*
> I go to London in order to shop for clothes.

Other constructions that use the infinitive are given in grammar reference section G2.

 5/2–5/4

5 🔺 Bitte schreib jetzt drei Sätze auf und mach drei neue Sätze, vielleicht für deinen Traumberuf.

6 💬 🔺 Sprich mit einem Partner und schreib einen Dialog auf.

A Was möchtest du werden?
B *Ich möchte ____ werden.*
A Warum?
B *Ich möchte ____ werden, um ____ zu ____ .*
A Und was möchtest du noch?
B *Ich möchte die Welt sehen/viele Leute treffen/mit Computern arbeiten…*
   Und du, was möchtest du werden?
A ____

7 🎧 Wer sagt was?

Beispiel *(1) Peter*

(1) Ich möchte viel Geld verdienen und oft Urlaub machen.
(2) Ich liebe Kinder, besonders kleine.
(3) Ich interessiere mich für Mathe und Naturwissenschaften und möchte in dem Bereich arbeiten.
(4) Ich möchte etwas Praktisches machen, habe Geduld und mag Elektrik.
(5) Ich möchte einen normalen Arbeitstag und keinen Stress.
(6) Ich möchte draußen arbeiten, aber nicht in der Bauindustrie.

2 Mein Arbeitspraktikum

1 📖 Lies bitte diese Texte.

Ich habe vor, nächstes Jahr ein Arbeitspraktikum in einer Autowerkstatt zu machen. Ich interessiere mich wahnsinnig für Autos: Mein Lieblingsauto ist ein VW Käfer. Ich muss wohl Kaffee kochen und Autos waschen aber ich lerne hoffentlich auch, wie man Autos repariert.

Christoph

Mein Betriebspraktikum mache ich nächste Woche in einer Buchhandlung. Ich bin eine leidenschaftliche Leseratte! Ich muss Kunden bedienen und sie beraten, wenn sie etwas Bestimmtes suchen. Ich habe vor, viele Bücher zu verkaufen! Die Auswahl ist ja schon enorm.

Helga

Nächsten Monat mache ich mein Arbeitspraktikum in einem Kindergarten. Nach der Schulzeit hoffe ich als Au-pair zu arbeiten, also brauche ich jetzt Erfahrungen. Ich bin sehr gern mit Menschen zusammen und ich freue mich darauf, mit den Kindern zu spielen und den Lehrern zu helfen.

Lukas

Weil ich mich sehr fürs Geld interessiere, habe ich die Absicht, mein Betriebspraktikum bei einer Bank zu erledigen. Hier lerne ich viel: Vielleicht arbeite ich mit einem Kollegen am Schalter, ich helfe den vielen Kunden, oder ich beantworte das Telefon usw.

Jens

Ende Mai mache ich ein Arbeitspraktikum bei einem Tierarzt. Ich freue mich darauf, weil ich Tiere unheimlich gern habe. In den letzten Sommerferien habe ich in einem Tierheim geholfen, um Erfahrungen zu sammeln. Wahrscheinlich lerne ich beim Tierarzt, die Tiere richtig zu behandeln.

Lara

a Wo machen diese Jugendlichen ihr Arbeitspraktikum? Finde das passende Bild für jede Person.

Name	Wo?	Warum?	Aufgaben?
Christoph	Autowerkstatt	interessiert sich für Autos	Autos waschen

b Was sind ihre Pläne? Mach jetzt Notizen.

2 📝 Schreib jetzt ein paar Sätze über deine Pläne für das Arbeitspraktikum.

Top-Tipp
Talking about your future plans

Ich habe vor,…	*nächste Woche*	*wahrscheinlich*
Ich hoffe,…	*nächste Monat*	*vielleicht*
Ich habe die Absicht,…	*nächste Jahr*	*wohl*
Ich freue mich auf…	*im Mai*	*hoffentlich*
	morgen	
	in 2 Tagen	

Adresse: @ http://www.sprachferien.at/DeutschArbeitspraktikum

> Explorer

Arbeitspraktikum in Wien

- **Willst du deine Deutschkenntnisse verbessern, deinen Wortschatz erweitern und dich besser in der Fremdsprache ausdrücken?**
- **Möchtest du Einblick in die Welt der Arbeit bekommen?**

Wir bieten folgende Bereiche für eine Praktikumsstelle in Wien an:

- **Tourismus: Restaurants, Hotels, Freizeit- bzw. Sportzentren, Reitställe**
- **Geschäfte: Musikladen, Sportgeschäft, Buchhandlung, Reisebüros**
- **Erziehung/Sozialbereich: Kindergärten, Volksschulen, Altersheime**
- **Landwirtschaft: Gartencenter, Bauernhof**
- **Büro**

Du wohnst bei einer netten Gastfamilie mit Vollpension. (Das ist die beste Art, Deutsch zu sprechen und Land und Leute besser kennen zu lernen!)

Hättest du Interesse daran, eine Gratisbroschüre zu bekommen? Gib bitte deine Interessen und Pläne an, damit wir dir entsprechende Infomaterialien schicken können.

Internet zone

3 Lies bitte diese Werbung aus dem Internet. Beantworte die folgenden Fragen.

(1) Nenne zwei Gründe aus der Anzeige, warum du vielleicht in Wien arbeiten möchtest.

(2) Wo kannst du dort wohnen?

(3) Was ist der Vorteil bei dieser Unterkunft?

(4) Du magst Sport. Wo möchtest du eine Praktikumsstelle?

(5) Und wenn du keinen Sport magst, aber gern draußen bist, wohin gehst du dann vielleicht?

(6) Du möchtest weitere Informationen. Wo findest du sie?

4 Hör bitte zu. Was macht Elizabeth in Wien? Mach Notizen.

(1) Arbeitspraktikum: wann? für wie lange? wo? warum?

(2) Gründe für den Aufenthalt in Wien?

(3) Arbeitsstunden?

(4) Aufgaben?

(5) Geld: was bekommt Elizabeth?

(6) Freizeitaktivitäten?

(7) Unterkunft?

(8) Meinung?

5 Mach jetzt eine Präsentation über dein Arbeitspraktikum. Du sollst erwähnen:

wann   für wie lange   wo   warum   Aufgaben

3 Nach dem Praktikum

„Na, wie war's? Was hast du gemacht?"

☑ **Talk about your work experience in the past**

1 📖 Kevin schreibt einen Bericht über sein Arbeitspraktikum für die Schulzeitung.

Ich habe 2 Wochen lang ein sehr interessantes Arbeitspraktikum in einer Metzgerei in England gemacht. Ich habe mich auf das Betriebspraktikum gefreut und es hat wirklich viel Spaß gemacht. Ich habe mein Englisch verbessert, weil ich so viel Englisch gesprochen habe. Ich habe auch gute Erfahrungen für meinen Traumberuf als Metzger gesammelt.

Die Stunden waren aber lang: Mein Arbeitstag hat schon um 9 Uhr morgens begonnen und hat erst um 6 Uhr abends geendet. Zu Mittag habe ich bloß eine Stunde Pause gehabt.

Die Arbeit war abwechslungsreich aber schon anstrengend: Im Geschäft habe ich die Kunden bedient und manchmal habe ich an der Kasse gearbeitet. Mindestens achtmal täglich habe ich Tee gekocht! Ich habe auch abgewaschen.

Ich habe von Dienstag bis Samstag gearbeitet. Abends bin ich zu müde gewesen, um etwas zu unternehmen. Am Sonntag und am Montag hatte ich frei: So habe ich mich ausgeschlafen und die vielen Sehenswürdigkeiten besichtigt.

Meine Kollegen sind freundlich und hilfsbereit gewesen. Sie haben mir viel geholfen. Leider habe ich kein Geld verdient und auch keine Trinkgelder bekommen.

Ich habe mich gut amüsiert und die ganze Erfahrung war toll! Das Praktikum war mir ein bisschen zu kurz: 3 Wochen wären viel besser gewesen.

a Wie war das Arbeitspraktikum?
Was hat Kevin positiv gefunden?
Was hat er negativ gefunden?
Mach Notizen.

Positiv ☺	Negativ ☹
hat Spaß gemacht	

b Füll jetzt bitte dieses Formular aus.

	Arbeitspraktikum der Klasse 10
Name	Kevin Schmidt
Wo?	
Wie lange?	
Grund für dieses Praktikum	
Routine	
Aufgaben	
Kollegen	
Meinung	

2a 🎧 Hör bitte zu. Magdalena, Evangelos und Angelika sprechen über ihr Arbeitspraktikum.

Was haben sie gemacht?
Was passt zusammen?

(1) (2) (3) (4) (5) (6)

b Hör noch einmal zu.
Füll jetzt bitte die Tabelle aus.

Name	Wo?	Warum?	Was (Aufgaben)?	Meinung	Andere Information
Magdalena					

3 💬 Wer ist das? **a** *A* beschreibt ein Arbeitspraktikum. *B* rät, welches es ist.

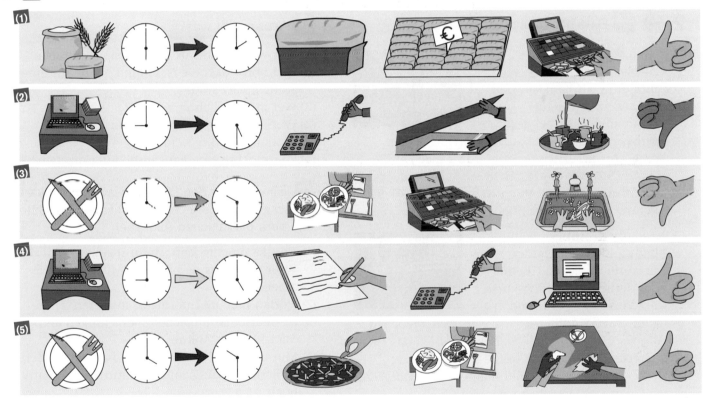

b 💬 Macht jetzt Interviews.

Beispiel **A** Wo hast du dein Arbeitspraktikum gemacht? **B** *Ich habe in einem Geschäft gearbeitet.*
A Was hast du gemacht? **B** *Ich habe die Kunden bedient.*
A Wann hast du gearbeitet? **B** *Ich habe die Tag von 09.00 bis 17.30 gearbeitet.*
A Wie hast du die Arbeit gefunden? **B** *Ich habe die Arbeit sehr langweilig gefunden.*
A Wie waren die Arbeitskollegen? **B** *Die Arbeitskollegen waren sehr freundlich.*

4 📝 Schreib jetzt einen Bericht über dein Arbeitspraktikum. Deine Meinung nicht vergessen!
Schreib ungefähr 75 Wörter. Du kannst die Details erfinden, wenn du kein Praktikum gemacht hast.
- Wo und wann hast du dein Praktikum gemacht?
- Was hast du gemacht und wie lange hast du jeden Tag gearbeitet?
- Wie hast du das Praktikum und deine Kollegen gefunden?

Thema 6 ...und in Zukunft?

1 Wie geht es weiter?

☑ **Discuss your plans for after your exams**

☑ **Learn to use the future tense**

1 📖 Hier sind ein paar wichtige Vokabeln. Bitte kombiniere das deutsche Wort mit einem englischen.

die Oberstufe
der Grundkurs   die Ausbildung
die Berufsschule   die Mittlere Reife
der/die Auszubildende   das Abitur
der Leistungskurs

A-levels   training
vocational school   minor subject
sixth form   major subject
trainee   GCSEs (German pupils leaving the Realschule or the Gymnasium at 16)

2 🎧 📖 Bitte hör zu und lies mit.

Lisa Ich werde die Schule verlassen und habe vor, eine Ausbildung als Bankkauffrau zu machen. Ich werde als Auszubildende bei der Sparkasse arbeiten und auch einen Tag in der Woche zur Berufsschule gehen. Das machen die meisten Schüler, die 16 bis 18 Jahre alt sind. Man lernt noch etwas mehr Englisch und auch Fächer, die für einen Beruf wichtig sind.

Elke Ich beabsichtige, mein Abitur zu machen. In der Oberstufe werde ich Chemie und Mathe als Leistungskurse wählen und Englisch und Biologie als Grundkurse. Als Wahlfach werde ich auf jeden Fall Erdkunde wählen, weil ich das interessant finde. Dann werde ich Pharmazie studieren. Hoffentlich sind meine Noten gut genug für einen Studienplatz an der Uni.

Kristian Also ich habe keine Lust mehr. Die Schule ist mir zu langweilig und ich möchte lieber etwas Praktisches lernen. Ich möchte eine Lehre als Automechaniker machen und werde am 1. September als Lehrling in einer VW-Werkstatt anfangen.

Sergej Ich plane, Lehrer zu werden und werde mich für die Hochschule in Köln bewerben, wenn es geht. Ich möchte an einer Hauptschule unterrichten. In der Oberstufe werde ich als Abifächer Deutsch, Sport, Geschichte und Musik nehmen.

3 💬 Wer macht was?

(1) Wer wird Mathe als Leistungskurs nehmen und hofft, dass die Noten gut genug für einen Studienplatz sind?
(2) Wer möchte Lehrer werden?
(3) Wer möchte mit der Schule aufhören und Automechaniker werden?
(4) Wer möchte eine Bankausbildung machen?

4 🎧 Bitte hör dir den Dialog zwischen Annika und Florian an. Was ist richtig, was ist falsch? Bitte korrigiere die falschen Aussagen.

(1) Annika möchte kein Abitur machen, weil ihr Vater will, dass sie nach der Mittleren Reife arbeitet.
(2) Florian möchte Informatik studieren.
(3) In Deutschland machen mehr Jungen als Mädchen das Abitur.
(4) Mit Abitur hat man bessere Chancen im Beruf.
(5) In Berlin ist die Zahl der Abiturienten relativ hoch.
(6) Nicht alle Abiturienten studieren.
(7) Annika hat in der Zeitung Jobinformationen gefunden.
(8) Sie denkt, dass Kauffrau für Marketingkommunikation der ideale Beruf ist.

5 💬 Macht Dialoge über eure Pläne. Was habt ihr vor?

A Was wirst du nach der Mittleren Reife machen?
B *Ich habe vor, mein Abitur zu machen, und du?*
A Ich werde einen Beruf erlernen.
B *Was wirst du machen und wie lange wird die Ausbildung dauern?*

A Welche Abifächer wirst du wählen?
B *Ich werde ____ als Leistungskurse und ____ als Grundkurse wählen.*

6 📖 Bitte lies den Zeitungstext und kombiniere die Sätze.

(1) Es gibt weniger Männer als Frauen in Deutschland…

(2) In Finnland ist die Abiturientenquote…

(3) In Mecklenburg-Vorpommern…

(4) Viele Abiturienten…

(5) Sehr viele von den Berliner Abiturienten…

(6) Die Zahl der Abiturienten ist in Deutschland…

a …nicht überall gleich.

b …wollen studieren.

c …die ihr Abitur machen.

d …sehr hoch.

e …machen eine Berufsausbildung.

f …machen nur Frauen das Abitur.

g …gibt es weniger Abiturienten als in Nordrhein-Westfalen.

h …gibt es viele Studenten.

Berlin — In der Bundesrepublik machen fast 40% aller Schüler Abitur. Die Abiturientenquote liegt bei Frauen höher als bei Männern, das heißt mehr Mädchen machen Abitur. In Finnland machen fast 80% aller Schüler ihr Abitur. Aber auch in Deutschland gibt es große Unterschiede. In Mecklenburg-Vorpommern haben 2003 nur 28% einer Altersstufe ihr Abitur gemacht, aber in Nordrhein-Westfalen waren es in dem Jahr 48%. Viele Abiturienten machen eine Berufsausbildung und studieren nicht. Die höchste Studentenquote ist bei den Schülern aus Berlin.

7 📝 Bitte schreib eine E-mail an deine Freundin über deine Pläne nach den Prüfungen.

Hallo Bettina,

Nächstes Jahr mache ich meine Prüfungen. Ich habe vor ———— . Ich werde ———— .

Grammatik

Das Futur (*the future*)

When you want to express what you are going to do in the future, you have several options in German:

- You can indicate what you are going to do by using a verb showing your intention (e.g. *Ich beabsichtige, Medizin zu studieren*/I intend to study medicine). This is known as 'future intent'.
- You can use the present tense, but you must indicate a 'time' — *am Donnerstag, im Sommer, nächste Woche* etc. (e.g. *Nächstes Jahr studiere ich Medizin*/ Next year I'll study medicine).
- You can use the future tense (*Ich werde Medizin studieren*/I will study medicine).

The future tense is formed from the verb *werden* and the infinitive, with any extra information placed in between *werden* and the infinitive.

ich	*werde*	*wir*	*werden*
du	*wirst*	*ihr*	*werdet*
er/sie/es/man	*wird*	*Sie/sie*	*werden*

(1) **Look again at Übung 2 and find two more examples of 'future intent'.**

(2) **Look again at Übung 2 and find four examples of the future tense.**

C4, F6

(3) **Complete these sentences with the correct form of *werden*.**

(a) Ich _____ Chemie wählen.

(b) Wir _____ eine Lehre machen.

(c) Du _____ keine Lehrstelle finden.

(d) Ihr _____ zur Berufsschule gehen.

(e) _____ sie (*she*) Englisch in der Oberstufe nehmen?

(f) Er _____ sofort arbeiten.

(4) **Change these sentences from the present tense into the future tense.**

(a) Sie verlässt die Schule.

(b) Wir lernen für das Abitur.

(c) Ihr sammelt praktische Erfahrung.

(d) Sie verbessert ihr Englisch

(e) Sie nimmt als Wahlfach Sport.

(5) **Below are three sentences in the future tense. Choose an expression of time and change them into the present tense.**

Ich werde nach Italien fliegen.
Nächste Woche fliege ich nach Italien.

(a) Er wird Automechaniker lernen.

(b) Wir werden Abitur machen.

(c) Du wirst die Berufsschule besuchen.

6/1

2 ...und nach dem Abitur?

☑ Talk more about your future plans

☑ Use adverbs to express probability

1 📖 Bitte lies, was diese Schüler sagen und achte auf die Wörter *wahrscheinlich, natürlich, auf jeden/keinen Fall, vielleicht, eventuell, möglicherweise*.

Diese Schüler möchten Abitur machen, aber was dann?

> *Ich habe in den Ferien ein Praktikum in einer Autowerkstatt gemacht. Das war ganz nett. Vielleicht mache ich das nach dem Abitur noch einmal. Nein, Automechaniker will ich auf keinen Fall werden, aber ich finde Maschinen interessant. Ich möchte eventuell Ingenieur werden und wenn meine Note in Mathe gut ist, will ich vielleicht Maschinenbau in München studieren. Möglicherweise werde ich mich auch um einen Studienplatz als Bauingenieur bewerben.*
>
> **Timo**

> *Ich werde direkt nach dem Abitur mit meiner Ausbildung als Computerfachfrau beginnen. Ich möchte so schnell wie möglich fertig sein und Geld verdienen.*
>
> **Sonja**

> *Mm, ich weiß es nocht nicht genau. Vielleicht plane ich ein Jahr im Ausland. Ich möchte etwas von der Welt sehen. Mein Vater hat Kollegen in Amerika, dort kann ich vielleicht wohnen. Vielleicht finde ich einen Job in einem Café oder so. Auf jeden Fall möchte ich mein Englisch verbessern, weil Englisch in der Berufswelt sehr wichtig ist.*
>
> **Annika**

> *Ich werde möglicherweise in einem sozialen Beruf arbeiten und vielleicht studieren, eventuell Sozialpädagogik. Ich werde wahrscheinlich ein soziales Jahr in einem Altenheim machen. Die Menschen dort erzählen viele Geschichten aus ihrer Jugend, die oft sehr lustig sind.*
>
> **Steffen**

> *Ich möchte Medizin studieren und vielleicht Kinderärztin werden. Wahrscheinlich werde ich in München studieren, wenn ich dort einen Studienplatz bekomme. Ich fange sofort im Wintersemester an, denn das Studium ist sehr lang.*
>
> **Bettina**

Wer macht was *vielleicht, auf jeden/keinen Fall, natürlich*?

Bitte sieh dir die Texte an und mach Notizen.

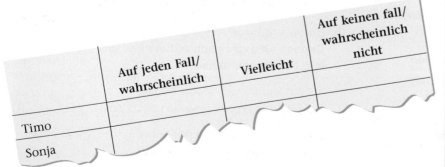

	Auf jeden Fall/ wahrscheinlich	Vielleicht	Auf keinen fall/ wahrscheinlich nicht
Timo			
Sonja			

C5

Grammatik

Adverbien (*adverbs*)

You can use adverbs to explain how likely something is to happen in the future. Look at the table opposite for examples and check that you know the meaning of each one. Remember: when you start a sentence with one of these, you need to invert the verb.

> *Ich werde in München studieren.*
> *Wahrscheinlich werde ich in München studieren.*

Look in the texts above and find three more adverbs that are used in this way.

🖱 6/2

2 💬 Bitte macht Dialoge. Du bist Timo oder Anna und du bist du selbst.

Beispiel

A Was machst du nach dem Abitur?

B *Ich werde wahrscheinlich eine Ausbildung machen.*

A Was wirst du machen?

B *Ich habe vor, Bankkaufmann zu lernen.*

A Und wie lange wird die Ausbildung dauern?

B *3 Jahre.*

A Und was wirst du dann machen?

B *Ich werde vielleicht bei der Deutschen Bank arbeiten.*

A Und was wirst du danach machen?

B _____

3 🏔 Bitte schreib zwei Pläne auf. Bitte nimm das Futur.

a Den Plan von Timo oder Anna:

Anna wird _____ . Sie wird vielleicht _____ .

b Deinen Plan:

Ich werde möglicherweise _____ . Wahrscheinlich werde ich _____ . Ich beabsichtige _____ . Ich habe eventuell vor _____ .

4 🎧 Bitte hör den drei Jugendlichen (Timo, Bettina und Annika) zu und suche das richtige Wort für die Lücken.

Timo muss für die _____ lernen. Er hat sich um einen _____ in München beworben, aber er weiß nicht, ob er dort studieren kann, weil er vielleicht in Mathe keine gute _____ bekommt.

Bettina hat vor, _____ zu studieren. Sie wird im Wintersemester _____, aber vorher _____ sie noch in Spanien Urlaub machen.

Annika plant ein Jahr im _____, um ihr Englisch zu _____ . Sie wird dort nicht _____, sondern eine _____ suchen.

3 Ich suche einen Job...

1 📖 Lies bitte diese Anzeige.

☑ **Apply for a job**
☑ **Understand *Sie* form of address**

Restaurant zum Hungrigen Mann

Freundliches Familienrestaurant sucht Mitarbeiter für die Sommerferien.

Sie
- haben Spaß am Kontakt mit Gästen.
- arbeiten gerne im Team.
- sind jung, motiviert, dynamisch.
- haben ein Flair für die Gastronomie.
- sprechen Deutsch und Französisch?

Abwechslungsreiche Beschäftigung an der Kasse, in der Küche oder direkt im Restaurant.

Sie sollten sich noch heute schriftlich bewerben bei

Frau Hana Huber
Restaurant Zum Hungrigen Mann
Seestraße 200
8820 Wädenswil (CH)

Grammatik

Du oder Sie? (du *or* Sie?)

D2

In German there are two modes of address (ways of talking to people): the formal *Sie* and the informal *du*. This causes confusion for English speakers as both of these words are translated by 'you'. The *du* form is always used by children and young people talking to each other, and for adults to talk to children and those younger than themselves. The *Sie* form is used when children and young people talk to adults not in their family, or when adults talk to each other in a formal situation such as a work meeting.

You will notice that the *Sie* form is used for the instructions in your exam, whereas the more informal *du* form is used for instructions in this book. *Sie* always begins with a capital letter, but *du*, and its plural form *ihr*, do not, unless they are the first word in a sentence.

 6/3

Was stimmt, der Anzeige nach?

(1) Diese Arbeitsstelle ist _____ .
fest/langweilig/provisorisch

(2) Teamarbeit ist _____ .
nötig/schlecht/unwichtig

(3) Der Mitarbeiter kann _____ .
Auto fahren/Fremdsprachen/kochen

(4) Man arbeitet _____ im Restaurant.
immer/nur/auch

(5) Man kann sich nur _____ bewerben.
telefonisch/per E-mail/per Brief

2a 📖 Lies bitte diesen Bewerbungsbrief.

Somerset, den 9. Mai

Sehr geehrte Frau Huber,

Ich habe Ihre Anzeige in der Zeitung gelesen und ich möchte mich um den Job als Mitarbeiterin in Ihrem Restaurant bewerben.

Ich habe schon Erfahrung, weil ich 2 Wochen Arbeitspraktikum in einem Restaurant in Wien gemacht habe. Ich habe auch einen Nebenjob in einem Café.

Ich glaube, ich werde diese Arbeit sehr interessant finden, weil ich gern mit Menschen zusammen bin und ich mich für eine Karriere als Köchin interessiere.

Ich komme aus England aber ich habe gute Deutschkenntnisse: Ich lerne Deutsch in der Schule und ich habe einen Aufenthalt in Österreich gemacht, um mein Deutsch zu verbessern.

Ich kann vom 8. Juli bis 30. August arbeiten.

Sie könnten mich zu jeder Zeit unter 00 44 1935 706696 erreichen.

Mit freundlichen Grüßen,

Elizabeth Smith

b 🖍 Beginne bitte, das Bewerbungsformular für Elizabeth auszufüllen.

Bewerbungsformular: Restaurant zum Hungrigen Mann

Name: ....

Vorname: ....

Alter: ....　Geburtsdatum: ....

Nationalität: ....

Adresse: ....

....

Telefon: ....

Schulausbildung: ....

....

Arbeitserfahrung: ....

Sprachkenntnisse (sehr gut/gut): ....

....

Eigenschaften: ....

....

Hobbys: ....

Warum möchten Sie bei uns arbeiten? ....

---

3 🎧 Hör bitte dem Vorstellungsgespräch gut zu. Jetzt füll das Bewerbungsformular komplett aus.

4a 📖 Lies bitte diese Anzeigen.

(1)

Für den Kindergarten
St. Maria von den Engeln
suchen wir vom **1. 7. bis zum 31. 8.**
für 20 Wochenstunden eine/n Mithelfer(in).

Sie
– arbeiten im Team und sind engagiert und kreativ
– sind zuverlässig und belastbar
– sind musikalisch und ideenreich

Bitte senden Sie Ihre Bewerbungsunterlagen an die Kath. Kirchengemeinde St. Margareta, Pastoratstr. 20, 50321 Brühl

(2)

Wir suchen nettes, fleißiges Zimmermädchen für unser Team ab sofort oder nach Vereinbarung. Hotel Ludwig, Köln, Nordrhein-Westfalen 0221/160540.

(3)

Wir suchen: Jungschauspieler
kurz gesagt, jede Art von Talent für Bühne, Film und Fernsehen.

Pro GmbH Casting, Goebenstr. 14, 50672 Köln

b 💬 Bitte macht ein Rollenspiel.

A hat ein Vorstellungsgespräch für einen Job (entweder (1), (2) oder (3)). *B* macht das Interview. Dann ist *B* dran.

B Wie heißen Sie? ....　A _____

B Wie alt sind Sie? ....　A _____

B Woher kommen Sie? ....　A _____

B Sind Sie Schüler(in)? ....　A _____

B Haben Sie Arbeitserfahrung? ....　A _____

B Was sind Ihre Eigenschaften? ....　A _____

B Was für Hobbys haben Sie? ....　A _____

B Haben Sie vielleicht Fragen? ....

A Was sind die Arbeitsstunden? ....　B _____

A Und wie viel werde ich verdienen? ....　B _____

5 🖍 Du möchtest dich um einen Job in Übung 4 bewerben. Schreib einen Bewerbungsbrief: Du kannst Elizabeths Brief adaptieren.

Schreib 75 bis 100 Wörter.

• Du möchtest dich um den Job als... bewerben. Wie heißt der Job?

• Hast du Erfahrung? Nenne Details.

• Wann kannst du arbeiten?

4 Im Büro

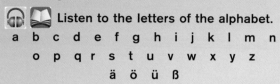
1a 📖 Lies diesen Zettel und beantworte die Fragen.

> Herr Schäfer von der Firma Hansen hat um 11 Uhr angerufen. Er möchte einen Termin ausmachen. Er kann sich am Freitag, den 14. März um 14.30 Uhr mit Ihnen treffen. Bitte rufen Sie ihn zurück. Seine Telefonnummer ist 0561 46 37 82.

(1) Wer hat angerufen?
(2) Um wie viel Uhr hat er angerufen?
(3) Was möchte er?
(4) Wann kann er sich mit dem Chef treffen?
(5) Was muss der Chef machen?
(6) Wie ist seine Telefonnummer?

b 🎧 Du arbeitest in einem Büro. Du hörst die Nachrichten auf Voicemail für den Manager ab. Füll die Lücken auf Deutsch oder mit Ziffern aus.

> (1) Frau **a** _____ hat um **b** _____ Uhr angerufen. Sie kann am **c** _____ Oktober nicht kommen. Bitte rufen Sie sie zurück. Ihre Telefonnummer ist 0632 **d** _____ 11 20.

> (2) Herr **a** _____ hat angerufen. Er hat eine Frage. Er wird Ihnen eine **b** _____ schicken.

> (3) Herr **a** _____ hat angerufen. Er muss den Termin am **b** _____ Juni ändern. Der 24. Juni um **c** _____ Uhr ist besser für ihn. Können Sie ihn bitte zurückrufen? Seine Nummer ist 0785 22 63 **d** _____.

Top-Tipp
Das Alphabet

🎧 📖 **Listen to the letters of the alphabet.**

a b c d e f g h i j k l m n
o p q r s t u v w x y z
ä ö ü ß

Grammatik
Fragen bilden (*forming questions*)

Inversion

You can form questions by inverting the verb. Start the sentence with the verb and put the subject second:

Haben Sie am Donnerstag Zeit?

Do you have time on Thursday?

Können Sie ihn bitte zurückrufen?

Can you ring him back please?

Question words

You can also form a question by starting the sentence with a question word. This will be followed by the verb and then the subject.

Wer hat angerufen?

Who has telephoned?

Wann kann sie kommen?

When can she come?

Wer?	Who?
Wo?	Where?
Wann?	When?
Was?	What?
Wie?	How?
Warum?	Why?
Wie viel(e)?	How much? How many?
Um wie viel Uhr?	(At) what time?
Welcher/welche/welches?	Which?

The question word *welcher* declines like *der/die/das* (see page 153).

2a  Lies dieses Gespräch mit einem Partner vor. *A* arbeitet im Büro. *B* ruft an.

b Macht Dialoge mit anderen Details.

A

> Guten Tag. Kann ich Ihnen helfen?

> Herr Schmidt am Apparat. Kann ich bitte Frau Hübner sprechen?

B

> Es tut mir Leid, aber Frau Hübner ist im Moment nicht da.

> Wann kommt sie wieder?

> Sie wird heute Nachmittag wieder im Büro sein.

> Kann sie mich bitte um 15 Uhr zurückrufen? Ich möchte einen Termin ausmachen.

> Ja, natürlich. Ich werde es ihr ausrichten. Wie ist Ihre Telefonnummer?

> Bitte schön. Auf Wiederhören.

> Meine Telefonnummer ist 0487 61 29 50. Viclen Dank. Auf Wiederhören.

3 Schreib eine E-mail an Frau Hübner mit den Informationen aus Übung 2. Du hast den Terminkalender von Frau Hübner vor dir. Schreib:

- wer angerufen hat
- wann er angerufen hat
- was er wollte

- was Frau Hübner machen soll.
- Schlag einen Termin vor, wann Frau Hübner sich mit Herrn Schmidt treffen kann.
- Stell Frau Hübner eine Frage über die Arbeit oder das Büro.

Nachricht					_ □ ✕
Datei	Edit	Überblick	Text formatieren	Werkzeuge	

An: Frau Hübner

Senden Betreff: Anruf von Herrn Schmidt

5300-jähriger Mann im Eis gefunden

Südtirol ist eine Region in Norditalien, wo fast 70% der Einwohner Deutsch sprechen. Viele Touristen fahren dorthin, um in den hohen Bergen zu wandern oder zu klettern. Im Sommer 1991 war es sogar oben auf den Bergen ungewöhnlich heiß. Ein deutscher Bergsteiger, Helmut Simon, und seine Frau Erika haben am 19. September eine Wanderung im Gebirge gemacht. Als sie einen Körper im Eis gefunden haben, haben sie die Polizei gerufen.

Dieser männliche Körper hat über 5000 Jahre im Eis in den Ötztaler Alpen gelegen! Journalisten haben ihm den Namen „Ötzi" gegeben. Wenn man Geschichte als Lieblingsfach mag, hat man viele Fragen: Wer war Ötzi? Wie hat er gelebt? Was hat er gegessen? Archäologen wissen schon: Er war etwa 1,60m groß und ungefähr 45 Jahre alt. Er hatte schulterlange, dunkle, lockige Haare und einen Bart. Als Kleidung hat er einen Mantel, eine Mütze und eine Art Hose getragen. Auch Schuhe aus Leder.

Was war er von Beruf? Bauer, Künstler, Fleischer vielleicht? Man hat Fleischreste in seinem Magen gefunden. Was hat seinen Tod verursacht? Eine Krankheit? Ein Unfall? Oder ist er durch Gewalt gestorben? An der linken Schulter war er verletzt. Streit mit einem Nachbarn oder mit einem Verwandten? So viele Fragen!

Um mehr über Ötzi zu lernen, muss man ins Südtiroler Museum in Bozen gehen. Dort liegt der Körper in einem kühlen Raum bei Temperaturen von minus 6 Grad Celsius.

1 📖 Sind diese Sätze richtig oder falsch? **Fünf** sind richtig. Korrigiere die falschen Sätze.

(1) Die Mehrzahl der Südtiroler spricht Italienisch.

(2) Im Sommer 1991 waren die Temperaturen höher als normal.

(3) Helmut Simon ist mit seiner Freundin gewandert.

(4) Ötzi ist seit über einem Jahrhundert tot.

(5) Der Körper im Eis war von einem Mann und nicht von einer Frau.

(6) Wir wissen nichts über Ötzis Aussehen.

(7) Ötzi ist als Jugendlicher gestorben.

(8) Als Ötzi lebte, trugen die Menschen keine Kleider.

(9) Wir wissen, dass Ötzi Tiere gegessen hat.

(10) Museumsbesucher können den Mann aus dem Eis in Italien sehen.

PROBLEMPUNKT Feste

Frage von Lukas99:

Hey, ich habe gehört, dass die Busse und Bahnen morgen streiken. Ich habe eine wichtige Mathe-Prüfung und komme normalerweise mit dem Bus zur Schule. Mathe will ich später an der Uni studieren und ich brauche eine gute Note! Meine Eltern haben kein Auto, also können sie mir nicht helfen. Schlimm, nicht? Was soll ich machen?

Antwort von SuperMax:

Furchtbar! Du bist fleißig und willst lernen, aber die Erwachsenen interessieren sich nicht dafür. Sie finden ihre eigenen Probleme wichtiger. Typisch! Ich würde mit dem Taxi zur Schule fahren. Sicher ist das teuer, aber es geht um deine Zukunft, oder? Weiß jemand, warum es diesen Streik überhaupt gibt?

Antwort von Überklug20:

Ich glaube, die Bus- und Bahnfahrer streiken, um einen höheren Lohn zu bekommen. Das kann ich ja verstehen. Sie wollen auch nicht zu viele Stunden an einem Tag arbeiten. Warum findest du das so schlimm? Es ist nur für einen Tag. Bleib einfach im Bett und entspanne dich morgen!

Antwort von Rosarot:

Also, du bleibst morgen zu Hause, ja? Und was erreichst du dann? Versuch doch irgendwie zur Schule zu gehen. Ruf doch einen Freund an. Vielleicht kannst du mit ihm fahren. Du musst diese Prüfung machen, sonst bekommst du eine schlechte Note. Kannst du nicht zu Fuß gehen – oder mit dem Rad fahren? Es ist egal, was andere Leute denken. Deine Noten sind wichtig!

2 📖 Finde diese Ausdrücke auf Deutsch.

> to study at university
> a good mark
> hard-working
> it's about your future
> to get a higher wage
> you must do this test

3 🏫 Welche Antwort findest du am besten und warum? Oder hast du eine bessere Idee? Schreib deine eigene Meinung an Lukas in ungefähr 50 Wörtern.

Einschulung

In Deutschland kommt ein Kind mit sechs Jahren in die Schule. Der erste Tag heißt die Einschulung. Das ist ein besonderer Tag für jedes Kind. Als Geschenk bekommen die Kinder in Deutschland, Österreich und in einigen Orten in der Schweiz eine Schultüte. Diese Tüte ist sehr groß, manchmal fast so groß wie das Kind selbst! Die Eltern können bunte Tüten in allen Farben kaufen oder sie machen sie zu Hause. In der Schultüte findet man Süßigkeiten, Puppen oder Spielzeuge und auch nützliche Dinge für die Schule wie Bleistifte, Radiergummis, Lineale.

St. Galler Kinderfest

In St. Gallen in der Schweiz feiern die Schulkinder das Kinderfest. Dieses Fest findet alle drei Jahre kurz vor den Sommerferien statt. Da das Wetter schön sein muss, weiß man das genaue Datum vorher nicht. Alle Schulen in der Stadt bleiben geschlossen. Die Schüler marschieren in einem langen Umzug zum Kinderfestplatz, wo sie singen und tanzen. Sie ziehen helle Kleider an, tragen Ballons, Blumen und Fahnen und essen Kinderfestbratwurst, eine Spezialität aus St. Gallen.

4 📖 Such für jede Lücke das Wort, das am besten passt.

(1) Bei der Einschulung ist ein Kind .... als fünf.
(2) Ein Kind .... am ersten Tag eine Schultüte.
(3) Die Schultüte ist .... mit Geschenken.
(4) Das Kinderfest findet nicht statt, wenn das Wetter .... ist.
(5) Am Kinderfesttag gibt es keinen .... an den Schulen.

älter	schlecht
bekommt	Schulhof
gibt	sonnig
jünger	Unterricht
leer	voll

🎧 Paper 1: listening

The question tests your ability to match what you hear to a visual stimulus or a written clue. The passage is in two parts.

Sie hören zweimal Informationen über die Schule und das Arbeitspraktikum. Schreiben Sie die Antworten **auf Deutsch** oder in Ziffern und kreuzen Sie die richtigen Kästchen an.

Meine Schule

1 Was ist Anjas Lieblingsfach? (Kreuzen Sie ein Kästchen an.)

A	
B	
C	

1913	1901 1066
	1989 1665
	1415 1492 1666
C	14 1929 1588

[1]

2 Wie viele Schüler gibt es in Ihrer Schule? .... Schüler.   [1]

3 Was findet Anja negativ? (Kreuzen Sie ein Kästchen an.)

A	
B	
C	

[1]

[PAUSE]

4 Wo hat Anja ihr Arbeitspraktikum gemacht? (Kreuzen Sie ein Kästchen an.)

A	
B	
C	

  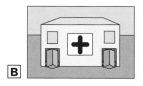 

[1]

5 Der Arbeitstag hat um .... Uhr begonnen.   [1]

6 Jeden Tag hatte sie .... Stunden frei.   [1]

7 Die Arbeit? (Kreuzen Sie ein Kästchen an.)

A	
B	
C	

[1]

[Total: 7]

Tips for success

- Try to predict the words you are listening for by looking at the pictures.
- *Ziffer(n)* means 'number(s)'. You might be listening for a number instead of a word.
- Don't leave any answers blank. If you are not sure, have a guess.

Paper 2: reading

This question tests your ability to pick out the main points and some details in a short text.

Lesen Sie den folgenden Brief. Suchen Sie dann die Antwort heraus, die am besten passt, und kreuzen Sie das richtige Kästchen an.

> Köln, den 14. Juli
>
> Liebe Tante Andrea,
>
> wie geht's dir? Ich bin froh, dass die Sommerferien endlich da sind. Die Schule war sehr stressig, weil ich Abitur gemacht habe. Hoffentlich werde ich gute Noten bekommen.
>
> Ich habe vor, Zahnarzt zu werden. Bis Mitte September werde ich als Kellner in einem Gasthaus arbeiten, um Geld zu verdienen. Danach werde ich an der Uni studieren.
>
> Mein Freund Axel hat einen Teilzeitjob in einem Reisebüro, aber er möchte in Zukunft Polizist werden. Er hilft gern anderen Leuten. Also wird ihm diese Arbeit gut passen.
>
> Dein
> Gerd

1 Gerd hat jetzt…

| A | | Prüfungen | B | | Stress | C | | Urlaub | [1] |

2 Gerd hat einen Sommerjob…

| A | | in einem Restaurant | B | | als Zahnarzt | C | | in einem Büro | [1] |

3 Nach den Ferien wird Gerd…

| A | | als Kellner arbeiten | B | | an der Uni studieren | C | | in einer Arztpraxis arbeiten | [1] |

4 Axel arbeitet…

| A | | an einem Bahnhof | B | | auf einer Polizeiwache | C | | in der Tourismusindustrie | [1] |

5 Axel ist sehr…

| A | | hilfsbereit | B | | fleißig | C | | hilflos | [1] |

[Total: 5]

Points to remember

- In the questions look out for words which have the same or similar meanings as those used in the text. For example, the word *Urlaub* (1C) has the same meaning as *Ferien* (as in *Sommerferien* in the text).
- If a key word appears both in the text and in the questions, check how it is used: *Zahnarzt* appears in the text and again in 2B, but becoming a dentist is his future ambition, not his summer job.

Thema 7 Unterwegs

1 Am Bahnhof

1 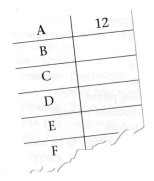 Lies bitte diese Informationen über den Bahnhof.

Was passt zusammen?
Füll die Tabelle aus.

A	12
B	
C	
D	
E	
F	

Bahnhof

Parken
Direkt unter dem Bahnhofsvorplatz befindet sich eine Tiefgarage **(A)**. Auch Fahrradabstellplätze **(B)**.

Fahrkartenverkauf
Es gibt sechs Fahrkartenschalter **(C)** und zwei Fahrkartenautomaten **(D)**.

Wartehalle (E)

Toiletten (F)

Service (G)
Auskunft bekommt man im Büro in der Schalterhalle.

Schließfächer
Die Schließfächer **(H)** befinden sich neben der Rolltreppe **(I)**.

Reisebedarf
Es gibt ein Café **(J)**, einen Kiosk **(K)** und eine Imbissstube **(L)**. Neben den Fahrkartenschaltern befindet sich auch eine Wechselstube **(M)**.

Taxis
Der Taxistandplatz **(N)** und der Busbahnhof **(O)** sind vor dem Bahnhof.

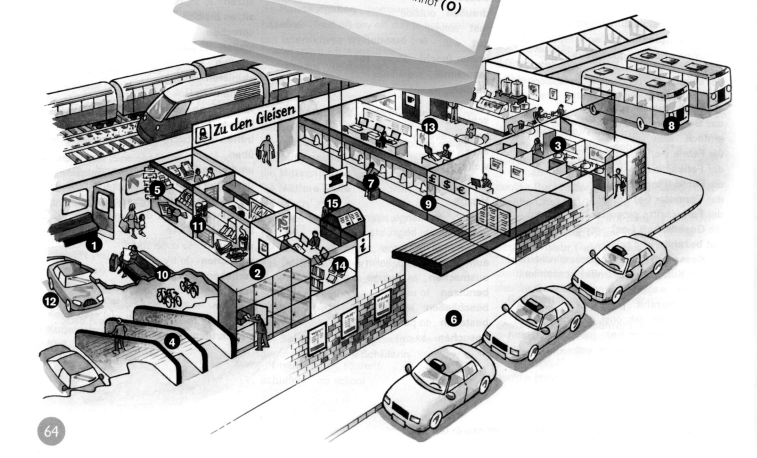

2a Lara und Jens sind im Auskunftsbüro am Bahnhof in Bad Reichenhall. Sie wollen nach Salzburg fahren. Bitte hör zu und lies mit.

Jens	Guten Tag. Wir möchten nach Salzburg fahren. Wann fährt der nächste Zug?
Angestellte	*Um 09:41 Uhr.*
Jens	Und wann kommt der Zug in Salzburg an?
Angestellte	*Um 10:07 Uhr.*
Jens	Müssen wir umsteigen?
Angestellte	*Nein, der Zug ist direkt.*
Jens	Von welchem Gleis fährt der Zug ab?
Angestellte	*Von Gleis 4.*

b Macht bitte Dialoge. *A* ist der Angestellte und *B* sucht Informationen.

Freilassing	10:47	11:07	→	🚂 2
München	11:19	13:05	→	🚂 3
Frankfurt	12:01	17:39	↻	AUGSBURG 🚂 1
Hamburg	14:09	16:35	↻	WILHELMSHÖHE 🚂 5

3a Am Fahrkartenschalter. Bitte hör zu und lies mit.

Jens	Ich möchte zwei Fahrkarten nach Salzburg, bitte. Zweiter Klasse.
Angestellte	*Einfach oder hin und zurück?*
Jens	Hin und zurück, bitte.
Angestellte	*Also zwei Rückfahrkarten nach Salzburg, zweiter Klasse. Das macht €18,40.*
Jens	Bitte schön und vielen Dank.

b Macht bitte Dialoge. *A* ist der Angestellte und *B* kauft Fahrkarten.

↔ × 1	→ × 2	↔ × 2	→ × 1
Freilassing 2Kl.	München 2Kl.	Frankfurt 1Kl.	Hamburg 2Kl.
€5,60	€56,00	€144,00	€61,00

4 Bitte hör zu und füll die Tabelle aus.

Top-Tipp
Ich möchte...

eine Einzelkarte nach...	→ × 1
einmal einfach nach...	→ × 1
zwei Einzelkarten nach...	→ × 2
zweimal einfach nach...	→ × 2
eine Rückfahrkarte nach...	↔ × 1
einmal hin und zurück nach...	↔ × 1
zwei Rückfahrkarten nach...	↔ × 2
zweimal hin und zurück nach...	↔ × 2
erster Klasse	1Kl.
zweiter Klasse	2Kl.

	Reiseziel	Abfahrt	Ankunft	Umsteigen	Gleis	Fahrkarte	Preis
(1)	Karlsruhe	10.15					

2 Wie komme ich zum Bahnhof?

1 🎧 📖 Hör zu und lies mit.

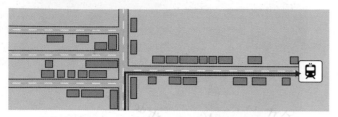

A Entschuldigung, bitte. Wie komme ich am besten zum Bahnhof?
B *Zum Bahnhof. Nehmen Sie die erste Straße rechts und dann gehen Sie geradeaus.*

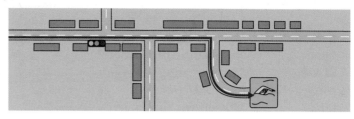

A Entschuldigen Sie, bitte. Wie komme ich zum Hallenbad?
B *Gehen Sie hier geradeaus, über die Ampel und nehmen Sie die zweite Straße rechts. Das Hallenbad ist um die Ecke.*

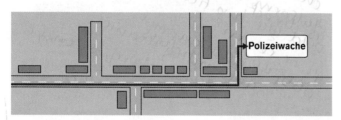

A Entschuldigen Sie, bitte. Wie komme ich zur Polizeiwache?
B *Das ist ganz einfach. Gehen Sie hier geradeaus. Nehmen Sie die dritte Straße links. Die Polizeiwache ist auf der rechten Seite.*

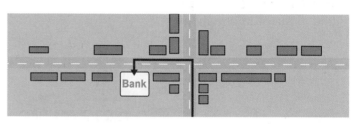

A Gibt es hier in der Nähe eine Bank?
B *Ja, gehen Sie geradeaus bis zur Kreuzung. An der Kreuzung gehen Sie links. Die Bank ist dann auf der linken Seite.*

2 💬 Macht die Rollenspiele zweimal: das erste Mal in der Sie-Form und das zweite Mal in der Du-Form.

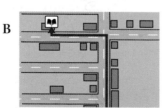

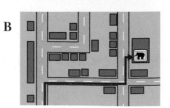

Grammatik

Der Imperativ

(*the imperative*)

F2

You use the imperative form of the verb to give someone instructions or orders.

The imperative of the polite form *Sie* is the same as the present tense, but you place the *Sie* after the verb:

Gehen Sie geradeaus. Go straight on.

Nehmen Sie die zweite Straße links.
Take the second road on the left.

To make the imperative of the *du* form, take off the *-(e)st* of the present tense:

gehen – du gehst → Geh geradeaus.
nehmen – du nimmst → Nimm die erste Straße rechts.

The *ihr* form is the same as the present tense: *geht, nehmt, macht.*

3 🎧 📖 Hör zu und lies mit.

A Ist der Bahnhof weit von hier?
B *Nein, etwa 5 Minuten. Gehen Sie am besten zu Fuß.*

A Ist die Polizeiwache weit von hier?
B *Ja. Am besten fahren Sie mit dem Bus, mit der Linie 7.* 🚌
A Wo ist die Haltestelle? Ⓗ
B *Um die Ecke.*

A Ist es weit bis zum Hallenbad?
B *Etwa ein Kilometer. Sie fahren am besten mit der U-Bahn. Linie 8.*
A Wo ist die nächste U-Bahn-Station? Ⓤ
B *Dort vorne, links.*

A Ist es weit?
B *Nein, nicht sehr weit. Aber Sie können mit der Straßenbahn fahren. Die Haltestelle ist dort drüben. Fahren Sie mit der Linie F.* 🚎 Ⓗ

Top-Tipp
zum/zur

m	**der** Markt	Wie komme ich **zum** Markt?	(zum = zu dem)
f	**die** Bibliothek	Wie komme ich **zur** Bibliothek?	(zur = zu der)
n	**das** Schloss	Wie komme ich **zum** Schloss?	(zum = zu dem)
pl	**die** Geschäfte	Wie komme ich **zu den** Geschäften?	

Der Berliner Hauptbahnhof

4 💬 Macht Dialoge.

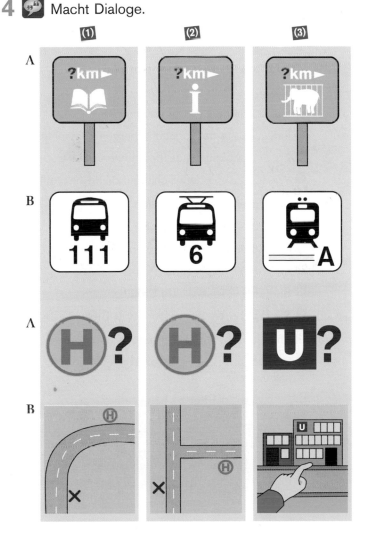

5 🎧 Hör bitte zu. Füll die Tabelle aus und markiere das Gebäude auf dem Plan.

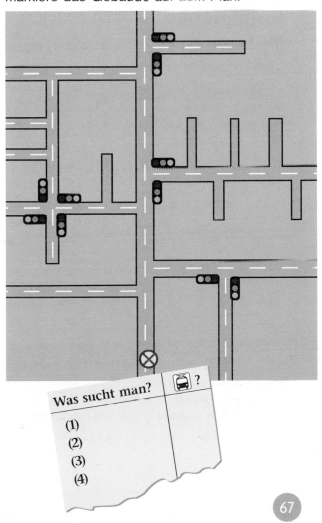

Was sucht man?	🚌 ?
(1)	
(2)	
(3)	
(4)	

3 Was kann man in Köln machen?

1 📖 Du bist im Verkehrsamt in Köln und hörst viele Fragen der Touristen.

Bitte verbinde die Bilder mit den Fragen.

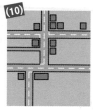
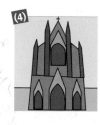

a Wo kann man hier gut einkaufen?

b Ist es weit bis zum Dom?

c Was läuft heute Abend im Theater?

d Welche Museen gibt es in Köln und wann sind sie geöffnet?

e Wo kann man heute Abend tanzen gehen?

f Wo kann man hier preiswert übernachten?

g Wo gibt es ein typisches Restaurant?

h Haben Sie einen Stadtplan von Köln?

i Wo sind die besten Geschäfte?

j Kann man auf dem Rhein Ausflüge mit dem Boot machen?

Grammatik

Modalverben *können, wollen, sollen*
(*three modal verbs*)

In order to say that you can, want or should/ought to do something, you use modal verbs. These verbs are followed by a second verb, which is in the infinitive and goes to the end of the sentence.

Here are the conjugations of three modal verbs:

	können (can/be able to)	**wollen** (to want)	**sollen** (should/ ought to)
ich	kann	will	soll
du	kannst	willst	sollst
er/sie/es/man	kann	will	soll
wir	können	wollen	sollen
ihr	könnt	wollt	sollt
Sie/sie	können	wollen	sollen

Any extra information is placed between the modal verb and the infinitive main verb.

e.g. Ich **kann** den Dom **sehen**. Ich **will** ein Museum **besuch**en. **Können** Sie um 19 Uhr **kommen**?

F1

(1) Fill in the gaps using forms of *können*.

a Ich _____ heute kommen.

b _____ Sie um 18 Uhr abfahren?

c Ihr _____ in der Jugendherberge übernachten.

d Er _____ nicht Deutsch sprechen.

e Wir _____ mit dem Schiff auf dem Rhein fahren.

(2) Make sentences using *wollen*.

a Ich – das Schokoladenmuseum – besuchen.

b den Stadtplan – wir – kaufen?

c du – das Buch – sehen?

d Sie (*she*) – essen – ein Brötchen.

e Sie (*you*) – buchen – hier – die Theaterkarten.

(3) Fill the gaps or make sentences using *sollen*.

a Sie (*you*) _____ nicht später als 22 Uhr ankommen.

b _____ wir die Karten hier kaufen?

c Du _____ nicht immer so laut sein.

d Ihr – noch – besichtigen – diese Kirche.

e Er – nicht immer – sein – so launisch.

2 📖 Bitte lies den Text und mach Notizen.

Köln ist eine sehr alte Stadt. Vor
2000 Jahren waren die Römer dort
und viele römische Ruinen und
ein interessantes Mosaik erinnern
an diese Zeit. Im Römisch-
Germanischen Museum kann man
Teller, Lampen, Schmuck, Glas aus
der Römerzeit ansehen. Das Museum
ist jeden Tag außer Montag von
10.00 bis 17.00 Uhr geöffnet. Der
Eintritt kostet für Schüler €3. Gleich
gegenüber ist der gotische Dom mit
vielen wunderschönen Fenstern.

Wenn man Schokolade mag, kann man das
Schokoladenmuseum besuchen, das am Rhein liegt. Auf
dem Rhein gibt es Schiffe und viele Touristen wollen
eine Rheinfahrt machen, wenn sie Köln besuchen.
Schiffe fahren täglich im Winter wie im Sommer
zwischen 8.00 und 15.30 an der Rheinpromenade in
der Nähe vom Dom ab.

Die „Hohe Straße" ist ideal zum Einkaufen. „Früh"
ist ein typisches Restaurant, wo man Kölsch* trinken
und zum Beispiel Kartoffelsalat mit Würstchen essen
kann. Es gibt eine Oper und viele Theater und natürlich
auch Nachtleben für die jungen Leute in Diskos und
Studentenkneipen.

*Kölsch — a special beer from Cologne

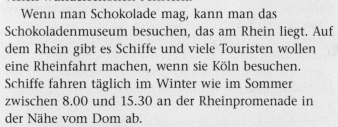

Geschichte	Museen	Restaurants/ Kneipen	Weitere Aktivitäten

3 💬 Denk an eine Stadt, wo du im Urlaub warst.

Bereite Antworten auf diese Fragen vor. Dann
mach Dialoge mit einem Partner/einer Partnerin.
- Beschreib diese Stadt.
- Was kann man dort machen oder sehen?
- Ist diese Stadt interessant für junge Leute?
  Warum/warum nicht?
- Was hältst du von dieser Stadt?

4 🎧 Du kommst abends in Berlin
an. Das Verkehrsamt ist schon
geschlossen.

Hör den automatischen Telefonbeantworter an und mach Notizen.

Telefon Verkehrsamt?	
Reichstag/ Öffnungszeiten?	
Fernsehturm/ Preis?	
Restaurant wo?	
Berlin und Umgebung	

5 🏰 Deine Freundin besucht deine
Heimatstadt. Schreib eine E-mail von
ungefähr 50 Wörtern auf Deutsch und
benutze Modalverben.
- Was kann sie dort machen?
- Was soll sie besuchen?
- Frag sie, was sie hier sehen will.

4 Wie reisen wir weiter?

☑ Learn about public transport in German-speaking countries

☑ Understand and use the genitive case

1 📖 Was passt zusammen? Kombiniere einen Buchstaben mit der richtigen Zahl.

(1) Fährst du gleich mit der Straßenbahn zum Stadion?

(2) Mit der U-Bahn bist du morgens schneller da.

(3) Ich fahre jetzt doch mit dem Bus. Es ist schon spät.

(4) Von Frankfurt starten mehr Flugzeuge als von Hamburg.

(5) Den Ärmelkanal überquert man mit einer Fähre.

Grammatik

A6, E4

Der Genitiv *(the genitive)*

The genitive case is used to express possession (similar to the -'s ending in English) and after certain prepositions. It is particularly used in **written** language. For information about the genitive endings, refer to the grammar reference section at the end of the book.

M *das Auto **des** Popsängers/meines Vaters*
the pop singer's car/my father's car

F *das Kleid **der** Popsängerin/meiner Mutter*
the female pop singer's dress/my mother's dress

N *die Puppe des Kindes/meines Babys*
the child's doll/my baby's doll

Note the '-s' or '-es' at the end of the **masculine** or **neuter** nouns.

The following prepositions require the genitive case:
außerhalb (outside of), *statt* (instead of), *trotz* (in spite of), *während* (during), *wegen* (because of):

*während **des** Unterrichts* (during lessons)
wegen meiner Erkältung (because of my cold)

🖱 7/1–7/4

2a 📖 Lies den Text und beantworte die Fragen.

Der Flughafen in Frankfurt

Der Frankfurter Flughafen, der Rhein-Main-Flughafen, ist der größte Flughafen des Landes. Frankfurt ist ein Verkehrsknotenpunkt. Das heißt viele Straßen, Fluglinien und Eisenbahnlinien kreuzen sich außerhalb und innerhalb der Innenstadt, weil Frankfurt sehr zentral in Europa liegt. Flugzeuge mit mehr als 280 Reisezielen in über 100 Ländern starten und landen jeden Tag. Trotz des regen Flugverkehrs sind die Flüge meistens pünktlich, aber 10–15% der Flüge landen während des Tages mit Verspätung. Wegen der Sicherheitskontrolle muss man seinen Mantel und oft seine Schuhe ausziehen, bevor man fliegen darf, und auch das Handgepäck muss während der Kontrolle durch den Scanner laufen. Trotz der vielen Angestellten, die dort arbeiten, sind die Wartezeiten oft lang.

(1) In welcher Stadt ist Deutschlands größter Flughafen?

(2) In wie viele Länder fliegen Flugzeuge von Frankfurt?

(3) Was liest du über die Lage der Stadt Frankfurt?

(4) Wie viel Prozent der Flugzeuge landen pünktlich?

(5) Was muss man immer ausziehen, während man durch die Sicherheitskontrolle geht?

(6) Warum muss man pünktlich an der Sicherheitskontrolle sein?

b 📖 Lies den Text und finde die richtige Zahl oder das richtige Datum für jeden Satz (1–4).

Kennst du die Wuppertaler Schwebebahn?

Wuppertal ist eine Stadt in Nordrhein-Westfalen. Fast die ganze Stadt liegt an der Wupper – das ist ein kleiner Fluss. Die Menschen dort haben ein interessantes Verkehrsmittel: seit 1901 fahren sie jeden Tag mit der Schwebebahn. Die Hochbahn hat 20 Haltestellen über 13 km und hängt über der Wupper. Man steigt auf einer Treppe ein. Sie ist ein sehr sicheres Verkehrsmittel – statt der Menschen war 1950 sogar der kleine Elefant Tuffi ein Passagier!

(1) Die Schwebebahn war ganz neu.
(2) Die Länge der Bahn über der Wupper.
(3) Die Zahl der Stellen, wo man einsteigen kann.
(4) Es gab einen ungewöhnlichen Fahrgast.

3 🎧 Hör das Gespräch an der Sicherheitskontrolle an und entscheide, welche Antwort richtig ist.

(1) Die Frau fliegt nach…
 a Köln
 b Wien
 c Rom

(2) Sie zeigt dem Angestellten…
 a ihren Laptop
 b ihren Pass
 c ihre Bordkarte

(3) Sie muss…
 a nur ihren Mantel ausziehen
 b nur ihre Stiefel ausziehen
 c ihren Mantel und ihre Stiefel ausziehen

(4) Im Handgepäck darf man…
 a keine scharfen Gegenstände mitnehmen
 b keine Flüssigkeiten haben
 c keine Sachen aus Metall einpacken

(5) Die Frau hat vergessen,…
 a dass ihr Mann den Rucksack gepackt hat
 b dass die Schere im Handgepäck war
 c dass sie einen Rucksack hat

(6) Sie muss…
 a nur die Schere wegwerfen
 b an der Sicherheitskontrolle bleiben
 c die Flüssigkeit und die Schere wegwerfen

4a 💬 Lies mit deinem Partner/deiner Partnerin den Dialog vor, der in Wien stattfindet.

Tourist Entschuldigen Sie bitte, wie komme ich zum Stephansdom?
Passant *Fahren Sie hier vom Flughafen mit der **S7** in Richtung Stadtmitte.*
Tourist Wo ist der Fahrkartenschalter?
Passant *Hier drüben **links**. Sie können die Karte auch am Automaten kaufen.*
Tourist Ich habe nur eine Kreditkarte.

Passant *Man kann auch eine Kreditkarte benutzen.*
Tourist Wo ist **die Haltestelle** zur U-Bahn?
Passant *Vor dem Kino.*
Tourist Entschuldigen Sie, ist die **S-Bahn** hier meistens pünktlich?
Passant *Na ja, **meistens** ist sie pünktlich.*
Tourist Nehmen Sie die S-Bahn oder die U-Bahn?
Passant *Ich fahre **lieber mit der U-Bahn**.*
Tourist Vielen Dank für Ihre Hilfe.

b 💬 Macht den Dialog noch einmal mit Wörtern aus der Liste unten statt der markierten Wörter.

neben dem Kaufhaus	U-Bahn
der Eingang	dort
hinter dem Bahnhof	fast immer
U3	nie
rechts	mit der S-Bahn

c 💬 Ein Tourist kommt in deine Stadt. Spiel Dialoge mit einem Partner. Wechselt euch ab.
 • Was kann man in deiner Stadt besuchen?
 • Fährst du mit dem Bus, mit der U-Bahn oder mit der Straßenbahn oder vielleicht fährst du mit dem Zug in die nächste Stadt?

5 📖✏️ Du wohnst in Wien. Deine Freundin/dein Freund aus Frankfurt möchte dich besuchen. Schreib eine E-mail.

Fernbus Wien – mehr fürs Geld

Reisen Sie bequem, günstig und schnell mit unseren modernen Fernbussen durch ganz Europa: zum Beispiel Frankfurt – Wien (Stadtzentrum) ab 35 Euro, dreimal täglich. Steigen Sie doch ein!

Infos und Tickets 0123 – 45 67 89

Wird deine Freundin/dein Freund mit diesem Fernbus fahren? Sie/er kann auch fliegen, oder mit dem Zug kommen.

Du holst sie/ihn im Stadtzentrum ab. Gib so viele Details an, wie du kannst. Du kannst etwas über den Flughafen sagen, die Sicherheitskontrolle erwähnen und wie man in Wien ins Stadtzentrum kommt.

Schreib mindestens 50 Wörter.

Thema 8 Ferien

1 Haben Sie Zimmer frei?

1 Hör zu und lies mit.

An der Rezeption

Guten Tag, kann ich Ihnen helfen?
Guten Tag, haben Sie ein Zimmer frei?
Möchten Sie ein Einzelzimmer oder ein Doppelzimmer?
Ein Doppelzimmer mit Dusche bitte, wenn es geht.
Wie lange möchten Sie bleiben?
Für zwei Nächte, bitte.
Es tut mir Leid, für zwei Nächte habe ich nur ein Zimmer mit Bad. Geht das?
Ja, das geht. Was kostet das Zimmer?
€40 pro Person für eine Nacht.
Ist das ein Zimmer mit Frühstück?
Ja, aber wir bieten auch Halbpension und Vollpension an. Pro Mahlzeit kostet das €12,50 extra.
Gut. Ja, wir nehmen das Zimmer, Halbpension bitte. Wann und wo können wir frühstücken?
Von 8 Uhr bis 10 Uhr in unserem Frühstücksraum. Gehen Sie durch diese Tür und nehmen Sie den Aufzug bis die zweite Etage.
Vielen Dank.
Bitte, hier ist Ihr Schlüssel, Zimmer 312. Haben Sie ein Auto?
Ja, wo ist der Parkplatz bitte?
Fahren Sie fünfzig Meter die Straße entlang und er ist dann links um die Ecke.

= zwei Nächte

Bitte lies den Text und finde alle Fragen.
Mach zwei Listen.

Fragen mit Fragewort	Fragen ohne Fragewort
Wo ist der Parkplatz?	Kann ich Ihnen helfen?

Hier sind die wichtigsten Fragewörter. Kennst du sie alle? Bitte schau im Wörterbuch nach.

wohin?   wann?   wem?   wen?

was?   wo?   warum?   wie?   wie viel?

woher?   wer?   wie lange?   wie viele?

Grammatik
Präpositionen mit dem Akkusativ
(*prepositions with the accusative case*)

The following prepositions are always followed by the accusative case:

bis durch für gegen ohne um entlang

Here are the accusative articles again:

m	f	n	pl
den	die	das	die
einen	eine	ein	—

(For the accusative of possessive adjectives — **meinen** etc. — see Thema 1, 'Verwandte und Tiere', page 6.)

e.g. *Ich gehe durch* } den Wald / die Stadt / das Feld

E1

(1) Read again the dialogue in Übung 1 and find the prepositions followed by the accusative.

(2) Insert the correct definite article:

Willkommen im Hotel. Wenn Sie durch —— Eingang gehen, der für —— Gäste ist, sehen Sie den wunderschönen Garten. Gehen Sie —— Gang entlang um —— Rezeption herum und Sie kommen zum Swimmingpool. Das Sprungbrett lehnt gegen —— Wand, weil der Pool sehr voll ist, aber ohne —— Sprungbrett macht es keinen Spaß.

 8/1

2 🗨 Bitte lest den Dialog in Übung 1 noch einmal. Jetzt seid ihr dran. Ihr bucht ein Hotelzimmer. Macht Dialoge an der Rezeption.

3a 📖 Bitte lies den Text.

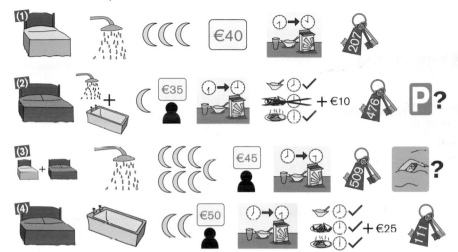

Willkommen im Schwarzwaldhotel
SONNENHOF

Lage
Mitten im Schwarzwald auf dem Land, etwa 20 km nördlich von Freiburg.

Einrichtung
Typisches gemütliches Schwarzwaldhaus mit Restaurant und mit typischer Schwarzwaldküche. Fernsehraum, Swimmingpool (Freibad), Hallenbad, Sauna, Solarium, Fitnessraum, Kinderspielplatz, Fahrradvermietung.

Zimmer
Gemütliche Zimmer mit traditioneller Ausstattung mit Bad/Dusche, WC, Balkon, Telefon, Minibar.

Sport und Unterhaltung
Vier Tennisplätze, Tischtennis, Nachtklub im Haus.

Ausflüge
Viele Ausflugsmöglichkeiten: die wunderschöne alte Universitätsstadt Freiburg mit ihrem historischen Zentrum, der Schwarzwald zum Wandern, Frankreich und die Städte Colmar und Straßburg im Elsass.

Ein erstklassiges Hotel mit sehr guter Küche in ruhiger Lage mit Sport- und Ausflugsmöglichkeiten.

Warum buchen Sie nicht heute?

b 📖 Welche drei Informationen über das Schwarzwaldhotel stehen *nicht* im Text?

c 🏰 Schreib eine E-mail an dieses Hotel (etwa 50 Wörter). Du möchtest ein Zimmer für eine Woche buchen.

- Schreib, wann du fahren willst.
- Gib deinen Namen an.
- Frag, was es kostet.

4 🎧 Bettina und Lisa wollen doch nicht mit ihren Eltern in dem Hotel wohnen und gehen zum Campingplatz. Hör zu und wähle a oder b für jede Information.

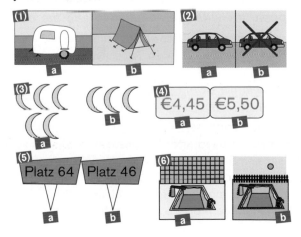

2 Wohin fährst du... und mit wem?

☑ Say where you spend your holiday and how you get there
☑ Say who you travel with
☑ Use prepositions that always take the dative case
☑ Use prepositions that can take the accusative or the dative case

1 📖 Welcher Kommentar passt zu welchem Bild?

① Ich verbringe meinen Urlaub mit meinen Freunden am Meer. Wir fliegen im Juli nach Mallorca.

② Wir sind mit dem Flugzeug mit unserer Tante nach Amerika geflogen. Dort haben wir bei meinen Großeltern gewohnt.

③ Wir bleiben in England. Wir mögen Cornwall und fahren im August mit dem Bus dorthin. Mein Onkel kommt auch mit.

④ Mein Vater und ich werden mit dem Auto von London nach Köln fahren.

⑤ Dieses Jahr fahre ich mit einer Freundin aus der Schule mit dem Zug nach Florenz.

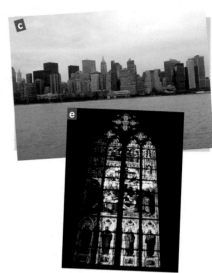

Grammatik

E2

Präpositionen mit dem Dativ
(prepositions with the dative case)

The following prepositions are always followed by the **dative** case:

ab aus außer bei gegenüber mit nach seit von zu

Here is a reminder of the article endings in the dative case:

m	f	n	pl
dem	der	dem	den
einem	einer	einem	—

8/2

Grammatik

E3

Präpositionen mit dem Akkusativ und mit dem Dativ
(prepositions with the accusative and the dative)

These prepositions are followed by either the accusative or the dative, depending on the context:

an auf hinter in neben über unter vor zwischen

Use the accusative if the preposition suggests movement from one place to another:

*Ich reise **in die** USA.*

Use the dative if the preposition suggests the location where someone or something is situated:

*Ich wohne **in den** USA.*

Which case is used after the prepositions in these sentences? Why?

(1) Nächsten Sommer werden wir eine Woche in der Türkei verbringen.
(2) Mein Freund fährt mit dem Auto in die Schweiz.
(3) Im Sommer fahre ich gern ans Meer.
(4) Machst du gern Urlaub an einem See?

 8/3, 8/4

2 Bitte macht Dialoge.

Wohin reist du diesen Sommer?
A Wohin reist du diesen Sommer?
B *Wir fahren nach Italien.*

| A Mit wem reist du? |
| B *Ich reise mit Freunden.* |

| A Wie kommst du dahin? |
| B *Wir fahren mit dem Auto.* |
| A Wann fahrt ihr? |
| B *Wir fahren im Juli.* |
| A Wie lange bleibt ihr? |
| B *Wir bleiben eine Woche.* |

Wohin bist du letzten Sommer gereist?
Wohin bist du letzten Sommer gereist?
Wir sind nach Italien gefahren.

| Mit wem bist du gereist? |
| *Ich bin mit Freunden gereist.* |

| Wie bist du dahin gekommen? |
| *Wir sind mit dem Auto gefahren.* |
| Wann seid ihr gefahren? |
| *Wir sind im Juli gefahren.* |
| Wie lange seid ihr geblieben? |
| *Wir sind eine Woche geblieben.* |

Ich reise…/ich bin…gereist/ ich bin…gefahren

- im Juli/August/April
- eine Woche/zwei Wochen in den Sommerferien/ Weihnachtsferien
- in den Osterferien

- mit meiner Familie
- mit Freunden/Verwandten
- mit der Klasse
- allein

- mit dem Auto
- mit dem Bus
- mit dem Zug
- mit dem Flugzeug
- mit der Bahn

- nach Frankreich/nach Italien/nach Spanien/ nach Österreich/nach Rom
- in die Schweiz/in die Türkei/in die USA
- in die Berge
- ans Meer
- zu meinem Onkel/zu meiner Tante/zu Verwandten

3 Bitte lies den Text. Die Sätze (1)–(8) stimmen nicht. Bitte korrigiere sie.

(1) Heinz ist 40 Jahre alt.
(2) Er radelt mit einem Freund.
(3) Australien hat er noch nicht besucht.
(4) Ohne Gepäck wiegt sein Rad 50 kg.
(5) Er schläft immer bei einer Familie.
(6) Er hat oft Probleme.
(7) Er möchte lieber bei seiner Familie sein.
(8) In Afrika hatte er Probleme mit seinem Rad.

Mit dem Fahrrad um die Welt

Heinz fährt seit mehr als 40 Jahren im Sommer wie im Winter mit dem Fahrrad um die Welt. Er möchte frei sein und fährt nicht mit Freunden, sondern immer allein. Von Kanada bis Australien hat er schon über 200 Länder besucht und ist mehr als eine halbe Million Kilometer geradelt. Er kommt aus Deutschland. Sein Rad ist nicht leicht, es wiegt 25 kg, dazu kommen noch ungefähr 50 kg Gepäck. Nachts schläft er in einem Zelt. Manchmal hatte er Probleme zum Beispiel mit einem Schwarm Bienen in Afrika. Er findet es nicht schade, dass er nicht oft bei seiner Familie sein kann, weil er frei sein muss, um mit dem Rad zu reisen.

4 Bitte hör gut zu und füll die Tabelle aus.

Wer?	Wohin?	Mit wem?	Wie?	Wie lange?
Florian				
Kerstin				
Lisa				
Timo				

5 Schreib eine E-mail an deine Freundin über deine Urlaubspläne. Schreib 80–90 Wörter und beantworte diese Fragen:

- Wohin wirst du fahren?
- Mit wem?
- Wie wirst du dorthin fahren?
- Wie lange wirst du bleiben?

3 Wo warst du und was hast du gemacht?

☑ Talk about what you did on holiday

☑ Learn more about the imperfect tense

1 🎧 📖 Bitte hör zu und lies mit.

Wer war das?
Finde die richtige Person für jedes Bild.

> Letzten Sommer bin ich für 2 Wochen mit meiner Freundin ans Meer geflogen. Ich habe jeden Tag am Strand gelegen und bin im Meer geschwommen. Ich habe auch ab und zu Volleyball gespielt. Wir hatten Glück, das Wetter war sehr sonnig und heiß. Der Urlaub war prima.
>
> **Angelika**

> Ich bin zu Hause geblieben. Das war aber nicht langweilig. Ich bin mit Freunden ins Freibad gegangen, oder ich habe im Garten gefaulenzt. Ich habe auch einen Film gesehen. Da war immer ganz viel los. Das Wetter war wechselhaft: Es hat manchmal geregnet, manchmal war es wolkig, aber es war auch teilweise schön warm.

> Im Winter bin ich mit meinen Eltern nach Österreich in die Berge gefahren. Wir sind mit dem Zug gereist und wir haben in einem Hotel gewohnt. Ich bin jeden Morgen Ski gefahren, manchmal sogar auf einer schwarzen Piste und am Nachmittag bin ich Snowboard gefahren. Das Wetter war fabelhaft, es war kalt aber sonnig und es gab viel Schnee.
>
> **Kevin**

> Meine Schwester und ich sind im April mit dem Auto aufs Land gefahren. Wir haben 5 Tage lang unsere Oma besucht. Es war sehr ruhig, aber wir hatten Zeit, uns zu entspannen. Manchmal sind wir spazieren gegangen, manchmal haben wir eine Radtour gemacht. Das Wetter war ideal: kühl und ein bisschen windig.
>
> **Magdalena**

> **Evangelos**

Grammatik F4
Das Imperfekt (the imperfect tense)

The imperfect is another way of talking about the past. Except for some common verbs, it is not usually used in speech. Two common verbs often used in the imperfect in spoken German are:

	sein (to be)	*haben* (to have)
ich	war (I was)	hatte (I had)
du	warst	hattest
er/sie/er/man	war	hatte
wir	waren	hatten
ihr	wart	hattet
Sie/sie	waren	hatten

The impersonal expression *es gibt* is also often used in the imperfect: *es gab* (there was/there were…). It is followed by the accusative:

> *Es gab einen schönen Strand.*

Read the texts in Übung 1 again. Identify all examples of the imperfect tense.

How would you say the following?
(1) The weather was cold.
(2) There were many tourists.
(3) They had a lot to do.
(4) I was tired.
(5) It was great! It wasn't boring at all.
(6) Did you have a single room? (formal and informal)
(7) The hotel had a swimming pool.
(8) The camp site was in the countryside.
(9) The hotel was dirty.
(10) I had a problem with my hotel room. The shower was broken.

Top-Tipp

**Wir haben gezeltet.
Wir haben auf einem
Campingplatz gewohnt.**

**Wir haben in
einem Wohnwagen
gewohnt.**

**Wir haben in einer
Jugendherberge
gewohnt.**

**Wir haben in einem
Ferienhaus gewohnt.**

**Wir haben bei
Freunden gewohnt.**

2 Macht Dialoge.

| Wie lange? | Wo? | Wo gewohnt? | Was gemacht? | Wetter? |

Beispiel

A Wo warst du in den Ferien?

B *Ich bin für eine Woche nach Spanien in
die Berge gefahren.*

A Wo hast du gewohnt?

B *Ich habe in einem Hotel gewohnt.
Es hatte ein Schwimmbad.*

A Was hast du gemacht?

B *Ich bin jeden Tag gewandert.*

A Und wie war das Wetter?

B *Es war ganz heiß.*

A Wie war der Urlaub?

B *Der Urlaub war ganz toll!*

A Wie bist du hingereist?

B *Ich bin geflogen.*

A Mit wem bist du gefahren?

B *Ich bin mit meinen Freunden dorthin gefahren.*

3 Hör bitte zu. Wie waren die Sommerferien?
Was hat Lara positiv gefunden und was hat sie
negativ gefunden? Füll die Tabelle aus.

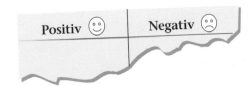

Positiv 😊	Negativ 😞

4 Du bist auf Urlaub. Schreib eine Postkarte
an eine Freundin zu Hause. Schreib ungefähr
50 Wörter. Sag ihr:

- wo du bist, mit wem und für wie lange
- wie das Wetter ist
- was du an drei verschiedenen Tagen schon
  gemacht hast
- was du noch machen willst

4 Ich möchte mich beschweren...

☑ **Make a complaint**

1 📖 Was ist das Problem? Finde für jedes Problem das passende Bild.

Beispiel **(1)** *e*

| 【1】 Das Zimmer ist zu laut. | 【2】 Es gibt keine Handtücher. | 【3】 Die Dusche ist kaputt. |

| 【4】 Der Fernseher funktioniert nicht. | 【5】 Es gibt ein Problem mit dem Bett. |

| 【6】 Ich habe keine schöne Aussicht. |

| 【7】 Das Schwimmbecken ist schmutzig. |

| 【8】 Das Essen ist kalt. | 【9】 Der Aufzug ist kaputt. |

| 【10】 Der Strand ist zu weit vom Hotel. |

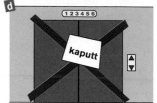

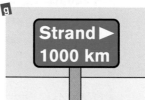

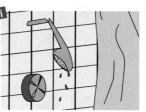

2 🎧 Hör bitte zu und füll die Tabelle aus. Was für Probleme haben diese Hotelgäste und was kann das Hotel machen?

	Welches Zimmer?	Problem(e)	Was kann das Hotel machen?
(1)	207	Zimmer ist zu klein	nichts
(2)			

Top-Tipp
Das Zimmer *Ich möchte mich beschweren...*

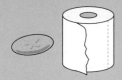

Es gibt { keine Lampe/Seife.
kein Toilettenpapier/Wasser.

Ich habe keine Aussicht.

Das Zimmer ist laut/klein/schmutzig.

Das WC ist kaputt.

Remember that *es gibt* needs to be followed by the accusative.

Es gibt
Ich habe } ein Problem mit { dem Fernseher.
der Lampe.

Das Radio funktioniert nicht.

Top-Tipp

Das Hotel *Ich möchte mich beschweren...*

Der Strand ist zu weit.   **Der Aufzug ist kaputt.**

Das Schwimmbecken ist schmutzig.   **Das Essen ist kalt/ schlecht/furchtbar.**

Top-Tipp

Im Geschäft *Ich möchte mich beschweren...*

Ich möchte mein Geld zurück.

Ich möchte ihn/ sie/es bitte umtauschen.

Ich möchte einen neuen/eine neue/ ein neues...

---

3 🗣 Lies die Gespräche. Macht Dialoge.

Im Hotel

A Was kann ich für Sie tun?

B *Ich möchte mich beschweren. Ich habe keine Handtücher in meinem Zimmer.*

A Das tut mir leid. Ich gebe Ihnen Handtücher. Ist sonst alles in Ordnung?

B *Nein, die Toilette ist kaputt.*

A Welches Zimmer ist das?

B *356.*

A Ich notiere. Man wird das WC reparieren.

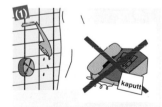 

Im Geschäft

A Ich habe letzte Woche diese Kuckucksuhr gekauft, aber sie funktioniert nicht.

B Das tut mir leid.

A Ich möchte sie bitte umtauschen.

B Haben Sie die Quittung?

A Ja, hier ist die Quittung.

B Also kein Problem. *Hier, bitte schön.*

4 🏰 Du hast gerade Ferien gemacht aber das Hotel war nicht gut. Du möchtest dich also beschweren. Schreib einen Brief an das Hotel.

5 🗣 Bereite Antworten vor. Finde neue Fragen. Übe die Fragen und Antworten mit einem Partner/einer Partnerin.

- Wie ist das Wetter auf dem Bild?
- Was tragen die Kinder?
- Wie sehen die Eltern aus?
- Was könnte die Familie machen?
- Wie wichtig ist das Wetter im Urlaub?

Thema 9 Gesundheit

1 Wie bleibe ich gesund?

1 📖 Schau die Bilder an und finde den richtigen Tipp.

Beispiel *(1)* *e*

Es ist egal wie alt du bist. Eine gute Gesundheit ist immer wichtig für ein gutes Leben. Die meisten Menschen wünschen sich deshalb auch Gesundheit. Um gesund zu bleiben, soll man...

(1) ...nur wenig Fett essen.
(2) ...kein Fastfood essen.
(3) ...nicht zu viel Schokolade essen.
(4) ...mehr Gemüse und Obst essen.
(5) ...kleine Portionen essen.
(6) ...frische Kräuter statt Salz nehmen.
(7) ...täglich einen Liter Wasser trinken.
(8) ...viel Sport treiben.

2 🎧 Hör diesen Jugendlichen (1–10) gut zu. Sind die Gewohnheiten gesund oder ungesund? Trage die Gewohnheit in die richtige Spalte ein. Füll die Tabelle *auf Deutsch* aus.

Gesund ☺	Ungesund ☹
1	

3  Lies bitte folgende Texte und dann füll die Tabelle aus.

> Neben der richtigen Ernährung treibe ich dreimal die Woche Sport. So bleibe ich gesund. Gesunde Kinder sind nicht nur körperlich fit. Sie können auch besser lernen.
>
> **Elizabeth**

> Ich frühstücke richtig, das heißt also gesund. Ich finde, mit leerem Magen in der Schule kann man nichts lernen. Wir brauchen Energie. Und die kommt von einer gesunden Ernährung.
>
> **Helga**

> Zu viel Zucker ist ungesund, und gesüßte Getränke löschen auch nicht den Durst. Ich trinke pro Tag mindestens einen Liter natürliche Flüssigkeit, zum Beispiel Kräutertee oder Mineralwasser.
>
> **Magdalena**

> Ich finde, regelmäßige Bewegung ist wichtig und hält fit. Deswegen laufe ich jeden Tag zur Schule.
>
> **Angelika**

> Der Schlaf ist sehr wichtig, weil sich der Körper beim Schlafen erholt. Wer immer zu wenig schläft, wird krank: Man fühlt sich schlapp und bekommt Kopfschmerzen. Ich schlafe regelmäßig 8 Stunden pro Nacht.
>
> **Lara**

	Was sie tut um gesund zu bleiben	Warum sie das tut
Elizabeth		
Helga		

4a Macht Dialoge. Wechselt euch ab!

Beispiel

A Letztes Jahr habe ich nie Tennis gespielt. Ich hatte keine Zeit.

B *Aber jetzt spielst du zweimal die Woche Tennis.*

(1) Vor 6 Monaten habe ich viel Kuchen gegessen. Ich war ungesund. Aber jetzt…

(2) Ich bewege mich täglich. Ich bin sehr fit. Aber letztes Jahr…

(3) Ich gehe jetzt nie spät ins Bett. Aber vor 3 Monaten…

(4) Ich habe immer viel Zeit im Internet verbracht. Aber jetzt…

(5) Seit 6 Monaten fahre ich mit dem Bus zur Schule. Aber vorher…

(6) Seit 3 Monaten rauche ich nicht. Ich lebe gesund. Aber früher…

(7) Zur Zeit stehe ich oft ganz früh auf. Aber letztes Jahr…

(8) Jetzt trinke ich nur fettarme Milch. Aber als ich jünger war…

b Mach jetzt eine Präsentation über Fitness und Gesundheit. Du sollst erwähnen:

- Wie du fit und gesund bleibst.
- Was du in der letzten Woche für deine Fitness und deine Gesundheit gemacht hast.
- Warum manche Leute nicht gesund sind.
- Deine Pläne für deine Fitness und deine Gesundheit im kommenden Jahr.

5 Für ein Schulprojekt sammelst du Informationen zum Thema: „Wie bleibe ich fit und gesund?". Mach jetzt eine Webseite, damit deine Mitschüler deine Tipps lesen können.

2 ...und was ist nicht so gesund?

☑ Talk about and give advice on unhealthy lifestyles

☑ Use the modal verbs *müssen* and *dürfen*

1 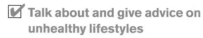 Bitte sieh dir die Bilder an. Was meinst du? Welcher Kommentar passt zu welchem Bild?

(1)

(2)

(3)

(4)

(5)

(6)

(7)

a Sie soll öfter Rad fahren.

b Er soll weniger Kaffee trinken.

c Er soll nicht so viele Zigaretten rauchen.

d Sie dürfen keine Drogen nehmen.

e Sie soll nicht so hart arbeiten.

f Er muss gesünder essen.

g Er muss jetzt ins Bett gehen.

h Man soll weniger Alkohol trinken.

i Sie muss früher aufstehen.

j Er muss mehr Sport treiben.

2  Bitte hör zu und mach Notizen. Was sagen Timo, Sonja und Lisa über ihre Familien?

Person?	Ernährung?	Rauchen/ Alkohol?	Sport?	Weitere Information?
Timos Vater				
Sonjas Mutter				

B8

Grammatik
Der Komparativ (*the comparative*)

To compare two things you use the comparative form of an adjective. This is formed by adding -er to the end of the adjective. A preceding vowel (a, u, o) sometimes takes an umlaut. The comparative can also be used as an adverb, e.g.:
Ich esse gesünder. I eat more healthily.

wenig	little	*weniger*	less
früh	early	*früher*	earlier
oft	often	*öfter*	more often
gesund	healthy	*gesünder*	healthier

Note:
viel	much	*mehr*	more

Grammatik
Modalverben: *müssen, dürfen*
(*modal verbs*)

You have already met three modal verbs: *können, wollen* and *sollen* (page 68). Here are two more: *müssen* and *dürfen. Müssen* is used to say what you have to do. *Dürfen* is used for what you are allowed to do.

	müssen (must/have to)	*dürfen* (may, to be allowed to)
ich	*muss*	*darf*
du	*musst*	*darfst*
er/sie/ es/man	*muss*	*darf*
wir	*müssen*	*dürfen*
ihr	*müsst*	*dürft*
Sie/sie	*müssen*	*dürfen*

Any extra information is placed between the modal verb and the infinitive main verb.

   *Sie **darf** kein Bier **trinken**.*

   *Sie **muss** zu viel **arbeiten**.*

Take care when making these verbs negative. *Du darfst nicht ausgehen* means 'You must not go out'. The sense

of *Du musst nicht ausgehen* is 'You don't have to go out' (followed perhaps by '...but you can if you want to').

What advice would you give to the following people? Use the familiar form (*du/ihr*) of *müssen* and *dürfen* and make more than one suggestion for each picture.

F1

3 💬 Schaut euch eure Notizen zu Übung 2 an. Was sagen die Kinder zu ihren Eltern und Lisa zu ihrem Bruder?
Bitte wechselt euch ab.

   Beispiel   *Du darfst nicht so viele Zigaretten rauchen.*

4 💬📖 Aus der Apothekenzeitschrift.

a Lest und diskutiert den Rat. Was macht jeder von euch?

   Beispiel   *Ich frühstücke jeden Tag.*

b Wie kann man die Information des Apothekers mit einem Modalverb (müssen, dürfen, sollen) ausdrücken? Bitte wechselt euch ab.

   Beispiel   *Sie müssen jeden Tag in Ruhe frühstücken.*

5 🏛 Deine deutsche Freundin in Hamburg hat Prüfungen und ist sehr gestresst. Schreib ihr eine E-mail von 80–90 Wörtern.
Was muss sie machen, um ein gesünderes Leben zu führen? Ihre Probleme:
- Sie isst nur Hamburger.
- Sie trinkt nur Cola.
- Sie schläft zu wenig.
- Sie macht keinen Sport.

Der gute Rat des Apothekers

So leben Sie gesünder:
- Frühstücken Sie jeden Tag in Ruhe.
- Trinken Sie weniger Kaffee und mehr Wasser oder Früchtetees.
- Schlafen Sie auf jeden Fall 7 Stunden pro Nacht.
- Rauchen Sie nicht und trinken Sie nicht regelmäßig Alkohol.
- Bleiben Sie an der frischen Luft, wenn Sie können.
- Essen Sie Obst.
- Waschen Sie sich oft die Hände.
- Arbeiten Sie nicht von morgens bis spät abends.

4 Was ist denn passiert?

☑ Find out about accidents and injuries
☑ Learn about the passive voice

1a 📖 🎧 Hör zu und lies die Texte mit.

(1) Skiläufer am Großglockner verunglückt

Am Sonntagnachmittag ist ein Skiläufer auf der Piste am Großglockner gegen einen Baum geprallt. Der 18-jährige junge Mann wurde mit dem Hubschrauber ins nächste Krankenhaus gebracht. Nach Angaben des Krankenhauses hat er sowohl Knochenbrüche als auch eine schwere Gehirnerschütterung. Er bleibt voraussichtlich bis zum Wochenende dort.

(2) Vorsicht! Grippevirus in Stuttgart

In Stuttgart sind in den letzten Tagen immer mehr Menschen an einem Grippevirus erkrankt. Das Gesundheitsamt empfiehlt die Grippeimpfung für ältere Menschen und für Kinder, die an Asthma leiden. Bei plötzlichen Grippesymptomen rufen Sie bitte Ihren Hausarzt an – er kann Sie beraten.

(3) Schwerer Zusammenstoß auf der A1

Hier ist der WDR 2 mit einer Verkehrsmeldung. Auf der Autobahn A1 in Richtung Köln-West 5 km Stau als Folge eines Autounfalls. Nach Angaben der Polizei sind mindestens acht Fahrzeuge betroffen. Ein Fahrer und ein Beifahrer im gleichen Auto hatten schwere Verletzungen, ein weiterer kam mit leichten Verletzungen davon. Bitte folgen Sie den Umleitungsschildern. Die A1 in Richtung Köln bleibt wahrscheinlich bis zum späten Nachmittag gesperrt.

(4) Feuer in der Küche

Bei einem Feuer in einer Restaurantküche wurde eine Person leicht verletzt. Nach Angaben der Feuerwehr, hat ein Koch im Restaurant 'Zum Seeblick' einen Karton neben einen heißen Grill gestellt und dann eine Kaffeepause gemacht. Ein Kellner hat den Brand entdeckt und die Feuerwehr gerufen. Der Schaden in der Küche beträgt zirka €5000.

b Welches Bild passt zu welchem Text?

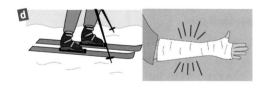

c In jedem Satz gibt es ein Wort, oder Wörter, die nicht zu dem Sinn des Texts passen. Korrigiere die falschen Aussagen.

(1) Ein ~~Krankenwagen~~ hat den Skiläufer ins Krankenhaus gebracht.

(2) Er bleibt bis ~~nächste Woche~~ im Krankenhaus.

(3) ~~Alle Erwachsenen~~ und auch Kinder, die an Asthma leiden, sollen in Stuttgart zum Impfen gehen.

(4) Wenn man Grippe hat, soll man sofort den Hausarzt ~~besuchen~~.

(5) Auf der Autobahn A1 ist ein Stau wegen ~~Straßenbauarbeiten~~.

(6) ~~Drei Personen~~ sind auf der A1 schwer verletzt und eine Person ist leicht verletzt.

(7) ~~Der Koch~~ hat den Brand sofort entdeckt.

(8) Man muss ~~mehr als~~ €5000 bezahlen, um die Küche zu reparieren.

G5

Grammatik
Das Passiv (*passive voice*)

The passive voice is used when the subject of the verb is not carrying out the action, but is on the receiving end of it. This means that a passive sentence often has an impersonal quality:

Mein Auto wird repariert.

We know the car is being repaired, but we do not know who is repairing it.

The passive is formed by using the verb *werden* as the auxiliary + past participle.

To avoid the use of the passive voice in German, the pronoun *man* (someone) is often used, with an active verb, e.g. *Man repariert mein Auto.*

Passive sentences occur in all tenses. In the past. the imperfect of *werden* can be used (*wurde*):

Mein Auto wurde letzte Woche repariert.

Find two passive constructions in the texts on page 86. They are both in the past.

2 Was passt zusammen? Kombiniert. Arbeite mit einem Partner.

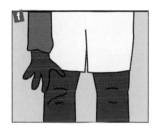

(1) Zwei Autos hatten auf der Straße neben dem Park einen Unfall.
(2) Die Feuerwehr ist gekommen.
(3) Sie ist beim Schlittschuhlaufen hingefallen.
(4) Ich habe im Garten gearbeitet und es gab viele Dornen an den Rosen. Mein Bein hat geblutet.
(5) Ich habe mir den Arm gebrochen.
(6) Die Frau ist gestolpert und ist jetzt verletzt.

3a Erzähl jetzt deinem Partner, was dir/deiner Familie passiert ist. Wo warst du?
● Wie war das Wetter?
● Wer hatte einen Unfall?
● Wann ist das passiert? (Jahreszeit, Datum, Uhrzeit)
● Was ist genau passiert?
● Wer konnte helfen?
● Wann war alles wieder in Ordnung?

Beispiel

Vor zwei Jahren waren wir in den Ferien in Österreich. Das Wetter war toll und wir hatten viel Schnee…

Top-Tipp

When you talk about a broken arm or leg you need to use the accusative for the limb (e.g. *den Arm*) and the dative for the pronouns *mir* and *dir*. The other pronouns (*sich, uns, euch*) are the same as those used with reflexive verbs. (See D3 in the grammar reference section.)

Beispiel: *Ich habe **mir das** Bein gebrochen.*

Füll die Lücken aus: Nimm das Reflexivpronomen im Dativ und den Artikel für den Körperteil im Akkusativ:

(1) Er hat _____ _____ Arm gebrochen.
(2) Ich habe _____ _____ Fuß gebrochen.
(3) Sie hat _____ _____ Bein gebrochen.
(4) Du hast _____ _____ Nase gebrochen.
(5) Haben Sie _____ _____ Knie gebrochen?

Mein Bruder ist ein guter Skiläufer… Die Piste war sehr steil… Er ist gestürzt und hat sich den Arm gebrochen… Ein Hubschrauber…

b Schreib jetzt deine Geschichte auf. Benutze die Punkte der Partnerarbeit in Übung 3a als Hilfe. Schreib ungefähr 50 Wörter.

10.11.89

Hurra!! Ein Loch in der Mauer

(1) Nach mehr als 28 Jahren hat die Berliner Mauer endlich ein Loch. Jubel und Erleichterung gab es gestern am Brandenburger Tor in Berlin. Nach den Ereignissen im letzten Sommer und den Herbstdemonstrationen in der DDR war es gestern Abend ganz unerwartet wieder möglich, problemlos die Grenze von Ost- nach Westberlin zu überqueren.

(2) Besonders viele junge Leute machten singend und jubelnd mit ihrem Trabi einen Ausflug nach Westberlin. „Wir kommen gleich zurück, Mensch ist das toll, wir wollen nur mal gucken, was es im Westen so gibt und schnell ein Bier trinken", sagte ein junger Mann, der gegen 23 Uhr mit vier Freunden im Auto die Grenze überquerte.

(3) In den letzten Monaten ist die Situation für DDR Staatschef Honecker immer schwieriger geworden, aber die Maueröffnung gestern Abend war für alle eine Überraschung.

(4) Bis 1961 konnten Deutsche aus der BRD und aus der DDR in Berlin leben und arbeiten. Viele Menschen wollten damals lieber in einem freien Land leben und verließen die DDR für immer.

(5) Die Reaktion der Regierung der DDR, die mit der Sowjetunion zusammen arbeitete, war der plötzliche Mauerbau über Nacht am 13. August 1961. Mehr als 28 Jahre lang, seit die Sektorengrenze damals plötzlich blockiert wurde, mussten die Berliner mit der schrecklichen Mauer leben, die ihre schöne Stadt bis gestern teilte.

(6) „Bei allem Jubel dürfen wir nicht vergessen, dass viele Menschen versuchten, über die Mauer zu fliehen und dabei erschossen wurden", sagte eine ältere Dame, die gerade aus der Oper kam.

1 📖 Welcher Abschnitt passt zu welchem Buchstaben?

a Die Mauer wurde plötzlich gebaut.

b Spät abends überqueren viele junge Leute die Grenze.

c Die politische Situation in der DDR war im Herbst 1989 sehr schwierig.

d Man kann wieder von Ostberlin nach Westberlin kommen.

e Jetzt sind alle Menschen froh, aber durch die Mauer sind viele Menschen getötet worden, die nicht mehr in Ostberlin leben wollten.

f Vor 1961 verließen viele Menschen die DDR, weil es kein freies Land war.

2 📖 ✏️ Beantworte die Fragen mit kurzen Antworten.

(1) Seit wann gab es eine Mauer zwischen West- und Ostberlin?

(2) Sieh das Datum des Artikels an: Wann genau konnte man die Grenze plötzlich überqueren?

(3) Was gab es im Herbst 1989 in der DDR?

(4) Wollten die jungen Leute im Trabi in Westberlin bleiben? Was wollten sie machen?

(5) Wie hießen die beiden Teile Deutschlands?

(6) Was haben einige Menschen nach dem Mauerbau 1961 versucht zu machen?

PROBLEMPUNKT **Feste**

Frage von Timo18:

Viele von meinen Klassenkameraden rauchen, obwohl man doch überall hört und liest, dass das sehr gesundheitsschädlich ist. An unserer Schule ist das Rauchen verboten. Wenn man 18 ist, darf man nicht mehr in der Pause in einer Ecke auf dem Schulhof rauchen. Außerhalb des Schulgeländes machen es natürlich viele Schüler. Wenn wir zu einem Popfestival gehen, rauchen meine Freunde Martin und Jonas manchmal fast eine ganze Schachtel Zigaretten und das ist doch zu viel! Sie sagen, „Das sieht doch cool aus!" Ich habe Angst davor, dass sie vom Nikotin abhängig werden oder noch schlimmer, härtere Drogen nehmen werden. Was soll ich machen?

Antwort von Schlafmütze:

Du sollst eine Schülerinitiative gegen das Rauchen an deiner Schule organisieren. Sprich mit deinem Schulsprecher oder mit deinem Klassenlehrer. An unserer Schule ist das Rauchen auch verboten. Wenn man weniger Gelegenheiten zu rauchen hat und sieht, wie uncool das ist, hört man oft damit auf.

Antwort von Spätzchen:

Du musst mit deinen Freunden sprechen und ihnen sagen, wie ungesund Zigaretten sind und wie gefährlich es ist, regelmäßig zu rauchen. Sag ihnen, dass du nicht mehr mit ihnen ausgehen möchtest, weil auch deine Kleidung und die Haare hinterher nach Rauch stinken.

Antwort von Grüne Tomate:

Sicher sind Zigaretten gefährlich – aber auch so teuer! Mach Pläne für einen Ausflug mit deinen Freunden, zu einem Popfestival vielleicht? Dafür muss man sparen. Dann rauchen Martin und Jonas sicher weniger, sonst können sie nicht mitkommen. Auf dem Festival könnt ihr dann die Musik und die Zeit mit Freunden genießen; dafür braucht man weder Zigaretten noch Drogen.

Karneval

Karneval, manchmal sagt man auch Fasching oder auch Fastnacht, feiert man vor dem Beginn der Fastenzeit, das heißt Ende Februar. Während der Fastenzeit essen und trinken viele Christen weniger Luxusartikel, vielleicht keine Schokolade, Kuchen oder Alkohol. Karneval, dagegen, ist eine große Party, wo man alles essen darf. Viele junge Menschen, aber auch die älteren, verkleiden sich, das heißt sie ziehen Karnevalskostüme an. Vielleicht sind sie Clown, Matrose oder Prinzessin oder tragen nur einen verrückten Hut. Oft gibt es Karnevalszüge, das sind bunt dekorierte Wagen, die durch die Stadt fahren und Musik spielen. Von dort werfen verkleidete Leute den Zuschauern Süßigkeiten zu.

Ostern

Ostern ist auch ein christliches Fest und findet im Frühling statt, meistens im April. Es ist kombiniert mit einer alten Tradition, den Frühling zu feiern.

Für die Kinder versteckt man Ostereier im Garten. Früher waren das gefärbte Hühnereier, heute sind es Schokoladeneier und Schokoladenosterhasen.

3 📖 Finde diese Wörter oder Ausdrücke im Text.

> classmates
> harmful to health
> outside the school grounds
> addicted
> opportunities
> people often stop doing it

4 🏛 Schreib deine Gedanken für das Forum auf. Schreib ungefähr 50 Wörter.
- Bist du einer Meinung mit Schlafmütze, Spätzchen oder Grüne Tomate?
- Warum/warum nicht?
- Versuch, etwas Neues zu sagen.

5 📖 Beantworte die Fragen mit kurzen Antworten.
1. (1) Was ist Karneval?
2. (2) Was machen viele Christen während der Fastenzeit nicht?
3. (3) Was essen sie in der Karnevalszeit? Warum?
4. (4) Was ist ein Karnevalskostüm?
5. (5) Was kann man vielleicht bekommen, wenn man einem Karnevalszug zuschaut?
6. (6) Was finden die Kinder zu Ostern im Garten?
7. (7) Was ist der Unterschied zwischen früher und heute?

🎧 Paper 1: listening

Sie hören zweimal ein Interview mit vier Jugendlichen, die über ihre Ferien sprechen. Während Sie zuhören, kreuzen Sie an, wenn die Aussage **richtig** ist.

Kreuzen Sie **nur 6** Kästchen an (✓ ✓ ✓ ✓ ✓ ✓).

Bevor Sie das Interview hören, lesen Sie bitte die Aussagen durch.

Richtig

Sara

(a) Sara war mit ihren Eltern im Urlaub. ☐

(b) Sie ist mit dem Flugzeug gereist. ☐

(c) Das Wetter war sehr heiß. ☐

Rüdiger

(d) Im Sommer hat Rüdiger Urlaub am Meer gemacht. ☐

(e) Die Familie hat auf einem Campingplatz übernachtet. ☐

(f) Seiner Meinung nach ist das Wetter im Urlaub sehr wichtig. ☐

Erika

(g) Erika ist im Sommer zu Hause geblieben. ☐

(h) Sie ist nach Amerika gefahren. ☐

(i) Wenn sie im Urlaub ist, fährt Erika nicht gern mit dem Bus. ☐

Patrick

(j) Patrick plant jetzt seinen Urlaub. ☐

(k) Die Gruppe wird mit dem Zug reisen. ☐

(l) Alle werden in Restaurants essen. ☐

[Total: 6]

Tips for success

- Read the sentences before the recording is played so that you have an idea of what to listen for.
- There are four speakers but you have to tick *six* sentences as true. This means it is not simply one per speaker.
- If you tick more than six boxes, you will lose marks.
- You probably won't hear exactly the same words as you read in the sentences. Listen out for synonyms such as *mit der Bahn* and *mit dem Zug,* which both mean 'by train'.

 Paper 2: reading

This question type requires you to choose words to fill the gaps in sentences so that they reflect what you have read in the text.

Lesen Sie den folgenden Text.

Leben Sie gesund?

Essen Sie richtig? Das Frühstück ist die wichtigste Mahlzeit des Tages. Trotzdem verlassen immer mehr Menschen das Haus mit leerem Magen. Haben Sie um 11 Uhr Hunger? Dann nehmen Sie lieber eine Banane oder einen Apfel ins Büro mit. Das ist viel besser als Schokolade oder Kekse.

Trinken Sie gern Kaffee? Vorsicht! Zwei Tassen am Tag sind genug, aber nur vor 18 Uhr. Sonst kann man nicht schlafen. Gehen Sie nicht zu spät, aber auch nicht zu früh, ins Bett. Zu lange schlafen ist auch nicht gesund.

Sport verbessert Ihre Lebensqualität. Fahren Sie normalerweise zur Arbeit? Lassen Sie den Wagen zu Hause und gehen Sie jeden Tag laufen oder spazieren. Sie werden nicht nur fit sein, sondern Sie werden auch Geld sparen.

Füllen Sie die Lücken aus mit dem Wort, das am besten passt.

Abend	langsam	ohne	nichts	Süßigkeiten
Obst	alles	Vormittag	regelmäßig	mit

Tips for success

- Look at the words in the box before you start reading and identify whether they are nouns, verbs, adjectives, adverbs or prepositions.
- Read the sentences and work out what kind of word you need to find.
- If the gap requires a noun, you might be able to work out which gender it needs to be or whether it is singular or plural. This might help you to eliminate words.
- You should find two possible alternatives for each gap. These might be opposites. Keep these in mind as you read the text.

1 Viele Leute essen .... , wenn sie aufstehen. [1]

2 Als Imbiss sollte man .... essen. [1]

3 Am besten trinkt man am .... keinen Kaffee. [1]

4 Sie sollten .... zu Fuß gehen. [1]

5 Es ist billiger, wenn man .... das Auto zur Arbeit kommt. [1]

[Total: 5]

Paper 3: speaking

In part 2 of the exam you give a presentation lasting for 1–2 minutes, which is followed by questions on what you have said. This part of the exam lasts for about 5 minutes.

Below is part of a sample presentation on the subject of holidays. Work through the tasks with a partner so that you can develop the techniques needed to create a good presentation.

Mein Urlaub

1 (a) Listen to the opening section of a student's presentation (paragraph A). Work with a partner and discuss how it could be improved.

Paragraph A

Use different sentence openings. Vary the word order. Use different pronouns and verb forms, e.g. *Wir haben in einem Hotel übernachtet.*

Link sentences with subordinate clauses, e.g. *…weil das Wetter dort schön ist.*

How did you travel? How long did you stay? E.g. Use *geflogen* instead of *gefahren; für eine Woche/zwei Wochen.*

Ich fahre gern in Urlaub.
Ich reise gern nach Spanien.
Das Wetter ist schön dort
und die Sonne scheint.
Ich bin letztes Jahr in den
Sommerferien nach Malaga
gefahren. Es war sehr schön.
Ich bin mit meiner Mutter und
meiner Schwester gefahren.
Ich habe in einem Hotel
übernachtet. Das Hotel war gut.
Ich bin zum Strand gegangen.
Ich schwimme gern und ich
liege gern in der Sonne.

Could you find more interesting adjectives? E.g. *Das Wetter war herrlich.*

Where was the hotel? E.g. *in der Nähe vom Strand, in der Stadtmitte.*

Add some time phrases, e.g. *jeden Tag.*

(b) Write out an improved version of this section using these tips.

2 Prepare a presentation in German about holidays using these headings. Remember to use what you have learned from the previous task.

Wie gefahren?	Wie lange?	Wohin?	Wo gewohnt?	Was gemacht?	Wetter?

When you have written your presentation, practise reading it out loud and time it. Swap with your partner and think up some questions to ask each other to prepare for the discussion.

Points to remember

Remember to include:
- a range of tenses and interesting adjectives (use a dictionary)
- subordinate clauses starting with *weil* (because), *da* (as, since), *obwohl* (although) etc., but remember to use correct word order
- *um…zu* clauses with an infinitive after *zu* (Grammar reference G2)
- linking words, e.g. *also* (so), *deshalb* (therefore), *dann* (then), *danach* (after that), but remember that these will affect the word order
- subjects other than just *ich*, e.g. *wir, meine Familie* etc., but remember to use the correct verb ending for different subjects
- a variety of sentence openings and time phrases, e.g. *jeden Tag* (every day), *normalerweise* (usually), *letztes Jahr* (last year), *nächstes Jahr* (next year), *oft* (often)

Paper 4: writing

In part 2 of the exam you have a choice of three tasks and you have to write 130–140 words in response to one of these. Work with a partner to decide what you would write for the following sample task and then write your own response before looking at the sample answer below.

---

1 Sie haben am Wochenende mit Ihrer Familie Ihren Geburtstag gefeiert. Heute sind Sie krank und Sie können nicht zur Schule gehen. Schreiben Sie eine E-mail an einen Schulfreund/eine Schulfreundin.
- Erklären Sie, warum Sie nicht in der Schule sind.
- Erzählen Sie, wie es bei Ihrer Geburtstagsfeier war.
- Sie waren gestern bei einer Ärztin. Was hat sie gesagt?
- Sagen Sie, was Sie zu Hause machen und wann Sie wieder zur Schule kommen werden.

Points to remember

In the writing and speaking exams you will need to understand instructions in German. They will use verbs in the imperative and could include the following:
- *Erklären Sie...* (Explain...)
- *Sagen Sie...* (Say...)
- *Erzählen Sie...* (Tell, talk about...)
- *Beschreiben Sie...* (Describe...)
- *Fragen Sie...* (Ask...)
- *Reagieren Sie...* (React...)

Sample student answer

Hallo Samira

Heute kann ich nicht zur Schule kommen, weil ich krank bin. Mir ist schlecht und ich habe Grippe. Ich habe Kopfschmerzen und meine Ohren tun weh. Am Samstag habe ich meinen Geburtstag gefeiert. Meine Familie und ich sind zuerst ins Kino gegangen und dann haben wir in einem Restaurant gegessen. Ich habe eine Pizza mit viel Käse gewählt. Das war total lecker! Gestern bin ich mit meiner Mutter zu einer Ärztin gegangen. Sie hat gesagt „Du musst im Bett bleiben!". Ich soll viel schlafen, viel Wasser trinken und Tabletten nehmen. Leider darf ich nicht ausgehen oder meine Freunde sehen. Ich finde es so langweilig hier, obwohl ich fernsehen und Musik hören kann. Natürlich kann ich auch den Computer benutzen! Hoffentlich kann ich am Donnerstag wieder zur Schule kommen.

Viele Grüße!

Nina

This is an example of a good answer using accurate German. In the exam this question is marked out of 30: communication (10), use of verbs (8) and other linguistic features (12).

2 (a) Work with a partner to find the features that make this a good answer. Make a list under each heading:

Communication	Use of verbs	Other linguistic features

(b) Consider what other good features the student could have included.

(c) Compare this version with your own and your partner's. Discuss which of the features you have each included and what you could have added to make it even better.

Travel

die **Abfahrt (-en)** departure
abfliegen to depart (by plane)
der **Abflug (¨-e)** departure (by plane)
die **Abreise (-n)** departure
abreisen to depart
ankommen to arrive
die **Ankunft (¨-e)** arrival
die **Ausfahrt (-en)** exit
der **Ausgang (¨-e)** way out, exit
das **Ausland** foreign countries, abroad
aussteigen to get off, alight
der **Ausweis (-e)** identity card
die **Autobahn (-en)** motorway
der **Bahnhof (¨-e)** (railway) station
der **Bahnsteig (-e)** platform
das **Benzin** petrol
bleifrei lead-free, unleaded
die **Bundesstraße (-n)** A-road
der **Busbahnhof (¨-e)** bus station
der/die **Busfahrer (-)/in (-nen)** bus driver
einfach single
einsteigen to get on
die **Einzelfahrkarte (-n)** single ticket
fahren to go, travel, drive
der/die **Fahrer (-)/in (-nen)** driver
die **Fahrkarte (-n)** ticket
die **Fahrt (-en)** journey
fliegen to fly
der **Flughafen (¨)** airport
der **Führerschein (-e)** driving licence
das **Fundbüro (-s)** lost-property office
der **Fußgänger (-)** pedestrian
der **Gegenstand (¨-e)** item
das **Gepäck** luggage
die **Gepäckaufbewahrung (-en)** left-luggage office
die **Geschwindigkeit (-en)** speed
das **Gleis (-e)** track, platform
die **Grenze (-n)** border
gute Reise safe journey
halten to stop
die **Haltestelle (-n)** stop
das **Handgepäck** hand luggage
die **Heimfahrt (-en)** journey home
hin und zurück return; there and back
im Ausland abroad
die **Karte (-n)** ticket
der **Kofferraum (-räume)** boot (of car)
der/die **Kontrolleur (-)/in (-nen)** inspector
kontrollieren to check
die **Landstraße (-n)** main arterial road
die **Maschine (-n)** aeroplane
das **Motor (-en)** engine
öffentlich public
die **Panne (-n)** breakdown, puncture
parken to park
per Anhalter fahren to hitchhike
der **Reifen (-)** tyre
die **Reise (-n)** journey
reisen to travel

die **Rückfahrkarte (-n)** return ticket
der **Schalter (-)** ticket office
schnell quick(ly), fast
die **Sicherheit** safety
starten to take off
der **Stau (-e)** traffic jam
die **Tankstelle (-en)** service station
die **Umleitung (-en)** traffic diversion
umsteigen to change (trains etc.)
der **Verkehr** traffic
die **Verkehrsmeldung** traffic news
verpassen to miss (train, bus etc.)
verspätet delayed
die **Verspätung (-en)** delay
volltanken to fill up (with fuel)
der **Zoll** customs

Directions

abbiegen to turn (off)
die **Ecke (-n)** corner
die **Einbahnstraße (-n)** one-way street
gehen to go, walk
geradeaus straight on
der **Kreisverkehr (-)** roundabout
die **Kreuzung (-en)** crossroads
links (on the) left
nächst next
die **Nähe (in der Nähe von)** near
rechts (on the) right
spazieren to walk
überqueren to cross over
weiterfahren to continue, drive on
wenden to turn
wie komme ich…? how do I get (to…)?

Means of transport

das **Auto (-s)** car
die **Bahn (-en)** train, railway
das **Boot (-e)** boat
die **Eisenbahn (-en)** railway
der **Eurotunnel** Channel Tunnel
die **Fähre (-n)** ferry
das **Fahrrad (¨-er)** bicycle
das **Flugzeug (-e)** plane
das **Mofa (-s)** moped
das **Motorrad (¨-er)** motorbike
das **Rad (¨-er)** wheel, bike
das **Schiff (-e)** ship
die **Straßenbahn (-en)** tram
die **U-Bahn (-en)** underground, tube
das **Verkehrsmittel (-n)** means of transport
der **Wagen (-)** car
zu Fuß on foot
der **Zug (¨-e)** train

Holiday activities

die **Aktivität (-en)** activity
baden to swim (in the sea)
der **Fotoapparat (-e)** camera
kosten to cost
das **Picknick (-s)** picnic
die **Postkarte (-n)** postcard

der/die **Reiseleiter (-)/in (-nen)** tourist guide
die **Sandburg (-en)** sand-castle
schicken to send
schwimmen to swim
sehen to see
die **Sehenswürdigkeit (-en)** tourist sight
sonnen (sich) to sunbathe
der **Wasserski** waterskiing
das **Windsurfbrett (-er)** windsurfing board

Holiday accommodation

der **Aufenthalt (-e)** stay
ausgebucht booked up, fully booked
auspacken to unpack
der **Balkon (-s)** balcony
besetzt occupied, taken, full
bleiben to stay
buchen to book
der **Campingplatz (¨-e)** campsite
das **Doppelbett (-en)** double bed
die **Dusche (-n)** shower
einpacken to wrap, pack
einschließlich including, inclusive
der **Empfang (¨-e)** reception
das **Formular (-e)** form
frei free, vacant, unoccupied
fünfzehn Tage a fortnight
die **Gebühr (-en)** charge, fee
die **Halbpension** half board
im voraus in advance
die **Jugendherberge (-n)** youth hostel
die **Klimatisierung (-en)** air conditioning
die **Miete (-n)** rent
mieten to rent, hire
die **Pension (-en)** guest house
der **Preis (-e)** price
reservieren to reserve
der **Schlafsack (¨-e)** sleeping bag
übernachten to spend the night, stay
die **Unterkunft (¨-e)** accommodation
die **Vollpension** full board
willkommen heißen to welcome
der **Zeitraum (ä-e)** period (of time)
das **Zelt (-e)** tent

Tourism

der **Abfahrtslauf** downhill skiing
abschicken to send, post
die **Ansichtskarte (-n)** picture postcard
die **Aussicht (-en)** view
beschreiben to describe
besichtigen to visit, look at, look round
besuchen to visit
die **Ferien** holidays
der **Hausberg (-e)** the 'local' mountain
der **Hügel (-)** hill
kennen lernen to get to know, meet
der **Koffer (-)** suitcase
die **Küste (-n)** coast, seaside
das **Land (¨-er)** country, countryside, land
der **Pass (¨-e)** passport

der/die **Reisende (-n)**   traveller
der **See (-n)**   lake
die **See (-n)**   sea
der **Sommer (-)**   summer
die **Sonnenbrille (-n)**   sunglasses
die **Sonnencreme (-s)**   sun cream
der **Stadtplan ("-e)**   street map
der **Strand ("-e)**   beach
die **Taschenlampe (-n)**   torch
der/die **Tourist (-en)/in (-nen)**   tourist
das **Touristenbüro (-s)**   tourist office
treffen   to meet (by prior arrangement)
die **Überraschung (-en)**   surprise
der **Urlaub (-e)**   holiday
verbringen   to spend (time)
vergessen   to forget
das **Verkehrsamt ("-er)**   tourist office
verlassen   to leave (a place)
der **Wechsel**   change
wechseln   to change

Parts of the body

der **Arm ("-e)**   arm
das **Auge (-n)**   eye
der **Bauch (Bäuche)**   stomach, tummy
das **Bein (-e)**   leg
die **Brust ("-e)**   chest
der **Finger (-)**   finger
der **Fuß ("-e)**   foot
das **Gesicht (-er)**   face
das **Hals ("-e)**   throat
die **Hand ("-e)**   hand
das **Herz (-en)**   heart
das **Knie (-)**   knee
der **Kopf ("-e)**   head
der **Magen (")**   stomach
der **Mund ("-er)**   mouth
die **Nase (-n)**   nose
das **Ohr (-en)**   ear
der **Zahn ("-e)**   tooth
die **Zehe (-n)**   toe
die **Zunge (-n)**   tongue

Accidents and ailments

die **Bauchschmerzen**   tummy ache
das **Blut**   blood
der **Durchfall**   diarrhoea
erbrechen   to vomit
das **Ereignis (-se)**   event
die **Erleichterung**   relief
erste Hilfe leisten   to give first aid
fallen   to fall
das **Fieber**   temperature, fever
gebrochen   broken
die **Gehirnerschütterung**   concussion
gestorben   dead
die **Grippe**   flu
die **Halsschmerzen**   sore throat
husten   to cough
jemanden erschießen   to shoot somebody
kaputt   broken
der **Knochenbruch (-brüche)**   broken bone

die **Kopfschmerzen**   headache
krank   ill, sick
krank fühlen (sich)   to feel ill, sick
die **Krankheit (-en)**   illness
leiden   to suffer
die **Magenschmerzen**   stomach ache
die **Ohrenschmerzen**   earache
das **Pflaster (-)**   plaster
prallen   to collide with, crash into
die **Rückenschmerzen**   backache
der **Sonnenbrand (-)**   sunburn
der **Stich (-e)**   sting, bite
stürzen   to fall (over/down)
unerwartet   unexpected
der **Unfall ("-e)**   accident
verletzen   to injure, hurt, wound
die **Verletzung (-en)**   injury
verunglücken   to have an accident
weh tun (sich)   to hurt (oneself)

Health issues

abnehmen   to lose weight
der **Alkohol**   alcohol
der/die **Arzt ("-e)/Ärztin (-nen)**   doctor
atmen   to breathe
ausruhen (sich)   to rest
besser gehen   to be better (healthwise)
erholen (sich)   to recover
erkältet sein   to have a cold
ernst   serious
gesund   healthy
die **Gesundheit**   health
gesundheitsschädlich   damaging to your health
im Bett bleiben   to stay in bed
die **Impfung (-en)**   vaccination
die **Hilfe**   help
die **Klinik (-en)**   clinic
der **Körper (-)**   body
das **Krankenhaus ("-er)**   hospital
der **Krankenpfleger (-)**   (male) nurse
die **Krankenschwester (-n)**   (female) nurse
der **Krankenwagen (-)**   ambulance
das **Medikament (-e)**   medicine
nehmen   to take
rauchen   to smoke
das **Rezept (-e)**   prescription
schlafen   to sleep
schlagen   to hit, knock
schwindlig   dizzy
die **Sprechstunde (-n)**   surgery, consultation
die **Spritze (-n)**   injection
der **Tabak**   tobacco
die **Tablette (-n)**   tablet
das **Taschentuch ("-er)**   handkerchief
die **Temperatur (-en)**   temperature
der **Termin (-e)**   appointment
übel   bad, nauseous
übergeben (sich)   to be sick, vomit
die **Übung (-en)**   exercise
der/die **Vegetarier (-)/in (-nen)**   vegetarian

der/die **Zahnarzt ("-e)/Zahnärztin (-nen)**   dentist
die **Zahnschmerzen**   toothache
die **Zigarette (-n)**   cigarette
zunehmen   to put on weight

Countries and continents

Afrika   Africa
Asien   Asia
Belgien   Belgium
Dänemark   Denmark
Deutschland   Germany
England   England
Europa   Europe
Frankreich   France
Griechenland   Greece
Großbritannien   Great Britain
Italien   Italy
Kanada   Canada
die **Niederlande**   Netherlands
Nordamerika   North America
Österreich   Austria
Polen   Poland
Schottland   Scotland
Schweden   Sweden
die **Schweiz**   Switzerland
die **Türkei**   Turkey
das **Vereinigte Königreich**   United Kingdom
die **Vereinigten Staaten**   United States

Nationalities

der/die **Amerikaner (-)/in (-nen)**   American
der/die **Belgier (-)/in (-nen)**   Belgian
der **Däne (-n)/die Dänin (-nen)**   Dane
der **Deutsche (-)/die Deutsche (-n)**   German
der/die **Engländer (-)/in (-nen)**   Englishman/woman
der/die **Franzose (-n)/Französin (-nen)**   Frenchman/woman
der/die **Holländer (-)/in (-nen)**   Dutchman/woman
der/die **Italiener (-)/in (-nen)**   Italian
der/die **Kanadier (-)/in (-nen)**   Canadian
der/die **Österreicher (-)/in (-nen)**   Austrian
der **Schotte (-n)/die Schottin (-nen)**   Scot
der/die **Schweizer (-)/in (-nen)**   Swiss
der/die **Spanier (-)/in (-nen)**   Spaniard
der **Türke (-n)/die Türkin (-nen)**   Turk
der/die **Waliser (-)/in (-nen)**   Welshman/woman

Geographical areas

die **Alpen**   the Alps
das **Bayern**   Bavaria
der **Bodensee**   Lake Constance
Köln   Cologne
München   Munich
der **Schwarzwald**   the Black Forest
Wien   Vienna

1 Was kann man in deiner Stadt machen?

☑ **Describe your town**
☑ **Say what you can do in your town**

1 📖 Bitte lies folgende Texte.

> Meine Stadt ist eine ziemlich große Touristenstadt mit ungefähr 80 000 Einwohnern. Es gibt viele Sehenswürdigkeiten. Wir haben den alten Dom in der Stadtmitte oder das Schloss Kyburg außerhalb der Stadt. Leider kommen zu viele Touristen im Sommer aber zum Glück gibt es den Stadtgarten mit einem Kinderspielplatz und dem Musikpavillon, wo man in Ruhe seinen Lunch essen oder die Zeitung lesen kann.

Angelika

> Ich wohne im Süden in einem kleinen Dorf auf dem Lande in der Nähe von Zürich. Die Landschaft ist malerisch aber das Dorfleben ist stinklangweilig, weil es nicht sehr viel für junge Leute gibt. Es gibt nur wenig Verkehr und man kann also ruhig spazieren gehen oder Rad fahren. Aber es gibt keine Unterhaltungsmöglichkeiten wie etwa ein Kino oder ein Sportzentrum. Wir haben bloß einen kleinen Laden.

Kevin

> Ich lebe in einer Kleinstadt an der Küste. Es gibt immer etwas Interessantes zu tun. Man kann die vielen Museen und Kunstgalerien besuchen oder ins Theater gehen. Wir haben auch verschiedene Feste, wo man sich gut amüsieren kann. Die öffentlichen Verkehrsmittel sind aber nicht so besonders und man muss also unbedingt ein Auto haben.

Evangelos

> Ich wohne in einer großen Industriestadt neben der Autobahn. Alles ist so schmutzig und es gibt viel zu viel Verkehr. Auf der anderen Seite ist immer viel los. Man kann ins Hallenbad gehen oder in den vielen Geschäften einkaufen und abends kann man im Nachtklub tanzen oder in ein Konzert gehen. In der Gegend gibt es einen Wald. Da kann man gut wandern.

Magdalena

a Welche Person ist das?

Beispiel 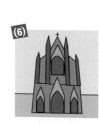 = *Magdalena*

 (1)
 (2)
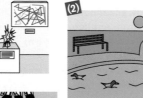 (9)
 (3)
 (4)
 (5)

(6)
(7)
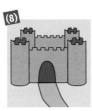(8)
(10)
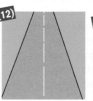(11)
(12)
(13) KAUFHAUS

b Was finden diese Jugendlichen positiv an ihrem Wohnort und was finden sie negativ?

Füll die Tabelle aus.

Name	Positiv 😊	Negativ ☹
Angelika	viele Sehenswürdigkeiten…	
Kevin		

2 🎧 Hör bitte zu. Christoph, Lara und Lukas reden über ihren Wohnort.

Was sagen sie? Mach Notizen.

Name:	Christoph
Wohnort:	Großstadt,...
Was es gibt:	Flughafen,...
Was man machen kann:	rudern,...

Top-Tipp

die Industriestadt — das Dorf — an der Küste — auf dem Land — im Norden — in der Nähe von

die Universitätsstadt — die Hafenstadt — die Großstadt — am Meer — neben der Autobahn — im Westen — Einwohner

3 a 💬 Macht Dialoge.

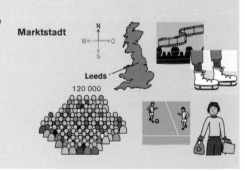

Beispiel

A Wo wohnst du?

B *Ich wohne in einer Marktstadt in Nordengland in der Nähe von Leeds. Es gibt 120 000 Einwohner.*

A Was gibt es in deiner Stadt?

B *Es gibt ein Kino und ein Eisstadion.*

A Was kann man dort machen?

B *Man kann Fußball spielen und einkaufen gehen.*

A Und wie findest du deinen Wohnort?

B *Ich finde meine Stadt toll, weil dort immer viel los ist.*

Marktstadt
Leeds
120 000

(1)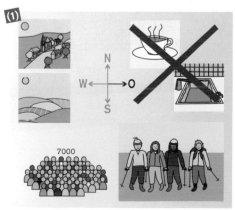

7000

(2)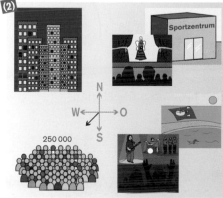

250 000

Sportzentrum

(3)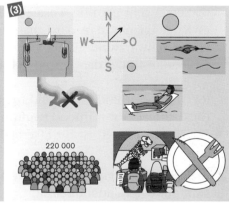

220 000

b Mach jetzt eine Präsentation über deinen Wohnort. Du sollst erwähnen:
- Wohnort
- Sehenswürdigkeiten (*es gibt...*)
- Unterhaltungsmöglichkeiten (*man kann...*)

4 🏰 Mach eine Broschüre über deinen Wohnort und deine Gegend für deutsche Touristen. Benutz deine Notizen aus Übung 3b.

2 ...und wie findest du deine Stadt?

✔ Give more detail about your home town and talk about your local area

✔ Use the verb *gefallen* to express likes and dislikes

✔ Revise other ways of expressing positive and negative opinions

1 📖 Was sagen Sergej, Florian und Elke?
Bitte lies die Texte. Was ist richtig und was ist falsch?
Bitte korrigiere die falschen Sätze.

Also ich komme aus Moskau und wohne jetzt in einem Hochhaus in Frankfurt. Die Stadt ist super! Frankfurt ist eine Großstadt und man kann eigentlich alles machen. Es gibt viele Sportmöglichkeiten, eine gute Fußballmannschaft, das gefällt mir alles, ich gehe gern ins Kino und spiele oft Fußball. Ich wohne gern hier. Natürlich gibt es auch Nachteile, wir haben keinen Garten und manchmal ist der Aufzug kaputt und wir müssen viele Treppen steigen.

Sergej

Wir wohnen auf dem Land in einem Bauernhaus im Schwarzwald. Klar der Schwarzwald ist Natur pur und viele Menschen machen hier Urlaub. Aber meiner Meinung nach ist es für junge Leute total langweilig. Hier ist nichts los, ein Spielplatz und ein Jugendklub am Samstagabend bis 23 Uhr, wir spielen Tischtennis, na super! Das nächste Kino ist in Freiburg, 45 km, die Busse fahren nach 19 Uhr kaum noch, und die Bushaltestelle ist im Ort, 15 Minuten zu Fuß von meinem Haus. Also ich mag es hier nicht. Wir haben einen Tennisplatz am Wald, das stimmt, und die Luft ist sauber...

Also ich wohne in einer Sackgasse in einer modernen Siedlung in Essen. Essen ist eine Großstadt und es gibt eigentlich viele Aktivitäten. Ich mache gern Sport und es gibt viele Sportklubs. Die Busse fahren regelmäßig in die Innenstadt und ich kann meine Freundinnen in einer Eisdiele oder zum Einkaufen treffen. Das gefällt mir. Unsere Siedlung ist am Stadtrand, sie liegt fast im Grünen. Das finde ich schön. Es gibt viele Bäume, ich denke, es ist super hier.

Elke

Florian

(1) Sergej wohnt in Moskau.
(2) Sergej geht gern ins Theater.
(3) Sergej glaubt, dass das Leben in Frankfurt gut ist.
(4) Im Schwarzwald gibt es viele Urlauber.
(5) Florian findet den Jugendklub ideal für junge Leute.
(6) Die Busverbindungen sind für Elke besser als für Florian.
(7) Elke macht mit ihren Freundinnen Sport.
(8) Die Stadt Essen ist für Elke nicht langweilig.

2 🎧 Sergej, Florian und Elke treffen sich auf einer Jugendfreizeit.
Du hast schon einige Informationen über Sergej, Florian und Elke.

Hör gut zu und kombiniere alle deine Informationen in dieser Tabelle.
Was ist positiv, was ist negativ an ihrem Heimatort?

Name	Wo? (Gegend/Stadt, Haus/Wohnung)	Positiv 😊	Negativ 😞
Sergej		Kino...	keinen Garten...

Grammatik

Das Verb *gefallen* (*the verb* gefallen)

You have already met two ways of expressing your opinion:

- the verb *mögen*
  Das mag ich.
  I like that.
  Das mag ich nicht.
  I don't like that.

- the word *gern*
  Ich wohne gern in Essen.
  I like living in Essen.
  Ich gehe nicht gern ins Kino.
  I don't like going to the cinema.

Go back to *Thema* 3, page 22, if you need to revise the above expressions or turn to the grammar section at the back of the book.

Another way to say that you like or dislike something involves the verb *gefallen*, which is followed by the dative:

*Die Stadt gefällt **mir**.* I like the town.
(The town is pleasing **to me**.)
*Die Stadt gefällt **dir**.* You like the town.
*Die Stadt gefällt **ihm**.* He likes the town.
*Die Stadt gefällt **ihr**.* She likes the town.
*Gefällt **Ihnen** die Stadt?* Do **you** like the town?
*Die Stadt gefällt **uns**.* We like the town.
*Die Stadt gefällt **euch**.* You like the town.
*Die Stadt gefällt **ihnen**.* They like the town.
*Gefällt **Ihnen** die Stadt?* Do **you** like the town?

Look in the grammar section at the back of the book if you have problems with the dative pronouns (page 155).

To express dislike simply add *nicht*:
  Die Stadt gefällt mir nicht.

Rewrite the following sentences using *gefallen*.

Example:
Ich mag die Stadt.
Die Stadt gefällt mir.

(1) Ich finde die Fußgängerzone gut.
(2) Ich mag die Brücke.
(3) Er findet das Kino langweilig.
(4) Wir mögen die Bibliothek nicht.
(5) Sie mag die Insel.

 10/1

3 💬 Macht Dialoge. Wechselt euch ab. Wie findest du deine Stadt?

A Wo wohnst du? Auf dem Land, in der Stadt, in einem Vorort?
B *Ich wohne...*
A Gefällt dir deine Stadt/dein Dorf?
B *Ja, die Stadt gefällt mir./Nein, das Dorf gefällt mir nicht.*
A Wo genau wohnst du?
B *Ich wohne in einem Haus am Stadtrand.*
A Was magst du dort?
B *Ich mag meinen Garten/den Spielplatz/die Disko/die Eisdiele/die Fußgängerzone.*
A Und was machst du nicht gern?
B *Ich fahre nicht gern mit dem Bus./Ich steige nicht gern Treppen.*
A Ist in deiner Stadt/deinem Dorf viel los?
B *Ja, da ist immer viel los./Nein, es ist langweilig.*

Top-Tipp
Was kann man noch sagen?

Meiner Meinung nach ist diese Stadt/dieses Dorf langweilig.

Ich finde diese Stadt/ das Dorf langweilig.

Hier ist nichts los/viel los.

Ich wohne gern/nicht gern hier.

Ich mag meine Stadt. Ich mag meine Stadt nicht.

Das ist ein Vorteil/Nachteil.

4 📝 Dein Brieffreund/deine Brieffreundin besucht dich.

Schreib eine E-mail über deine Stadt (100 Wörter).
- Schreib, was man in deiner Stadt machen kann (drei Sachen).
- Schreib, ob die Stadt dir gefällt (warum/warum nicht?).
- Frag ihn/sie, wie seine/ihre Stadt ist.

3 Großstadt, Kleinstadt?

☑ Discuss and understand the advantages and disadvantages of living in a big or a small town

1 📖 Was passt zum Leben in der Großstadt und was zum Leben in einer Kleinstadt? Mach zwei Listen.

In der Großstadt	In der Kleinstadt

a Die Luft ist sauber.

b Es gibt viel Natur.

c Das Theater ist gleich um die Ecke.

d Abends fahren keine Busse.

e Man kann schön spazieren gehen.

f Manchmal ist es sehr laut.

g Nirgends kann ich mein Auto parken.

h Ich habe einen großen Garten mit Blick auf die Berge.

i Hier gibt es nur ein kleines Lebensmittelgeschäft.

j Der Verkehr geht mir auf die Nerven.

k Mit der U-Bahn bin ich schnell in meinem Büro.

l Ich hole frische Milch vom Bauernhof.

m Die Kinder können auf der Straße spielen.

n Einkaufen kann man hier schlecht.

o Hier braucht man ein Auto, sonst ist es schwierig.

p Ich finde es gut, dass die Kinder jeden Tag Kühe, Schafe und Pferde sehen.

q Ich brauche kein Auto, die Straßenbahn hält vor dem Haus.

r Hier ist es sehr ruhig und es gibt keine Probleme mit Drogen und Alkohol.

s Die Kinder haben viele Freizeitmöglichkeiten: Tennisklub, Sportverein, Musikschule, alles ist im Zentrum.

t Es gibt viele verschiedene Schulen in der Nähe.

2 💬 Diskutiert die Vorteile und die Nachteile von Großstadt und Kleinstadt. Bitte seht euch die Bilder unten an und benutzt die Liste aus Übung 1. Wer macht den schönsten Satz?

A Möchtest du in einer Kleinstadt wohnen?

B *Nein, ich wohne lieber in der Großstadt, weil das Theater gleich um die Ecke ist, obwohl der Verkehr mir auf die Nerven geht.*

Top-Tipp

Ein Vorteil ist...

Ein Nachteil ist...

Man kann/ kann nicht...

Es gibt.../es gibt keinen, keine, kein...

Man hat...

Man braucht.../ braucht keinen, keine, kein...

10/2

Großstadt

Kleinstadt

3 📖 ✏️ Bitte lies beide Texte und beantworte die Fragen.

(1) Wo arbeiten viele Menschen in Leverkusen?

(2) Wie kann man in Büsum Geld verdienen?

(3) Was gibt es in beiden Orten, in Leverkusen und in Büsum?

(4) Nenne zwei Aktivitäten, die man als Tourist in Büsum machen kann.

(5) Nenne zwei Vorteile des Lebens in Leverkusen.

(6) Was ist vielleicht ein Nachteil in Leverkusen?

(7) Nenne zwei Vorteile des Lebens in Büsum.

(8) Was ist vielleicht ein Nachteil in Büsum?

(9) Wo möchtest du lieber wohnen, in Leverkusen oder in Büsum und warum?

Leverkusen liegt am Rhein in Nordrhein-Westfalen und hat ungefähr 160 000 Einwohner. Es ist eine Industriestadt. Seit 1863 gibt es dort die Firma Bayer, heute ein großer Chemiekonzern, der viele Arbeitsplätze hat.

Leverkusen liegt verkehrsgünstig, Autobahnen, Flugverbindungen und die Deutsche Bahn sind direkt vor der Tür. Es gibt dort ein Theater, Kinos, viele internationale Restaurants und viel Sport, besonders der Fußballklub Bayer Leverkusen, der ein modernes Stadion hat, das Bayarena heißt. Man kann auch gut einkaufen.

Es gibt auch viele Schulen und eine große Musikschule. Das Bergische Land ist ganz in der Nähe, dort kann man gut wandern und auch die historische Stadt Köln ist nicht weit.

Büsum ist ein kleiner Seeort an der Westküste von Schleswig-Holstein. „Moin" sagt man dort, nicht „Guten Morgen". Es ist ein Fischerort und hat nur ungefähr 4800 Einwohner. Es ist ein Nordseebad und im Sommer kommen viele Touristen mit dem Auto oder mit dem Zug dorthin. Am Strand stehen 2500 Strandkörbe, das sind große Sitze für Touristen. „Büsum erfrischt" ist das Motto des Seebades. Die Luft ist gesund, man kann einen Hafenbummel machen oder eine Wattwanderung*, wenn Ebbe** ist.
Es gibt eine Surfschule, viele Restaurants und Boutiquen.

* Wattwanderung – *a walk along the mudflats*
** Ebbe – *low tide*

4 🎧 Bitte hör die Radiodiskussion über das Leben in einer Großstadt oder Kleinstadt an und mach eine Liste von den Vorteilen und den Nachteilen, die du hörst.

Großstadt		Kleinstadt	
Vorteile	Nachteile	Vorteile	Nachteile

5 ✏️ Wo möchtest du lieber wohnen, in einer Kleinstadt oder einer Großstadt? Mach ein positives Poster und schreib einige Sätze entweder über die Vorteile des Großstadtlebens oder über die Vorteile des Kleinstadtlebens und zeig es in deiner Klasse.

4 Meine Kindheit in Berlin

☑ Talk about childhood
☑ Revise talking about the past
☑ Revise personal pronouns

Otto, seine Tochter Helga und seine Enkeltochter Marisa sind alle in Berlin aufgewachsen. Was für eine Kindheit hatten sie?

Ottos Kindheit

Otto: Kind der 50er Jahre

Ich war in den fünfziger Jahren ein Kind in Berlin und das war eine schwere Zeit für uns in Deutschland, weil es kurz nach dem Krieg war. Wir hatten nicht viel Geld. Ich habe mit meinen Eltern und meinen Großeltern in einer Wohnung gewohnt und Luxus wie heute war unbekannt! Wir hatten zum Beispiel keine Heizung und das Haus war im Winter unglaublich kalt. Ich hatte drei Geschwister und ich war der jüngste – alle haben mich geliebt und sie haben oft mit mir zusammen zu Hause gespielt. Wir hatten Spielzeuge, zum Beispiel kleine Soldaten, Autos und Puppen. Und wir haben viel gelesen, weil es damals bei uns keinen Fernseher gab. Ich habe die Schule mit 15 Jahren verlassen und habe sofort gearbeitet. Für mich war die Idee, weiter in der Schule zu bleiben, gar nicht möglich. Ich habe Geld verdient und das war uns wichtig. Damals sind nicht so viele Schüler bis 18 in der Schule geblieben.

1  Lies den Text und beantworte die Fragen.

(1) Ungefähr wie alt ist Otto jetzt?
(2) Wie viele Generationen haben bei Otto im Haus gewohnt?
(3) Wie viele Kinder gab es in der Familie?
(4) Mit wem hat Otto oft als Kind gespielt?
(5) Was war für die Kinder damals nicht möglich?
(6) Mit welchem Alter hat Otto die Arbeit begonnen?

2a 🎧 Hier spricht Helga über ihre Kindheit in der DDR. Hör zu und kreuze die **sechs** richtigen Aussagen an.

Beispiel Helga ist in Berlin geboren.	✗
(1) Als Kind hat sie in der DDR gelebt.	
(2) Sie ist in Westberlin aufgewachsen.	
(3) Das war in den 90er Jahren.	
(4) Ihre Mutter hat gearbeitet, als Helga sehr klein war.	
(5) Sie ging als Baby zur Kinderkrippe.	
(6) Im Kindergarten gab es keinen Platz für Helga.	
(7) Im Kindergarten hat es viel Spaß gemacht.	
(8) Sie durfte nicht Mitglied der Jungen Pioniere sein.	
(9) Als Kind hat sie viel Zeit in der Natur verbracht.	
(10) Helga hatte ein unglückliches Familienleben als Kind.	
(11) Sie ist mit ihrer Familie nie auf Urlaub gefahren.	
(12) Als Teenager hat sie andere Länder besucht.	

b 📖 Mach Recherche online. Wie war das Leben in der DDR, besonders für Kinder?

3 🎧 Hier spricht Marisa über ihre Kindheit im 21sten Jahrhundert. Hör zu und entscheide, welches Wort oder welche Wortgruppe am besten passt.

(1) Marisa hat immer **a** auf dem Land **b** im Stadtzentrum **c** in einem Dorf gewohnt.

(2) Sie war **a** drei **b** fünf **c** sechs Jahre alt, als sie zum ersten Mal in die Schule ging.

(3) Als Kind hatte sie **a** keine **b** nicht genug **c** viele Spielzeuge.

(4) Sie ist mit ihren Eltern **a** ins Ausland **b** nach Ostdeutschland **c** in den Norden gefahren.

(5) Für ihren Großvater war eine Reise ins Ausland nicht **a** möglich **b** erlaubt **c** billig.

(6) Marisa möchte **a** mehr Spaß **b** mehr Geld **c** Geschwister haben.

(7) Marisa erklärt, dass viele deutsche Kinder heute **a** zwei **b** viele **c** keine Geschwister haben.

4 ✏️ Schreib drei Sätze: *Als ich Kind war...*, *aber jetzt...*

Beispiele

Als ich Kind war, habe ich Milch getrunken, aber jetzt trinke ich Cola.

Als ich Kind war, hatte ich viele Spielzeuge, aber jetzt habe ich einen iPad.

5 💬 Erzähl einem Partner/einer Partnerin von deiner Kindheit. Benutze die Phrasen unten. Kannst du eine Minute sprechen?

- Als ich klein war,...
- Damals...
- Einmal...
- Im Winter/Im Sommer/Zu Weihnachten/ Zu meinem Geburtstag/Manchmal
- Zu Hause/In der Schule/In der Nähe von uns/ Bei meinen Großeltern
- Ich habe gespielt/getragen/gegessen...
- Ich bin gegangen/gefahren/geschwommen...
- Es war/Es gab...
- Ich hatte/Wir hatten...
- Ich war/Wir waren...

Grammatik

Personalpronomen (*personal pronouns*)

You are familiar with personal pronouns such as *ich* and *du* in the nominative case, but they are also used in the accusative and dative cases, as listed below:

Nominative	Accusative	Dative
ich	*mich*	*mir*
du	*dich*	*dir*
er	*ihn*	*ihm*
sie	*sie*	*ihr*

(See Grammar D1 for the rest of the table.)

Use the nominative case when the pronoun stands for the subject of the sentence:

Ich *wohne in der Stadtmitte.*
Sie *ist Einzelkind.*

Use the accusative case when the pronoun stands for the direct object of the sentence:

Meine Eltern lieben **mich**.
Hast du **ihn** *gesehen?*

Use the dative case when the pronoun stands for the indirect object of the sentence, often translated as 'to' or 'for' in English:

Das war **mir** *wichtig.*
Hat er **dir** *geschrieben?*

(A) Choose the correct pronoun for each sentence.

(1) Hast **du/dich/dir** immer in Berlin gewohnt?

(2) Ich mag meinen Vater, ich liebe **er/ihn/ihm**.

(3) Was ist **sie/ihr** lieber? Cola oder Wasser?

(4) Meine Mutter arbeitet und ich sehe **sie/ihr** nur abends.

(5) Mein Großvater? **Er/Ihn/Ihm** ist Berliner.

Be careful when you use pronouns with prepositions that are followed by the accusative or dative case. For example, a pronoun used after *für* must be in the accusative case (see page 156, E1). After *mit* use the dative case (see page 156, E2).

Sie hat ein Geschenk **für ihn**.
Ich gehe gern **mit dir** *auf die Party.*

(B) Re-read Otto's text and find the German for 'for me' and 'with me'.

(C) Translate into German:

(1) for you
(2) against me
(3) with him
(4) at her house (use *bei*)
(5) without you

1 Klamotten kaufen

1a 🎧 📖 Bitte hör zu und lies mit. Was ist anders? Korrigiere die Fehler.

☑ Shop for clothes

☑ Describe items of clothing

☑ Use *dieser, welcher* and the question words *was für*

Im Kleidungsgeschäft

Verkäuferin	Guten Tag! Kann ich Ihnen helfen?
Angelika	*Ich suche einen Pullover.*
Verkäuferin	Welche Größe haben Sie?
Angelika	*38.*
Verkäuferin	Und was für eine Farbe möchten Sie?
Angelika	*Grün, bitte.*
Verkäuferin	Ich habe diesen grünen Pullover in Größe 38.
Angelika	*Was kostet er?*
Verkäuferin	€28.
Angelika	*Ich möchte bitte den Pullover anprobieren. Wo ist die Umkleidekabine?*
Verkäuferin	Da vorne links.
Angelika	*Nein, der Pullover ist leider zu eng. Haben Sie vielleicht Größe 40?*
Verkäuferin	Ja, also bitte.
Angelika	*Ja, dieser Pullover passt mir gut. Ich nehme diesen Pullover.*
Verkäuferin	Kommen Sie zur Kasse. Wie wollen Sie zahlen?
Angelika	*Mit Bargeld, bitte.*
Verkäuferin	Gut. Behalten Sie die Quittung und dann können Sie den Pullover umtauschen, falls es ein Problem gibt. Also, schönen Tag noch. Auf Wiedersehen.
Angelika	*Auf Wiedersehen.*

b Wie sagt man das auf Deutsch? Suche im Dialog nach.

2 🎧 Hör bitte zu. Was wollen diese Leute kaufen (1–4)?

Füll die Tabelle aus.

	Was?	Größe?	Farbe?	Preis?	Weitere Informationen?
(1)					
(2)					

3 💬 Macht bitte Dialoge.

Beispiel

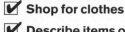

A Ich suche eine Jacke.
B *Welche Größe?*
A 36.
B *Und was für eine Farbe möchten Sie?*
A Blau, bitte.
B *Ich habe diese blaue Jacke in Größe 36.*
A Was kostet sie?
B *€42.*
A Könnte ich die Jacke anprobieren?
B *Ja, die Umkleidekabine ist vorne links.*
A Diese Jacke ist zu klein. Haben Sie Größe 38?
B *Ja, also bitte.*
A Ja, diese Jacke passt mir gut. Ich nehme sie. Wo ist die Kasse?

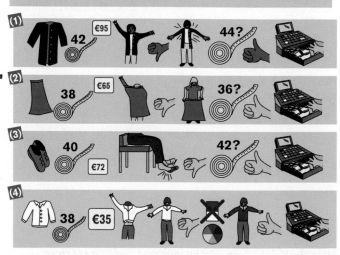

Grammatik

Was für ein *(what sort of)*, welcher *(which)*, dieser *(this/these)*, jener *(that/those)*

Was für (ein) is used to ask 'what?' or 'what sort of?'. When *was für* is followed by *ein*, remember that *ein* changes its form according to case and gender of the noun being used. (See Grammar reference A4 if you cannot remember how *ein* changes.) The case depends on the function of the noun.

> *Was für **ein** Geschäft ist das?*
> (*Geschäft* is the subject, so nominative)
> What sort of shop is that?
> *Was für **einen** Rock möchten Sie?*
> (*Rock* is the direct object, so accusative)
> What sort of skirt would you like?

You met the word *welcher/welche/welches/welche* as a question word on page 54. It is used to ask 'which?'. It follows the same pattern as *der*:

	m	**f**	**n**	**pl**
Nominative	*welcher Pullover*	*welche Farbe*	*welches Hemd*	*welche Schuhe*
Accusative	*welchen Pullover*	*welche Farbe*	*welches Hemd*	*welche Schuhe*
Dative	*welchem Pullover*	*welcher Farbe*	*welchem Hemd*	*welchen Schuhen*

> ***Welches** Kleid hast du gekauft?*
> Which dress did you buy?

In welchem Geschäft hast du das Kleid gekauft?
In which shop did you buy the dress?

Use *was für* when there is a wider choice on offer and *welcher* when the choice is more limited.

Dieser corresponds to the English 'this' ('these' in the plural). *Jener* means 'that' ('those' in the plural). They also follow the same pattern as *der* (see Grammar reference A3).

> ***Dieses** Kleid passt mir gut.*
> This dress fits me well.
> *Ich habe **jene** Schuhe gekauft.*
> I bought those shoes.
> ***Diesen** Pullover mag ich nicht.*
> I don't like this jumper.

Put the following sentences into German.

(1) Which T-shirt do you like?
(2) I like this T-shirt. It costs only €16.
(3) What sort of clothes do you like wearing?
(4) Which shoes did you buy?
(5) These shoes are too tight. Have you got these shoes in size 42, please?
(6) Which shop has got a sale?
(7) What sort of car does he drive?
(8) I think that blue blouse is horrible.
(9) Which skirt do you have to wear for school?
(10) What sort of presents did you buy for your parents?
(11) What sort of person is she?
(12) I bought those trousers in this shop.

11/1, 11/2

4 Mach eine Mode-Broschüre auf Deutsch.

- Beschreib ein anderes Kleidungsstück.
- Gib Details wie Größen, Preis und Farben an.
- Benutz Wörter wie *dieser/jener* und Adjektive.
- Schreib ungefähr 50 Wörter.

Beispiel

Streifenjeans

Topmoderne Streifenjeans in bequemer 5-Taschen-Form!

Aktueller
Wash-Out
Effekt

€29.99

Größe
Alle Größen ein Preis
Ab Größe 34 bis Größe 54

Farbe:
blau   grau
oder schwarz

Material:
70% Baumwolle
25% Polyester
5% Elasthan

Länge ab ca. 108 cm

2 Das sind die Skier, die €200 kosten

1 🎧 📖 ✏️ Bitte hör zu und lies mit.

Timo	Hallo Sonja, na, wie geht's?
Sonja	*Gut, danke, was macht dein Computerhobby?*
Timo	Ich habe einen neuen Computer, den ich erst vor 2 Tagen bekommen habe.
Sonja	*Super, wo hast du ihn gekauft?*
Timo	In dem PC-Geschäft, das erst vor 2 Monaten geöffnet hat.
Sonja	*Ach ja, in der Gartenstraße, der Laden, der riesige Fenster hat.*
Timo	Genau der! Da will ich jetzt hin und gucken, ob ich das Spiel finde, das ich suche.
Sonja	*Du hast es gut, ein neuer PC! Ich habe immer noch den alten, den mein Vater von der Arbeit mitgebracht hat. Niemand dort will einen Computer, der schon 7 Jahre alt ist. Hast du eigentlich noch andere Hobbys?*
Timo	Also Computer ist mein Haupthobby, aber ich mag auch Haustiere und Rockmusik, die Toten Hosen und so. Ich suche noch einen kleinen CD-Spieler, den ich mir leisten kann. Mein alter macht komische Geräusche, er ist wohl fast kaputt.
Sonja	*Du kannst die CDs ja auch auf dem PC hören, da hast du ja das neueste Modell, das es gibt.*
Timo	Und du, wie ist es bei dir mit anderen Hobbys?
Sonja	*Ich treffe mich gern mit meinen Freunden. Dann gehen wir oft in die Eisdiele, die jetzt dort am Marktplatz ist oder ist das kein Hobby?*
Timo	Doch, machst du auch Sport?
Sonja	*Ich gehe manchmal mit Bettina in die Eishalle. Sie hat mir die Schlittschuhe geschenkt, die sie nicht mehr braucht. Sie hat neue gekauft, die moderner und schneller sind.*
Timo	Da bist du sicher ziemlich fit…ich muss jetzt weiter, sonst macht das Geschäft zu, bevor ich nach dem Computerspiel gucken kann…

Das ist der Mann, der gut Ski läuft.

Das ist die Frau, die im Juli in Spanien Urlaub macht.

Das ist das Kind, das so gut Geige spielt.

a Was stimmt und was stimmt nicht? Bitte korrigiere die falschen Aussagen.

(1) Timo bekommt seinen Computer in 2 Tagen.
(2) Das PC-Geschäft ist neu in der Stadt.
(3) Sonja möchte auch einen neuen Computer.
(4) Timo hat auch einen neuen CD-Spieler.
(5) Sonja kann Schlittschuh laufen.
(6) Sonja hat neue Schlittschuhe gekauft.

b Sucht die Relativsätze in dem Dialog und macht eine Liste in der Gruppe.

D4

Grammatik

Relativpronomen (*relative pronouns*)

Relative pronouns are used to link two sentences. When two sentences are joined together, there must be a comma between the two clauses.

- A relative clause usually begins with a relative pronoun.
- Relative pronouns also exist in English (that, who, which etc.).
- In German relative pronouns send the verb to the end of the sentence.
- Unlike in English, you cannot omit the relative pronoun in German.

Example 1

Der Mann heißt Walter. Er spielt gut Tennis.
The man is called Walter. He plays tennis well.

Since *Der Mann* and *er* refer to the same person you can turn the two sentences into one. This is done by means of a relative pronoun. The masculine relative pronoun in this sentence would be *der* (for the other forms see the table opposite).

*Der Mann, **der** gut Tennis spielt, heißt Walter.*
The man who plays tennis well is called Walter.

The relative pronoun must agree in number and gender with the noun to which it refers. The case of the relative pronoun, however, depends on the role it plays in the relative clause, as shown in the next example.

Example 2

Der Hund ist klein. Ich möchte den Hund.
The dog is small. I would like the dog.

In the second sentence the dog is in the accusative case, so its 'role' in the sentence is different from in the first example (see page 151 for the accusative case).

Because *Hund* is masculine and in the accusative case in the relative clause, you have to use *den* to link the two sentences.

*Der Hund, **den** ich möchte, ist klein.*
The dog which/that I want is small.

The relative pronoun can be combined with a preposition. In this case normal case and word order rules apply:

Der Freund, mit dem ich spiele, wohnt in Köln.
The friend I play with lives in Cologne.

Below is a list of the nominative, accusative and dative forms of the relative pronouns:

	m	f	n	pl
Nominative	der	die	das	die
Accusative	den	die	das	die
Dative	dem	der	dem	denen

In this sentence the relative pronoun is *was*:

Alles, was ich kaufe, ist billig.

See page 156 for more about *was* as a relative pronoun.

Can you link the following sentences with a relative pronoun?

(1) Der Lehrer wohnt in Berlin. Er kauft einen Ferrari.

(2) Meine Großmutter kocht gern Schnitzel. Sie ist sehr alt.

(3) Meine Freundin hat kein Haustier. Sie liebt meinen Hund.

(4) Das Kind isst zu viele Süßigkeiten. Es kauft gerade 200g Schokolade.

11/3, 11/4

2  Bitte macht Dialoge und wechselt euch ab.

a A Guten Tag, was möchtest du?
   B *Haben Sie Skier?*
   A Ja, welche? (*welchen*/masculine, *welche*/feminine, *welches*/neuter, *welche*/plural)
   B *Ich möchte die Skier, die €200 kosten.*
   A Gut, hier sind die Skier, die €200 kosten.
   B *Vielen Dank.*

b Was kaufst du für dich? Bitte macht Dialoge.

3 Schreib eine E-mail an deinen Freund/ deine Freundin über deine Hobbys und was du dafür* kaufen musst. Nimm mindestens dreimal ein Relativpronomen. (**for it/them*)

Thema 12 Essen und Trinken

1 …und was soll ich einkaufen?

☑ Revise food items
☑ Revise how to form plurals

1a 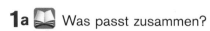 Was passt zusammen?

Beispiel   *(1) e*

Wenn du Probleme hast, schau bitte im Wörterbuch nach!

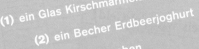
(1) ein Glas Kirschmarmelade
(2) ein Becher Erdbeerjoghurt
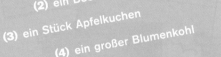
(3) ein Stück Apfelkuchen
(4) ein großer Blumenkohl

(5) ein Kilo Zwiebeln
(6) vier Bananen
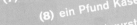
(7) ein Paket Kaffee
(8) ein Pfund Käse
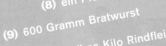
(9) 600 Gramm Bratwurst
(10) ein halbes Kilo Rindfleisch
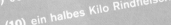
(11) eine Dose Gemüsesuppe
(12) sechs Scheiben Schinken
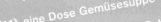
(13) eine Tüte Kartoffelchips
(14) eine Flasche Rotwein

(15) ein Kasten Mineralwasser
(16) ein kleines Weißbrot
(17) eine Packung Waschpulver
(18) eine Tüte Bonbons
(19) eine Schachtel Pralinen
(20) eine Tafel Schokolade
(21) ein Liter Milch
(22) eine Tube Senf

a 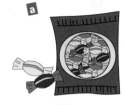   b    c

d 0.5 kg   e    f

g 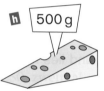   h 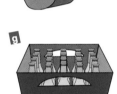 500 g   i

j 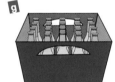 1kg   k    l 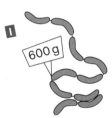 600 g

m    n Waschpulver 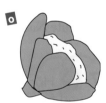   o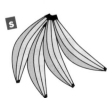

p   q  Joghurt   r Milch 1L 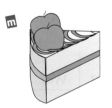   s

t    u Senf   v

b Schreib eine Einkaufsliste von 10 Produkten, die du auf dieser Seite **nicht** siehst. Benutz ein Wörterbuch!

Einkaufsliste

A2

Grammatik

Mehr über den Plural (*more about the plural*)

The best way to remember the plural form is to learn it together with each noun in the singular. Note that there are many exceptions to the rules given below and previously on page 4.

- Plural **masculine nouns** usually end in -e and sometimes an umlaut is added to the vowel in the stem. (Weak masculine nouns are an exception. See A7 in the Grammar reference section.)
  der Tisch – die Tische, der Baum – die Bäume

  Masculine nouns that end in -*el*, -*en* or -*er* may appear the same in the plural:
  der Lehrer – die Lehrer, der Schlüssel – die Schlüssel

  but some may take an umlaut:
  der Bruder – die Brüder

- Plural **feminine nouns** usually end in -n or -en.
  die Frau – die Frauen, die Blume – die Blumen

- Plural **neuter nouns** usually end in -e or -er (where appropriate there is also an umlaut).
  das Spiel – die Spiele, das Buch – die Bücher

- **The plural ending -s is used only for nouns that come from foreign languages.**
  das Auto – die Autos, das Kino – die Kinos, das Restaurant – die Restaurants

(1) **Look again at the list of food items in Übung 1. Note any plurals you can find.**

(2) **What is the plural form of the following nouns?**
die Zitrone
die Karotte
das Ei
der Kuchen
die Flasche
die Schachtel
die Dose
die Packung
die Tüte
das Brot
der Saft

(3) **Check your answers in the glossary at the back of the book. Discuss with a partner the rules for setting out plurals in a dictionary.**

---

2 🎧 Was kaufen die Leute? Bitte hör zu und füll die Tabelle aus.

Jede Person kauft mehrere Produkte. Wo ist die Person?
- Auf dem Markt?
- In der Bäckerei?
- Im Süßwarengeschäft?
- Im Supermarkt?
- In der Metzgerei?

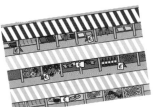

Person	Geschäft?	Was kauft er/sie?	Wie viel kauft er/sie?	Preis?
Person 1				

3 💬 Nach der Schule hast du für deine Eltern eingekauft. Du hast aber einiges vergessen! Schick deiner Mutter ein SMS. Sag ihr in etwa 50 Wörtern:
- was du am Markt (drei Sachen) and in der Bäckerei (zwei Sachen) gekauft hast
- warum du nicht zum Supermarkt gegangen bist
- was sie noch kaufen muss (vier Sachen)

2 Ich hätte gern ein langes Brot…

1 💬 Jetzt seid ihr dran. Was möchtet ihr kaufen?
Macht Dialoge:

a in einem Supermarkt in Österreich (Euros)

b in einem Supermarkt in der Schweiz (Schweizer Franken)

✔ Practise shopping transactions

✔ Revise definite and indefinite articles in the nominative and accusative cases

✔ Revise adjective endings in the nominative and accusative cases

Du sagst:	Der Verkäufer/die Verkäuferin sagt:
Ich möchte…	Kann ich dir/Ihnen helfen?
Ich hätte gern…einen großen Kuchen, eine kleine Dose Ananas, ein langes Brot.	Bitte schön?
Haben Sie…?	Sonst noch etwas?
Das ist alles.	Ist das alles?
Das wär's.	Das macht/kostet €20,45 (zwanzig Euro fünfundvierzig).
Was kostet das/macht das?	Das macht/kostet CHF 10,50 (zehn Franken fünfzig).

Verkäufer(in)	Guten Tag, bitte schön?
Kunde/Kundin	*Ich möchte… . Ich hätte gern… .*
Verkäufer(in)	Sonst noch etwas?
Kunde/Kundin	*Ja, haben Sie… ? Ich möchte… .*
Verkäufer(in)	Ist das alles?
Kunde/Kundin	*Ja, was macht das?/Was kostet das?*
Verkäufer(in)	Das macht/kostet…
Kunde/Kundin	*Tschüs.*

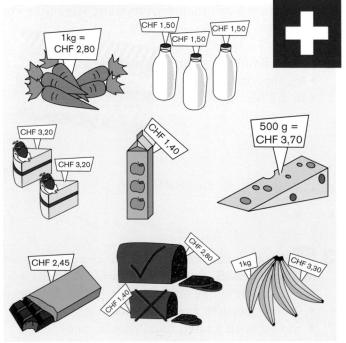

2 📖 🏛 Du planst eine Party für zehn Freunde. Hier ist die E-mail von deiner besten Freundin.

Hallo!

Das ist ja toll, dass bei dir am Samstag eine Party steigt!

Sind deine Eltern da, oder gehen sie aus?

Was essen wir und was trinken wir? Willst du wirklich alles kaufen?

Alle essen gerne Pizza und Salat natürlich. Kuchen, Torte oder Schokolade sind auch gut.

Schreib mal, was du kaufst! Oder sollen wir auch etwas mitbringen, Cola, Chips oder so?

Bis Samstag!

Gruß

Sabine

Schreib eine Antwort an Sabine (ungefähr 150 Wörter) mit folgenden Informationen:

- was deine Eltern am Samstag machen werden
- welche Lebensmittel und Getränke du für die Party schon gekauft hast und welche du noch kaufen musst
- was Sabine und ihre Freunde mitbringen sollen
- wie man sich an der Party amüsieren wird

Liebe Sabine,

Grammatik

B2, B3

Wiederholung von Adjektivendungen im Nominativ und Akkusativ

(revision of adjective endings in the nominative and accusative)

Do you remember the nominative forms of the definite and indefinite articles? (see page 150)

Here they are again, along with adjectives in the same cases (see page 152).

m	f	n	pl
der rote Apfel	*die gelbe Banane*	*das gute Fleisch*	*die schönen Erdbeeren*
ein roter Apfel	*eine gelbe Banane*	*ein gutes Fleisch*	*schöne Erdbeeren*

Only the masculine form changes in the accusative case:

den roten Apfel   einen roten Apfel

Ich möchte den kleinen Kuchen/einen roten Apfel/einen großen Blumenkohl.

🔖 12/1

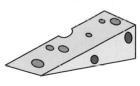

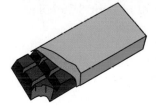

3 ...und wo gehen wir essen?

1 📖 Welches Bild passt?

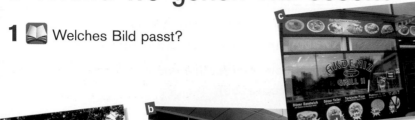

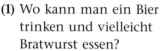

☑ Order meals in a restaurant and learn how to make a complaint

☑ Express preferences in your choice of meals

☑ Revise the present tense of *geben, essen* and *nehmen*

☑ Use the dative to express your likes and dislikes

(1) Wo kann man ein Bier trinken und vielleicht Bratwurst essen?

(2) In welchem Restaurant kann man Frühlingsrolle essen?

(3) Wo kann man gut gegrilltes Fleisch essen?

(4) Ich möchte nur ein Eis, wo kann man Eis essen?

(5) Ich möchte nur einen schnellen Kaffee.

(6) Ich esse am liebsten Fisch.

(7) Ich möchte in einem kleinen Hotel Schnitzel und Pommes essen.

(8) In welchem Restaurant möchtest du am liebsten essen?

2 📖 ✏️ Bitte sieh die Speisekarte an und beantworte die Fragen und benutze die richtige Form der Verben *essen* und *nehmen*. Du kannst in allen Sätzen beide Verben benutzen.

(1) Thomas hat nicht viel Hunger und isst gern Käse. Was kann Thomas nehmen? Er nimmt...

(2) Lisa möchte Fisch und ein kaltes Getränk, aber sie hat nicht viel Geld. Was kann sie essen und trinken?

(3) Kerstin ist Vegetarierin und möchte etwas Kaltes, aber kein Brötchen. Was ist gut für sie?

(4) Herr Schneider hat viel Appetit. Er möchte eine warme Vorspeise, isst gern Fleisch und Reis und er liebt Schokolade. Was ist vielleicht sein Menü?

(5) Frau Schneider macht eine Diät, sie möchte abnehmen, aber sie möchte, wie ihr Mann, Vorspeise, Hauptgericht und Nachspeise essen. Was wählt sie?

HOTEL AM MARKT

Speisekarte

Für den kleinen Appetit/Vorspeisen

Tomatensuppe mit Brot	€ 3,20
Champignonsuppe mit Brot	€ 3,80
Kartoffelsalat mit Würstchen	€ 5,20
Tomaten mit Mozzarella und Basilikum	€ 5,90
Käsebrötchen	€ 2,95
Schinkenbrötchen	€ 3,45

Vegetarische Speisen

Spaghetti mit Tomatensoße	€ 5,10
Bunter Salatteller	€ 6,75
Käseomelette mit Schwarzbrot	€ 6,20

Hauptgerichte

Bratfisch mit Pommes Frites	€ 6,35
Lachs mit Kartoffeln und Salat	€ 8,65
Currywurst mit Brötchen und Salat	€ 6,30
Wiener Schnitzel mit Kartoffeln und Gemüse	€ 9,50
Ungarischer Gulasch mit Reis	€ 9,70

Nachspeisen

Gemischtes Eis	€ 2,50
mit Sahne	€ 2,75
Obstsalat	€ 2,90
Schokoladencreme	€ 2,40
mit Sahne	€ 2,65

Getränke

Coca-Cola 0,25 l	€ 1,50
Fanta 0,25 l	€ 1,50
Apfelsaft 0,2 l	€ 1,70
Glas Weißwein/Rotwein 0,2 l	€ 2,25
Bier (Pils) 0,5 l	€ 2,00
Tasse Kaffee	€ 1,20
Glas Tee mit Zitrone	€ 1,10

3a 🎧 Bitte hör zu und kreuze an. Wer sagt was?

	Gast	Kellner
Haben Sie noch einen Tisch frei?	X	
Ja, hier in der Ecke?		
Nein danke, aber die Rechnung bitte.		
Was kann ich Ihnen zu trinken bringen?		
Das Fleisch ist zu kalt.		
Ich hätte gern den ungarischen Gulasch.		
Noch ein Bier bitte.		
Ja, sofort.		

b 🎧 Was isst/trinkt der Mann, was isst/trinkt die Frau?

Mann	Frau	Weitere Informationen

4 💬 Macht Dialoge in der Gruppe. Hört noch einmal den Dialog in Übung 3. Ihr braucht einen Kellner/eine Kellnerin und Gäste. Nehmt die Speisekarte aus Übung 2.

Kellner/Kellnerin („Bedienung")

Hier ist die Speisekarte.

Was möchten Sie trinken?

Möchten Sie bestellen?

Was kann ich für Sie tun?

Was nehmen Sie?

Was essen Sie?

Schmeckt es Ihnen?

Hier ist...

Ja, das geht/natürlich.

Gast

Haben Sie einen Tisch für zwei/drei/vier/fünf... Personen?

Ich nehme/ich esse/ich möchte/ich hätte gern...

Wir möchten bestellen.

Geht das?

Das Fleisch ist zu kalt, die Suppe ist zu salzig, die Cola ist zu warm, das Eis schmeckt (mir) nicht.

Das Essen schmeckt gut.

Die Rechnung, bitte/ich möchte zahlen.

Stimmt so. (*Keep the change.*)

5 📷 Schreib eine Einladung an einen Freund/eine Freundin. Du möchtest mit ihm/ihr im Hotel am Markt (Speisekarte in Übung 2) essen.
- Wann (Zeit, Tag, Datum) trefft ihr euch?
- Wo trefft ihr euch?

Erklär dem Freund, was man dort essen kann und wie viel es ungefähr kosten wird.

C2

Grammatik
Wiederholung von *gern/lieber/ am liebsten*

- To say you **like** eating (drinking/doing) something, place *gern* after the verb.
- To say you **prefer** something, place *lieber* after the verb.
- To express your **favourite** choice, use *am liebsten* after the verb.

*Ich esse **gern** Kartoffeln.* I like eating potatoes.
*Ich esse **lieber** Nudeln.* I prefer eating pasta.
*Ich esse **am liebsten** Reis.* I like eating rice best of all.

Choose three food items and put them in your order of preference.

G1

Grammatik
Das Verb *schmecken* (*to taste*)

Like the verb *gefallen* (see page 99) the verb *schmecken* (to taste) takes the dative case.

*Schmeckt **dir** das Eis?* Does the ice cream taste good to you? Do you like the ice cream?
*Das Eis schmeckt **mir**.* I like the ice cream.
*Das Eis schmeckt **mir** nicht.* I don't like the ice cream.

 12/2

F1

Grammatik
Starke Verben im Präsens (*strong verbs in the present tense*)

Some verbs with an 'e' in the stem (e.g. *geben, nehmen, essen*) change the 'e' to an 'i' in the second and third person singular **in the present tense** (see page 3).

geben (to give)			
ich	*gebe*	*wir*	*geben*
du	*gibst*	*ihr*	*gebt*
er/sie/es/man	*gibt*	*Sie/sie*	*geben*

Similarly for *nehmen* and *essen*:
du nimmst　　　　　*du isst*
er/sie/es/man nimmt　　*er/sie/es/man isst*

 12/3

115

4 Gesund essen

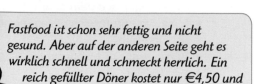

☑ Talk about healthy eating
☑ Understand a recipe
☑ Use subordinating conjunctions

1 📖 Lies bitte diese Texte.

Fastfood ist schon sehr fettig und nicht gesund. Aber auf der anderen Seite geht es wirklich schnell und schmeckt herrlich. Ein reich gefüllter Döner kostet nur €4,50 und nach dem Essen bist du wirklich satt.

Angelika

Häufig essen Kinder zu viel und zu süß. Überall locken süße Snacks und Softdrinks für Zwischendurch. Aber Süßigkeiten enthalten viel Zucker. Daher soll man Süßwaren nur sparsam essen, damit man nicht dick wird.

Magdalena

Obst und Gemüse enthalten nur wenig Kalorien und helfen dir dabei, dein Immunsystem zu schützen. Täglich fünf Portionen Obst und Gemüse — am besten drei Portionen Gemüse und zwei Portionen Obst — sind ideal, damit du gesund bleibst.

Lukas

Man soll nur wenig Fett essen, damit das Risiko einer Herzkrankheit gering bleibt. Fleischwaren enthalten leider zu viel Fett. Auch soll man mäßig Milchprodukte, Ei, Fleisch und Fisch essen, dafür aber viel Vollkornbrot, Nudeln, Kartoffeln und Reis.

Jens

a Wer sagt das? Trage den richtigen Namen ein.

(1) Kuchen und Kekse lieber lassen.	
(2) Du hast keinen Hunger nach der Mahlzeit.	
(3) Wenig Wurst essen.	
(4) Viele Apfelsinen und viel Kohl essen.	
(5) Imbisse sind preisgünstig.	
(6) Spaghetti essen.	

b Was soll man essen? Was soll man nicht essen? Warum? Füll die Tabelle aus.

Du sollst lieber essen	Warum?	Du sollst lieber *nicht* essen	Warum?

2 🎧 Hör bitte zu.

Fastfood: Was ist positiv und was ist negativ? Mach Notizen auf Deutsch.

Vorteile von Fastfood 👍	Nachteile von Fastfood 👎

3 💬 Sieh dir dieses Bild an und beantworte die Fragen:
- Was siehst du auf dem Bild?
- Was machen der Mann und der Junge?
- Was wird das Kind vielleicht essen?
- Kaufst du gern solches Essen?
- Meinst du, dass du eine gesunde Diät hast? Warum/warum nicht?

4 Lies bitte dieses Rezept. Finde die deutschen Ausdrücke.

Gemüsepfanne

Mittagessen-Rezept von Cordelia (17) aus Hildesheim, Niedersachsen (Deutschland)

Zutaten

1–2 Zwiebel
(in Würfel schneiden)
2 Stangen Lauch
(in Scheiben schneiden)
250 g Karotten
(in Würfel schneiden)
100 g Sellerie
(in Scheiben schneiden)
1–2 kleine Zucchini
(in Würfel schneiden)
1 Paprikaschote
(in Streifen schneiden)
100 g Kartoffeln
(in Würfel schneiden)
¼ Liter Gemüsebrühe, evtl. Salz
⅛ Liter Wasser

So geht's

Gemüse waschen, putzen und klein schneiden. Mit etwas Margarine in einer Pfanne anbraten. Salz, Gemüsebrühe und Wasser dazugeben und ca. 25 Min. kochen lassen.

Tipp

Du kannst anstatt Kartoffeln auch Reis nehmen. Dazu kochst du ca. 100 g Reis mit etwas Salz in einem Extra-Topf und gibst ihn zum Gemüse dazu. Alles zusammen dann noch ca. 5 Min. auf kleiner Flamme kochen lassen.

Kann ich nur weiterempfehlen, schmeckt ausgezeichnet gut. Ich wünsche allen einen guten Appetit, und ich würde mich über eine E-mail freuen, damit ich weiß, ob es geschmeckt hat, oder nicht. Cordelia969390@aol.com Danke!

Grammatik H4

Damit (*so that, in order that*)

Damit is a subordinating conjunction meaning 'in order that'. You have already met some subordinating conjunctions:
   e.g. *weil, wenn, dass, als*

Subordinating conjunctions send the verb to the end of the subordinate clause. The two clauses must be separated by a comma.
   *Man soll viel Obst essen, **damit** man gesund **bleibt**.*
   You should eat lots of fruit so that you stay healthy.
   ***Damit** man nicht dick **wird**, soll man wenig Fett essen.*
   So that you don't get fat, you should eat little fat.

Note that **so dass** means **as a result** or **with the result that** and is another subordinating conjunction:
   *Er hat immer viel Obst und Gemüse gegessen, **so dass** er jetzt top gesund ist.*
   He has always eaten lots of fruit and vegetables with the result that he is now very healthy.

Complete these sentences:
(1) Damit man fit bleibt,…
(2) Er isst immer gesund,…
(3) Wir essen keinen Döner,…
(4) Kuchen soll man nur selten essen,…
(5) Man soll keine Cola und Limo trinken,…

Other conjunctions are **bevor** and **nachdem**.

5 Hast du ein Lieblingsgericht? Schreib das Rezept auf Deutsch auf!

12/4

Heute schauen wir ins Leben der Familie Erkan in Berlin Kreuzberg. Cevat und seine Frau Sezin sind Restaurantbesitzer. Sie haben zwei Kinder. Ihre Tochter Gülcan geht in die Schule (Klasse 10). Ihr Sohn Günay ist sechs Jahre alt.

Ein Tag im Leben der Familie Erkan

Cevat: Es war immer mein Traum, ein eigenes Restaurant zu haben und hier in Kreuzberg, wo so viele deutsch-türkische Familien leben, ist das genau richtig! Ich serviere fast nur türkische Spezialitäten. Heute bin ich, wie fast jeden Tag, um fünf Uhr morgens zum Markt gegangen. Ich brauche immer eine Menge frisches Obst und Gemüse, Fleisch und Gewürze[1]. Heute werden wir etwa 80 Mittagessen servieren, und dann wird's gleich wieder losgehen, da wir das Abendessen vorbereiten müssen! Heute gibt's Köfte, das heißt türkische Hackbällchen[2] aus Lamm, und auch Menemen (das ist Rührei mit Tomaten und Paprika[3]). Wie jeden Tag, backen wir auch Fladenbrot und Süßigkeiten wie Baklava, eine Art Kuchen mit türkischem Honig und Pistazien.

Sezin: Ich arbeite meistens im Restaurant, aber heute bin ich als Touristenführerin tätig. Viele Leute sind dieses Wochenende für den Karneval der Kulturen nach Berlin gekommen und wollen auch das Viertel ein bisschen sehen. Kreuzberg ist ein faszinierender Stadtteil für Kunst und Kultur und die Stimmung ist entspannt und auch multikulturell.

Gülcan: Ich wohne unheimlich gern in Kreuzberg, das eine Mischung meiner zwei Kulturen bietet: deutsch und türkisch. Fast ein Drittel der Bewohner sind nicht-deutscher Herkunft und man hört oft Türkisch auf der Straße. Dieses Wochenende ist der Karneval der Kulturen, ein viertägiges Fest, das für seine Originalität und Fantasie bekannt ist. Es wird Umzüge und Kostüme geben und Musik, Tanz, Kunst und Akrobatik aus aller Welt. Es ist nicht besonders türkisch, aber ich finde, dass Kreuzberg genau die richtige Umgebung ist, die Kulturen der Welt zu feiern.

[1] Gewürze – *spices*
[2] Hackbällchen – *meatballs*
[3] Paprika – *peppers*

1 Lies den Text, dann beantworte die Fragen auf Deutsch.

(1) Was hat Cevat heute auf seiner Einkaufsliste?
(2) Warum hat Cevat heute Morgen viel Arbeit?
(3) Was wird man heute im Restaurant essen? (Nenne zwei Hauptspeisen und eine Nachspeise.)
(4) Warum ist es interessant, in Kreuzberg als Touristenführer zu arbeiten?
(5) Welche Sprachen spricht wohl Gülcan?
(6) Wie heißt das Fest, das bald stattfinden wird?
(7) Aus welchen Ländern kommen die Künstler, die beim Fest mitmachen?

2 Stell dir vor, du hast einen Tag in Kreuzberg verbracht. Schreib etwa 150 Wörter darüber für dein Tagebuch. Gib folgende Informationen:

• Was hast du gemacht und gesehen?
• Was hast du gegessen?
• Was war deine Meinung zu diesem Stadtteil?
• Möchtest du in Kreuzberg wohnen? Warum/ Warum nicht?

PROBLEMPUNKT Feste

Frage von Gülcan2000:

Eine Klassenkameradin von mir wohnt in einem Wohnblock, wo es auch eine Familie aus Syrien gibt. Das Leben muss schwer für sie sein und ich möchte wenn möglich irgendwie helfen. Sie haben vier Kinder und zwei sind Teenager, wie ich. Hat jemand eine Idee? Was könnte ich machen?

Antwort von sowasAnna:

Selam[1], Gülcan2000! Ich bin auch Türkin. Na ja, eigentlich bin ich deutsch, aber wenn ich bei meinen Großeltern bin, die fast nur türkisch sprechen, verstehe ich, dass man sich nur in einer Kultur zu Hause fühlt, wenn man die Sprache kann. Ich glaube, du sollst hingehen und mit den Familienmitgliedern ein bisschen auf Deutsch reden. Dann können sie ein paar Wörter lernen.

Antwort von meintraumleben:

Wo gehen die Teenager zur Schule? Wie machen sie ihre Hausaufgaben? Vielleicht könntest du helfen? Geh mit deinen Hausaufgaben zu ihnen. Ihr könnt dann zusammen arbeiten und du kannst ihnen zeigen, was sie machen müssen.

[1] Selam – Turkish for 'Hi there'

3 Finde diese Ausdrücke auf Deutsch.

> talk a bit of German
> you can show them what to do
> actually I'm German
> life must be hard for them
> you can work on it together
> a girl in my class

4 Welche Lösung findest du am besten und warum? Hast du andere Ideen? Schreib eine Antwort an Gülcan. Schreib ungefähr 50 Wörter.

5 Lies den Text über Eid, dann schreib ein passendes Wort in jede Lücke.

(1) Etwa 4,5 Millionen Muslime wohnen in ....
(2) Für sie heißt das wichtigste Fest im Jahr ....
(3) Das Fest findet nach dem .... statt.
(4) Vor Eid soll man ....
(5) Am ersten Tag des Festes geht man oft in die ....
(6) Nach dem Gottesdienst gibt es ein riesiges ....
(7) Für die Kinder gibt es ....

Eid Mubarak!

Eid Mubarak! So begrüßt man andere Leute während des islamischen Festes Eid. In Deutschland wohnen etwa 4,5 Millionen Muslime, viele aber gar nicht alle, von türkischer Herkunft. Andere stammen aus Pakistan, Iran und Afghanistan.

Das dreitägige Fest heißt Eid-ul-fitr und findet am Ende von „Ramadan" statt. Während des Ramadan fasten viele Muslime, das heißt, sie essen während des Tages nicht, sondern nur abends. „Eid" bedeutet „Fest" und „ul-fitr" bedeutet, dass man nicht mehr fastet. Das Fest findet im Spätsommer oder im Herbst statt.

Für Eid kommen alle zusammen, und das beginnt oft mit einem Gottesdienst in der Moschee. Nachher begrüßt man alle und man isst mit der ganzen Familie zusammen. Viele tragen neue Kleider und manche schmücken auch das Haus. Die Kinder bekommen Geld und Geschenke. Die Kinder sagen alle, dass Eid einer der wichtigsten Tage im ganzen Jahr ist.

Eid hat eine Verbindung mit Weihnachten und Ostern. Die Geschenke und das Festessen gehören zu Weihnachten, und die Fastenzeit kann man mit den 40 Tagen vor Ostern vergleichen.

6 Beantworte die Fragen auf Deutsch.

(1) Wie begrüßt man seine Freunde und Familie zu Eid?
(2) Woher stammen die meisten Muslime, die in Deutschland wohnen?
(3) Wie nennt man die muslimische Fastenzeit?
(4) Was kaufen wohl viele kurz vor Eid?
(5) Warum sind die Kinder zu Eid besonders glücklich?

🎧 Paper 1: listening

Before you listen to the conversation, work with a partner to discuss what you have to do for both parts. Work together to predict which word might replace the word that has been crossed out in part A. If it is a noun, remember that it must be the right gender.

Sie hören zweimal ein Gespräch mit Andrea in zwei Teilen (A und B).

Teil A

In jedem Satz gibt es ein Wort, Wörter oder eine Ziffer, die nicht zu dem Sinn des Gesprächs passen. Hören Sie gut zu und schreiben Sie jedes Mal das richtige Wort **auf Deutsch**.

1 Am Samstag Nachmittag war Andrea im ~~Supermarkt~~. .... **[1]**

2 Sie wollte ein Geschenk für ihre ~~Freundin~~ kaufen. .... **[1]**

3 Andrea hat eine blaue ~~Jacke~~ gekauft. .... **[1]**

4 Das Geschenk hat ~~dreißig~~ Euro gekostet. .... **[1]**

5 Das Kleidungsstück war zu ~~groß~~. .... **[1]**

[*PAUSE*]

Teil B

Jetzt hören Sie zweimal den letzten Teil des Gesprächs mit Andrea. Hören Sie gut zu und beantworten Sie die Fragen **auf Deutsch**.

6 Was hat Andrea für sich selber gekauft? .... **[1]**

7 Was hat sie zu Mittag gegessen? .... **[1]**

8 Was isst sie nicht gern? .... **[1]**

9 Um wie viel Uhr ist sie nach Hause gekommen? .... **[1]**

[Total: 9]

Points to remember

- Read through the sentences and questions before you start listening so that you know what to listen for.
- In part A one word is crossed out as it is incorrect according to what you hear. You have to write the correct word. You do not need to copy out the rest of the sentence.
- The answers to questions 1–5 will be one word each, which you will hear on the recording.
- In part B you do not need to use full sentences in your answers.

Paper 2: reading

Hanna macht eine Klassenfahrt nach Wien und schickt diesen Brief an ihre Eltern. Lesen Sie den Brief und beantworten Sie die folgenden Fragen **auf Deutsch**.

Wien, den 9. April

Liebe Mama, lieber Papa,

diese Stadt ist so schön! Überall hört man Musik und die Innenstadt ist sehr sauber. Wir haben heute den Dom besucht und morgen werden wir in die Oper gehen. Ich habe noch nie eine Oper gesehen, also finde ich das sehr spannend.

Wollt ihr wissen, wie das Essen ist? Sehr lecker! Wir frühstücken immer um halb acht in der Jugendherberge und es gibt eine sehr große Auswahl: Brot, Butter, Wurst, Honig, Marmelade, Joghurt... Jeder findet etwas, was ihm schmeckt.

Direkt um die Ecke ist ein Supermarkt, wo wir jeden Tag Brötchen mit Schinken oder Käse fürs Mittagessen kaufen. Unsere Lehrerin, Frau Henkel, kauft kleine Flaschen Wasser oder Saft für uns, aber wir Schüler müssen sie im Rucksack tragen. Gestern sind wir am Abend in ein Restaurant gegangen und haben unsere Mahlzeit von der Speisekarte bestellt. Die meisten aus der Klasse wollten etwas essen, was in Österreich typisch ist. Also haben sie Schnitzel mit Pommes bestellt. Aber ich habe Hähnchen mit Kartoffeln genommen, weil das mein Lieblingsgericht ist.

In zwei Tagen werden wir nach Hause zurückfahren. Die Reise wird sechs Stunden dauern und das wird langweilig sein. Wir werden schon um fünf Uhr aufstehen, weil der Zug sehr früh vom Hauptbahnhof abfährt. Das finde ich nicht so gut. Obwohl wir Wien nicht verlassen wollen, werde ich froh sein, euch wiederzusehen.

Bis dann!

Hanna

1 Warum mag Hanna die Stadt Wien? [1]

2 Wo wird sie zum ersten Mal hingehen? [1]

3 Warum findet Hanna das Frühstück gut? [1]

4 Warum gehen die Schüler in den Supermarkt? [1]

5 Wer muss die Getränke tragen? [1]

6 Warum haben viele Schüler Schnitzel gegessen? [1]

7 Wie findet Hanna Hähnchen mit Kartoffeln? [1]

8 Was wird Hanna langweilig finden? [1]

9 Was findet Hanna nicht so gut? [1]

10 Wann wird Hanna glücklich sein? [1]

[Total: 10]

Points to remember

- Remember you must write all answers *in German*, but you don't need to use full sentences.
- If you change your mind about an answer, make sure you have crossed it out and made it clear which answer is correct.
- Don't leave any answers blank. If you're not sure of an answer, have a guess.
- Remember that the questions are answered in order in the text, so if you know the answers to questions 3 and 5, you know roughly where to look for the answer to question 4.

Paper 3: speaking

The sample answer below is a good presentation about a student's home town.

🎧 Before you listen to the recording, cover up the lower half of the page. Follow the text as you listen and think about how the speaker makes what she is saying sound more interesting. Turn to the checklist on page 92 to see what you should include in a presentation. Can you find examples of these items here?

Heute werde ich über meine Stadt sprechen. Ich wohne in Hamburg, die eine sehr große Industriestadt in Norddeutschland ist. Hier wohne ich seit acht Jahren. Als ich jünger war, habe ich in einem kleinen ruhigen Dorf auf dem Land in der Nähe der Ostseeküste gewohnt. Das war schön, weil ich mit meinen Freunden am Strand gespielt habe. Aber Hamburg gefällt mir besser, da die Stadt größer ist und weil es so viel zu tun gibt. Zum Beispiel fahre ich gern Rad, und am Fluss gibt es sichere Radwege bis zum Hafen.

Ich wohne mit meiner Familie in einem modernen Wohnblock am Stadtrand, wo ich auch zur Schule gehe. Am Abend fahre ich oft mit meinem Bruder in die Stadtmitte, um ins Kino oder in ein Konzert zu gehen. Die Bus- und S-Bahnverbindungen sind super und für Schüler und Studenten gar nicht teuer. Wenn Touristen nach Hamburg kommen, gibt es viele Sehenswürdigkeiten. Zum Beispiel kann man den Hafen von einer Fähre besichtigen, das Rathaus besuchen, den Fischmarkt ansehen und Spaziergänge durch die Innenstadt machen. Wir haben verschiedene Einkaufszentren, obwohl ich mich für Geschäfte nicht so sehr interessiere.

What questions do you think the examiner might now ask to start a discussion? Discuss your ideas with a partner before looking at the questions below.

🎧 Listen to the student answering questions about her presentation. Do you think her answers are good? Has she included opinions, reasons and a range of tenses and structures?

1 Was kann man in Hamburg machen, wenn man sich für Sport interessiert?

2 Was gibt es für Kulturfans?

3 Ist Hamburg die größte Stadt in Deutschland?

4 Was sind die Vor- und Nachteile des Großstadtlebens?

5 Was kann man in Hamburg besonders essen oder trinken?

6 Möchten Sie auch in Zukunft in Hamburg wohnen? Warum, oder warum nicht?

Tips for success

- Check that the written form of your presentation is accurate before you attempt to learn it by heart.
- To learn the presentation, use strategies such as rewriting it with gaps instead of words and then gradually increasing the number of gaps until you are just left with the first word of each sentence. Practise saying it out loud as often as possible.
- It can help to record your presentation on your phone or on a digital recorder and keep playing it back.
- Don't speak too fast, and use expression so that your presentation doesn't sound monotonous.

Paper 4: writing

In this task you will focus on how to improve a piece of writing in order to get high marks.

Schreiben Sie 130–140 Wörter **auf Deutsch**.

Letzte Woche haben Sie Ihr Portemonnaie mit Ihrem ganzen Geld in der Stadtmitte verloren. Schreiben Sie einen Artikel darüber.

- Erklären Sie, wo Sie waren und warum Sie dort waren.
- Wann konnten Sie das Portemonnaie nicht finden? Wie haben Sie reagiert?
- Beschreiben Sie, was Sie gemacht haben, um es zu finden.
- Erzählen Sie, was am Ende passiert ist.

Here is a student's answer, which is accurate but would not get a good mark. Why not? Read it and then discuss the questions below with a partner.

1 Is it the right length?

2 Have all the bullet points been addressed?

3 Does it sound interesting?

4 Has the student used a variety of linguistic features?

5 Can you suggest ways of improving it?

Sample student answer

Ich war letzte Woche in der Stadtmitte[1]. [2]Ich habe mein Portemonnaie verloren. Meiner Meinung nach war das schlimm[3]. Es war ein großes Problem[4]. [5]Ich habe es[6] gesucht aber ich habe es[7] nicht gefunden. Also war ich sehr traurig[8]. [9]Ich bin zum Fundbüro gegangen. Der[10] Mann da hatte es nicht[11]. Ich bin[12] nach Hause gegangen[13]. Meine Mutter war böse[14]. Am nächsten Tag hat[15] eine Frau angerufen. Sie hatte mein Portemonnaie gefunden[16].

A good answer might contain all of the following words, phrases or clauses. Decide where you could add them to the text, e.g. 1–(h). Rewrite the text including these words but remember to change the word order where necessary.

- **(a)** höfliche
- **(b)** weil ich kein Geld für die Fahrkarte hatte
- **(c)** und ich wusste nicht, was ich machen sollte
- **(d)** und ich habe geweint
- **(e)** Als ich in der U-Bahn war,
- **(f)** zum Glück
- **(g)** aber ich habe ihm meine Telefonnummer gegeben
- **(h)** um zum Fußballspiel zu gehen
- **(i)** und ich war sehr froh
- **(j)** dort
- **(k)** weil mein ganzes Geld im Portemonnaie war
- **(l)** leider
- **(m)** dass ich das Geld verloren hatte
- **(n)** Zuerst bin ich zur U-Bahnstation zurückgegangen und
- **(o)** danach
- **(p)** zu Fuß

Points to remember

- You must address all the four bullet points and all the details within each point.
- Include details, reasons and opinions to make your writing sound more interesting.
- Write as close to the word limit as possible.

Childhood

bevorzugen to prefer
erzählen to tell (a story)
gefallen to like, please
gern (haben) to like
die Geschwister (pl) brothers and sisters, siblings
hassen to hate
die Jugendgruppe (-n) youth group
der/die Jugendliche (-n) young person
Junge Pioniere Young Pioneers (DDR youth organisation)
die Kinderkrippe (-n) nursery/creche
laufen to run
lieben to love
lieber (haben) to prefer
mögen to like
schlafen to sleep
die Schule verlassen to leave school
das Spiel (-e) game
das Spielzeug (-) toy

Urban life

die Ampel (-n) traffic light
der Aufzug ("-e) lift
befinden (sich) to be located, be found
die Bibliothek (-en) library
die Brücke (-n) bridge
die Burg (-en) castle
der/die Dieb (-e)/in (-nen) thief
der Dom (-e) cathedral
der/die Einwohner (-)/in (-nen) inhabitant
die Etage (-n) floor, storey
der Fahrstuhl ("-e) lift
das Freibad ("-er) open-air swimming pool
der/die Fußgänger (-)/in (-nen) pedestrian
die Fußgängerzone (-n) pedestrian precinct
das Gebäude (-) building
die Gegend (-en) area
das Geschäft (-e) shop, business
der Hafen (") port, harbour
das Hallenbad ("-er) indoor swimming pool
im Ausland abroad
die Kathedrale (-n) cathedral
der Laden (") shop
langsam slow(ly)
langweilig boring
der Marktplatz ("-e) market square
der Ort (-e) place
der Palast ("-e) palace
der Parkplatz ("-e) car park
der Platz ("-e) square, space
die Polizei police
die Polizeiwache (-en) police station
der/die Polizist (-en)/in (-nen) police officer
das Rathaus ("-er) town hall
das Schloss ("-er) castle
schön beautiful, lovely
das Schwimmbad ("-er) swimming pool

die Sehenswürdigkeit (-en) sight, place of interest
die Stadt ("-e) town
die Stadtmitte (-n) town centre
der Stock ("-e) floor, storey
die Straße (-n) road, street
die U-Bahn underground
der Verkehr traffic
das Viertel (-) district, quarter
der Vorort (-e) suburb
weit far
der Zeitungskiosk (-e) newspaper kiosk/ stand

Rural life

angeln to go fishing
auf dem Lande in the country
der/die Bauer (-)/in (-nen) farmer
der Bauernhof ("-e) farm
der Baum ("-e) tree
der Berg (-e) mountain
die Blume (-n) flower
das Dorf ("-er) village
der Fluss ("-e) river
das Gasthaus ("-er) inn
die Kuh ("-e) cow
die Landschaft landscape, scenery, countryside
leise quiet
malerisch picturesque
die Mücke (-n) midge, mosquito, gnat
das Pferd (-e) horse
ruhig quiet, peaceful
das Schwein (-e) pig
der See (-n) lake

Current affairs and social issues

der Angriff (-e) attack
arbeitslos unemployed
besprechen to discuss
der Bundestag German parliament
der (Bürger)krieg (-e) (civil) war
die Droge (-n) drug
der Drogenkonsum drug-taking
entdecken to discover
der/die Forscher (-)/in (-nen) researcher
gefährlich dangerous
die Grenze (-n) border
der/die Kanzler (-)/in (-nen) chancellor
der/die König (-e)/in (-nen) king/queen
die Kleidung (-en) clothes
die Kultur culture
die Medaille (-n) medal
die Menschenrechte human rights
die Olympischen Spiele Olympic Games
die Rakete (-n) rocket
die Seuche (-n) epidemic
der/die Soldat (-en)/in soldier
der/die Spion (-e)/in (-nen) spy
streiken to strike

verboten forbidden
weiche Drogen soft drugs
der Wohnblock (-s) block of flats
zusammenarbeiten to work together

Services

anrufen to ring, phone, give a call
arbeiten to work
ausfüllen to complete, fill in
die Auskunft information
bekommen to receive, get
bleiben Sie bitte am Apparat please stay on the line
der Briefkasten (") letter box
die Briefmarke (-en) postage stamp
das Call-Center (-s) call centre
danken to thank
die Deutsche Post German postal service
es tut mir leid I'm sorry
der Fehler (-) mistake, fault
der Feuerwehrmann ("-er)/die Feuerwehrfrau (-en) firefighter
füllen to fill (a form)
das Fundbüro (-s) lost-property office
das Informationsbüro (-s) information office
der Notanruf (-e) emergency call
das Postamt ("-er) post office
schicken to send
die Sparkasse (-n) savings bank
die Tasche (-n) bag
treffen to meet up
vergessen to forget, leave behind
verlieren to lose
wählen to dial, choose
die Wechselstube (-n) bureau de change

Meals and snacks

das Abendessen (-) evening meal, dinner
das Essen food
frisch fresh, cool
das Frühstück (-e) breakfast
geräuchert smoked
das Gericht (-e) dish
der Geschmack ("-e) flavour
guten Appetit! enjoy your meal!
das Hauptgericht (-e) main course
der Imbiss (-e) snack
Kaffee und Kuchen coffee and cake (afternoon snack)
kühl cool
lecker delicious, tasty
die Mahlzeit (-en) meal
das Mittagessen (-) lunch
die Nachspeise (-n) dessert
das Rezept (-e) recipe
süß sweet
das Tagesgericht (-e) today's special
trinken to drink
die Vorspeise (-n) starter

Drinks

das **Bier (-e)** beer
das **Getränk (-e)** drink
der **Glühwein** mulled wine
der **Kaffee** coffee
das **kohlensäurehaltiges Getränk (-e)** fizzy drink
die **Milch** milk
das **Mineralwasser** mineral water
der **Saft (¨-e)** juice
der **Sprudel** sparkling mineral water
der **Tee** tea
das **Wasser** water
der **Wein (-e)** wine

Food

die **Ananas (-)** pineapple
der **Apfel (¨)** apple
die **Apfelsine (-n)** orange
die **Aprikose (-n)** apricot
der **Aufschnitt** assorted sliced cold meals
die **Birne (-n)** pear
der **Blumenkohl (-e)** cauliflower
die **Blutwurst (¨-e)** black pudding
der **Bonbon (-s)** sweet
die **Bratkartoffeln** fried potatoes
die **Bratwurst (¨-e)** fried sausage
das **Brot (-e)** bread
das **Brötchen (-)** bread roll
das **Butterbrot (-e)** sandwich
der **Champignon (-s)** mushroom
die **Chip (-s)** crisp
das **Ei (-er)** egg
der **Eintopf (¨-e)** stew
das **Eis (-)** ice, ice cream
die **Ente (-n), das Entenfleisch** duck
die **Erbse (-n)** pea
die **Erdbeere (-n)** strawberry
das **Fladenbrot (-e)** flatbread
das **Fleisch** meat
die **Frühstückscerealien** breakfast cereals
das **Gebäck** biscuits, pastries
das **Gemüse** vegetable(s)
das **Gewürz (-e)** spice
die **Gurke (-n)** cucumber, gherkin
das **Hackbällchen (-)** meatball
das **Hähnchen (-)** chicken
das **Hammelfleisch** mutton
die **Himbeere (-n)** raspberry
der **Honig** honey
das **Kalbfleisch** veal
der **Karpfen (-)** carp
die **Kartoffel (-n)** potato
der **Käse (-)** cheese
die **Kirsche (-n)** cherry
der **Knoblauch** garlic
der **Kohl (-e)** cabbage

das **Kotelett (-s)** chop, cutlet
der **Kuchen (-)** cake
der **Lachs** salmon
das **Lammfleisch** lamb
die **Lebensmittel** food, groceries
die **Leberwurst (¨-e)** liver sausage
die **Marmelade (-n)** jam
die **Meeresfrüchte** seafood
die **Melone (-n)** melon
die **Muscheln** mussels
die **Nudeln** pasta, noodles
das **Öl** oil
die **Pastete (-n)** paté
der **Pfannkuchen (-)** pancake
der **Pfeffer** pepper
der **Pfirsich (-e)** peach
die **Pflaume (-n)** plum
der **Pilz (-e)** mushroom
die **Pommes (frites)** chips, fries
die **Pute (-n)** turkey
das **Rindfleisch** beef
die **Sahne** cream
der **Salat (-e)** lettuce, salad
das **Salz** salt
das **Sauerkraut** pickled cabbage
der **Schinken** ham
das **Schnitzel (-)** escalope
die **Schokolade (-n)** chocolate
das **Schweinefleisch** pork
das **Senf** mustard
der **Speck** bacon
die **Speise (-n)** meal, food
das **Spiegelei (-er)** fried egg
die **Suppe (-n)** soup
die **Süßigkeiten** sweets
der **Thunfisch** tuna
die **Tomate (-n)** tomato
die **Torte (-n)** flan, gâteau
die **Traube (-n)** grape
die **Wurst (¨-e)** sausage
die **Zitrone (-n)** lemon
der **Zucker** sugar
die **Zwiebel (-n)** onion

Shopping and money matters

die **Abteilung (-en)** department
ausgeben to spend (money)
die **Auswahl (-en)** selection, choice
bestellen to order
billig cheap
Einkäufe machen to do one's shopping
einkaufen to buy
einkaufen gehen to go shopping
das **Einkaufszentrum (Einkaufszentren)** shopping centre
die **Größe (-n)** size
der **Hut (¨-e)** hat
die **Kasse (-n)** till, cash desk, checkout

kaufen to buy
das **Kleingeld** loose change
kosten to cost
der/die **Kunde (-n)/in (-nen)** customer, client
das **Leder** leather
die **Münze (-n)** coin
öffnen to open
das **Portemonnaie (-s)** purse, wallet
der **Preis (-e)** price
preiswert good value, inexpensive, cheap
die **Rechnung (-en)** bill
das **Schaufenster (-)** shop window
der **Schaufensterbummel (-)** window shopping
die **Schlange (-n)** queue, snake
schließen to close
der **Schlussverkauf (¨-e)** end of season sale
sparen to save
die **Tasche (-n)** bag
das **Taschengeld** pocket money
teuer expensive
die **Tüte (-n)** bag
verkaufen to sell
der/die **Verkäufer (-)/in (-nen)** sales assistant

Shops

die **Apotheke (-n)** chemist's shop (dispensing)
die **Bäckerei (-en)** baker's shop
der **Buchhandlung (-en)** bookshop
die **Drogerie (-n)** chemist's (non-dispensing)
die **Handlung (-en)** shop
das **Kaufhaus (¨-er)** department store
die **Konditorei (-en)** cake shop
der **Laden (¨)** small shop
die **Metzgerei (-en)** butcher's shop
das **Schmuckgeschäft (-e)** jewellery shop
das **Schreibwarengeschäft (-e)** stationery shop
das **Süßwarengeschäft (-e)** sweet shop
das **Warenhaus (¨-er)** department store

Quantities

die **Dose (-n)** tin, can
das **Drittel (-)** third
das **Dutzend (-e)** dozen
ein bisschen a bit
die **Flasche (-n)** bottle
genug enough
die **Hälfte (-n)** half
das **Kännchen (-)** jug, pot
mehrere several
die **Packung (-en)** pack, packet
die **Schachtel (-n)** box, packet
das **Stück (-e)** piece
viel(e) a lot of, many, much
das **Viertel (-)** quarter
wenig(e) few, little

Thema 13 Medien

1 Gehen wir lieber ins Kino?

1 📖 Lies bitte die Programmvorschau.

> ☑ **Talk about television programmes**
> ☑ **Make arrangements to go out**
> ☑ **Talk about films**

TV HEUTE

Schneller finden, was Sie wirklich interessiert

Programmvorschau für heute Abend

	ARD①	**ZDF**	**RTL**
20.00	**Sportschau live** Weltreiterspiele: Dressur Mannschaft Finale	**Safari in Kenia** Doku	**Unter uns** Serie
20.30	**Das Quiz mit Jörg Pilawa** Quizsendung	**SOKO Classics** Krimiserie — Niemand ist eiskalt	**Gute Zeiten, schlechte Zeiten** Seifenoper
21.00	**Tagesschau** Nachrichten **ARD-Wetterschau** Wetterbericht	**heute** Nachrichten	**Guten Abend RTL** Nachrichtenmagazin — Moderation: Janine Steeger
21.30	**Harald Schmidt** Talkshow Gast: Axel Stein	**Die Pferdeinsel** Fr. Abenteuerfilm (synchronisiert)	**Musikanten Dampfer** Volksmusik

Was passt zusammen?   **Beispiel** **a** = *Harald Schmidt: Talkshow, 21.30 ARD*

2 🎧 Hör bitte zu. Was sehen diese Leute (Angelika, Kevin, Magdalena, Evangelos) im Fernsehen? Schau die Vorschau an und füll die Tabelle aus.

	Interessiert sich für	Sendung	Uhrzeit	Sender
Angelika				

3 💬 Macht Dialoge.

Beispiel A Ich möchte eine Talkshow sehen.
B *Wie wäre es mit „Harald Schmidt"?*
A Wann kommt das?
B *Um 21.00 Uhr im ARD.*

4a  Lies die folgenden Informationen.

Kino am Altmarkt

Garfield 2 (OV)

FSK AB 0

80 Min.

Mittwoch 17.30
20.15

Monster House (OV)

FSK AB 6

90 Min.

Mittwoch 20.00
22.15

Alle Karten nur €7

vom 01.09 bis 02.09

R CKFESTIVAL

auf der Freilichtbühne
in **LANDSBERG**

01.09
Ute Freudenberg
Lift, Stefan Diestelmann
Die Klosterbrüder
Pankow, Monokel

02.09
K....!
Stern Combo Meissen
Jürgen Kerth (Projekt Ostblues-Band)
Renft, Cäsar,
Dirk Michaelis

Einlass 18.30 Uhr
Beginn 20.00 Uhr
Alle Karten €35

Theater
am Stadtgarten

Freitag: 20.15

Rote Nase
Eine Tragödie von Franziska Lehmann

Samstag: 20.00

Der Besuch der alten Dame
Eine tragische Komödie von Friedrich Dürrenmatt

Sonntag: 20.30

Ein Sommernachtstraum
Eine Komödie von William Shakespeare

Karten: €25, €35, €45
Studenten und Schüler alle Plätze €15

b 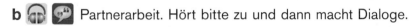 Partnerarbeit. Hört bitte zu und dann macht Dialoge.

A Wollen wir heute Abend ins Kino?
B *Was läuft?*
A Garfield.
B *Was ist das für ein Film?*
A Das ist ein Trickfilm.
B *Wann beginnt der Film?*
A Um 20.15.
B *Was kostet der Eintritt?*

A €7.
B *Gibt es Ermäßigungen für Schüler?*
A Nein, alle Karten kosten €7.
B *Ja, gut. Wann und wo treffen wir uns?*
A Um Viertel vor acht, vor dem Kino.
B *Bis später, dann.*

5 Lies bitte diese Beschreibung des Filmes „Herr der Diebe".

Welche vier Sätze sind richtig?

(1) Die Geschichte findet in Italien statt.
(2) Die reichen Menschen helfen den armen Kindern.
(3) Der Hauptcharakter ist ein namenloser Jugendlicher.
(4) Zwei Kinder hatten Probleme mit ihren Eltern.
(5) Zwei Männer wollen die Kinder finden.
(6) Es ist ein Film für alle Altersgruppen.

6 Schreib 130–150 Wörter über einen Film, den du neulich gesehen hast.
- Was für ein Film war es und was war die Geschichte?
- Wie hat dir der Film gefallen? Warum?
- Gehst du gern ins Kino oder machst du lieber etwas anderes in deiner Freizeit?

In Venedig gibt es eine Kinderbande, die die reichen Menschen bestiehlt. Sie verteilt das Geld unter den armen Kindern der Stadt. Anführer ist ein 15-Jähriger, aber niemand weiß, wer er ist. Es ist der „Herr der Diebe". Eines Tages kommen zwei Kinder zu der Bande, weil sie vor gemeinen Stiefeltern fliehen. Die Bande findet dann ein Karussell mit Zauberkräften. Danach suchen sowohl der böse Barbarossa als auch ein Detektiv die Kinder. Der Film ist wirklich sehenswert, für Klein und Groß geeignet.

2 Was liest du so?

☑ Talk about what you like to read
☑ Learn more about the imperfect tense
☑ Learn more about the pluperfect tense

1 📖 Bitte ordne in die richtigen Kolonnen ein.

Zeitung	Zeitschrift	Buch

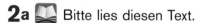

BRAVO

Kölner Stadt-Anzeiger

DIE ZEIT

Die Nacht von Lissabon

Der Pfad im Schnee

Lisa

DER ZAUBERBERG

Brigitte

★ stern

Süddeutsche Zeitung

FUSSBALL TECHNIK & TAKTIK

BUNTE

Tintenherz

DER SPIEGEL

Harry Potter und der Halbblutprinz

b 📖 🏰 Warst du schon einmal bei einer live Show oder in einem Musical, bei einem Fußballspiel, im Theater oder im Kino? Schreib einen kleinen Text darüber.

Tim Bendzko

Ich war beim Konzert von Tim Bendzko in Köln. Es war einfach Wahnsinn! Ich kann es noch gar nicht glauben, dass ich ihn live gesehen habe. Nur schade, dass es so schnell vorbei war! Die Karten waren natürlich ziemlich teuer und ich habe lange dafür gespart, aber es war der schönste Tag meines Lebens. Danke an Tim Bendzko für diesen supertollen geilen Auftritt.

2a 📖 Bitte lies diesen Text.

Ein Krokodil im Rhein

Es gibt sogar im Rhein Krokodile. In der Nähe von Speyer hat ein Radfahrer ein Krokodil gesehen, als er in die Büsche ging, weil es keine Toilette gab. Das Tier bewegte sich nicht, aber als der Radfahrer Erde nach ihm warf, riss es das Maul auf und erschreckte ihn.

Eine Zoologin glaubt, dass es im Rhein genug Nahrung (zum Beispiel Fische) für das Krokodil gibt und dass das Tier nicht gefährlich ist, weil es vor Menschen fliehen wird. Wahrscheinlich hat ein privater Halter das Tier zum Rhein gebracht, weil es zu groß war.

Bitte beantworte die Fragen.

(1) Wer hat das Krokodil gesehen?
(2) Was, glaubst du, hat der Mann in den Büschen gemacht?
(3) Warum hat das Krokodil das Maul aufgerissen?
(4) Wieso kann das Krokodil im Rhein leben?
(5) Woher kommt das Krokodil?
(6) Wo kann man diesen Text vielleicht lesen?

3 🎧 Was lesen die Jugendlichen? Bitte hör gut zu.

	Was liest er/sie?	Weitere Informationen
Timo		

Top-Tipp
Was liest du gern?

Horoskop
historische Romane   Krimis   Lokalzeitung
Sciencefictionromane   Autobiografien   Fachzeitschriften
wahre Geschichten   Modezeitschriften   Problemseiten
Fernsehprogramm   Horrorgeschichten   Liebesromane
Tageszeitung   Zeitschriften   Comichefte   Sportseite
Biografien   Reisebücher   Sachbücher   Internet

*Ich **lese** oft Horrorgeschichten.*
*Modezeitschriften **mag ich nicht.***
*Ich **mag** Liebesromane.*
*Ich **lese** auch gern Comichefte.*
*Sachbücher **lese** ich nie.*
*Historische Romane **mag ich auch nicht.***
*Ich **lese lieber** die Sportseite.*

F4

Grammatik

Das Imperfekt von *wollen, geben*
(*the imperfect tense* of wollen, geben)

When you describe an event in the past, you normally use the perfect tense (see page 38, and grammar section page 158), but it is also possible to use the imperfect tense. You have already seen the imperfect tense in forms such as *ich hatte* or *ich war*.

The imperfect tense is often used in written texts, as is the perfect tense. It is purely usage that defines these two tenses: there are no rules to tell you when you should use one or the other. In speaking and in letters, it is preferable to use the perfect tense.

The following table lists:

- the regular forms of a verb in the imperfect (*wollen*). You add the endings to the stem of the verb. The first and the third person singular are identical
- the forms of an irregular (strong) verb (*geben*). In these verbs the first and third person singular are also identical

wollen (to want)				*geben* (to give)			
ich	*wollte*	*wir*	*wollten*	*ich*	*gab*	*wir*	*gaben*
du	*wolltest*	*ihr*	*wolltet*	*du*	*gabst*	*ihr*	*gabt*
er/sie/es/ man	*wollte*	*Sie/ sie*	*wollten*	*er/sie/es/ man*	*gab*	*Sie/ sie*	*gaben*

A list of irregular verbs is given in the grammar section (pages 164–165).

(1) Look again at the 'Krokodil' text in Übung 2. Find all the verbs that are in the perfect/imperfect and future tenses.

(2) Read the following story and fill in the missing verbs from the list below:
war besuchte hatte
wohnte hörte wollte fragte

Rotkäppchen

Es ____ einmal ein kleines Mädchen, das Rotkäppchen hieß. Rotkäppchen ____ eine Großmutter, die im Wald ____ . Rotkäppchen liebte die Großmutter und ____ sie oft. Nun war die Großmutter krank und Rotkäppchen ____ ihr Kuchen und Wein bringen. Sie ging durch den Wald, als sie den Wolf traf. Er ____ sie: „Wohin gehst du? Nimm der Großmutter doch diese schönen Blumen mit." Als Rotkäppchen später zum Haus der Großmutter kam, hatte der Wolf die Großmutter schon gefressen und fraß auch noch das Rotkäppchen. Der Jäger ____ den Wolf im Haus der Großmutter und konnte beide retten.

 13/1, 13/2

F5

Grammatik

Das Plusquamperfekt
(*the pluperfect tense*)

The pluperfect tense is used to describe an event that happened before the time of the imperfect tense.

Look again at the 'Rotkäppchen' story. When the girl arrived (imperfect tense), the wolf had already eaten (pluperfect tense) the grandmother:

Als Rotkäppchen später zum Haus der Großmutter kam, hatte der Wolf die Großmutter schon gefressen.

The pluperfect is formed from elements that you already know: the imperfect tense of *haben* or of *sein* (for verbs of movement, e.g. *kommen*) plus the past participle (see page 160).

essen (to eat)				*kommen* (to come)			
ich	*hatte gegessen*	*wir*	*hatten gegessen*	*ich*	*war gekommen*	*wir*	*waren gekommen*
du	*hattest gegessen*	*ihr*	*hattet gegessen*	*du*	*warst gekommen*	*ihr*	*wart gekommen*
er/sie/es/man	*hatte gegessen*	*Sie/sie*	*hatten gegessen*	*er/sie/es/man*	*war gekommen*	*Sie/sie*	*waren gekommen*

4 💬 Was liest du? Bitte diskutiert in der Gruppe.

A Was liest du?
B Ich lese oft ____ , aber ____ mag ich nicht.
C Warum nicht?

B Weil das langweilig/zu stressig/____ ist. Und du, was liest du gern?
A Ich mag ____ , ____ lese ich auch gern, aber ____ lese ich nie.
C Nein, das mag ich auch nicht. Ich lese lieber ____ .

3 Ich brauche meinen Computer und mein Handy…

☑ Talk about the internet, e-mails and mobile phones
☑ Revise the future tense

Webtipps des Monats

a Sprachen lernen? Kein Problem!

Unter www.lingoland.net kannst du eine neue Sprache lernen, an einem Sprachen-Quiz teilnehmen, eine eigene Homepage bauen und im Europa-Atlas Informationen zu vielen Ländern erfahren.

b Du bist krank? Was ist mit dir los?

Fragen zu bestimmten Krankheiten? Kein Problem. Die Bibliothek von www.medizity.de gibt dir Anwort! MediZity ist die Medizinstadt für junge Menschen im Internet. Teste auch dein Wissen im Online-Fitnessstudio.

Willkommen in MediZity.de, der Medizinstadt für Kids im Internet!

c Wie funkioniert die Werbung?

www.mediasmart.de erklärt, warum es Werbung überhaupt gibt, wer sie macht, wie sie funktioniert. Hier lernst du eine Menge. Zeige dann in einem Test, was du gelernt hast und vielleicht bekommst du sogar ein Werbediplom.

1 📖 ⛰ Lies bitte diese Webtipps.

a Welches Wort passt zu welcher Website?

Beispiel Fitness	**b**
(1) Reklame	
(2) Gesundheit	
(3) Jugendliche	
(4) Frage-und-Antwort-Spiel	
(5) Fernsehen, Zeitungen	

b Welche Website wäre geeignet?

Beispiel Du interessierst dich für eine Karriere als Werbefachmann.	**c**
(1) Du möchtest nach Spanien fahren und dich mit den Spaniern unterhalten.	
(2) Du musst viel husten und alle Speisen erbrechen.	
(3) Du möchtest wissen, warum es so viele Slogans im Radio und Plakate im Bus gibt.	
(4) Du lernst leidenschaftlich gern Erdkunde.	
(5) Du möchtest deine Fitness verbessern.	

c Hast du einen Webtipp? Schreib bitte fünf Punkte über deine Lieblingswebsite.

2   Lies bitte diese beiden E-Mails.

DIE INTERNAUTEN-ZEITUNG
Die Online-Zeitung für Jugendliche

Von: julia0692@gmx.de
An: redaktion@internauten.de
Betr: E-mail-Freundschaft

Hey! Ich heiße Julia, bin 16 und komme aus Deutschland. Ich spreche Deutsch (sehr gut), Englisch (miserabel) und Französisch (geht).
Ich suche E-mailfreunde, denen ich auf Englisch schreiben kann, was dich nicht hindert, mir auf Deutsch zu schreiben. Ich löse gern Rätsel, tanze und bin täglich im Internet: Ich chatte gern, lese Online-Zeitungen, schreibe eine Menge E-mails! Ich schicke auch SMS, wenn ich unterwegs bin. Wenn du Lust hast, schreib mir eine Mail.

DIE INTERNAUTEN-ZEITUNG
Die Online-Zeitung für Jugendliche

Von: oliver_schmidt@yahoo.de
An: redaktion@internauten.de
Betr: E-mail-Freundschaft

Ich bin Oliver, komme aus Österreich und möchte mit dir Kontakt aufnehmen – am besten auf Deutsch, im Englischen bin ich nicht so gut! Werde im Oktober 16. Chatten im Internet mag ich nicht besonders aber Recherchen mache ich sehr gern: Meine Lieblingswebsite ist Die Wikipedia. Das ist eine Enzyklopädie. Ich schreibe auch E-mails. Wenn ich nicht zu Hause bin, simse ich. Außerdem spiele ich Querflöte und singe seit 10 Jahren im Chor. Ich warte auf deine E-mail.

a Füll diese Tabelle aus.

b Schreib jetzt so eine E-mail über dich.

Name:	Julia	Oliver
Alter:		
Wohnort:		
Fremdsprachen:		
Hobbys:		
Internet:		
Handy:		

3 Hör bitte diesem Interview zu.
Was sagt Herr Imgrund über Handys?

(1) Gib einen Vorteil und zwei Nachteile von Handys.
(2) Wann schicken Jugendliche SMS?
(3) Bei Jugendlichen, wer finanziert das Handy?
(4) Wieso haben die Jugendlichen Geldschulden?
(5) Wann sollte man das Handy benutzen?
(6) Warum ist Herr Imgrund kein Handyfan?
(7) Wie war die Situation vor 20 Jahren anders?
(8) Ist er optimistisch für die Zukunft? Begründe deine Antwort!

4 Mach jetzt eine Umfrage zum Handy in der Klasse. Dann mach eine Präsentation über die Ergebnisse.
- Wie oft, wo und wofür benutzen die Schüler ihr Handy?
- Gibt es Schüler, die kein Handy haben?
- Was hast du interessant gefunden?

F6

Grammatik
Mehr über das Futur (*more about the future tense*)

In the interview in Übung 3, Herr Imgrund uses the future tense to talk about what will happen:

Int: *Wie **wird** es wohl in Zukunft **aussehen**?*
HI: *Wir **werden** nicht mehr persönlich mit anderen Menschen **reden**. Wir **werden** isoliert **sein**. Das Handy **wird** uns einsam **machen**.*

Put the following sentences into the future tense (see page 160 for full details).
(1) Es gibt keine Bücher mehr.
(2) Das Internet ist sehr wichtig.
(3) Wir schreiben keine Briefe mehr.
(4) Er liest nur noch Online-Zeitungen.
(5) Jeder Mensch hat ein Handy.
(6) Ich schicke viele E-mails.
(7) Sie bekommen mindestens zehn SMS pro Tag.
(8) Chattest du jeden Tag?

 13/3, 13/4

4 ...und wer ist ein Superstar?

Berühmte Leute in der Musik

1a Bitte lies diese Texte.

Ludwig van Beethoven

wurde 1770 in Bonn geboren. 1792 zog er nach Wien. Er schrieb neun Sinfonien, die neunte ist weltbekannt. Er komponierte auch Klavierkonzerte und viele Sonaten für Streichinstrumente (Violine, Cello usw.). Leider war er am Ende seines Lebens fast taub und konnte seine Musik nicht mehr hören. Er starb 1827 in Wien.

Die Scorpions

sind eine Hard-Rockband aus Hannover. Sie schrieben das offizielle Lied der EXPO 2000 „Moment of Glory" und spielten mit den Berliner Philharmonikern (das berühmteste klassische Orchester in Deutschland) in einer Klassik-Meets-Rock CD. Die Scorpions spielten auch mit Nationalorchestern anderer Länder. Ein bekanntes Album ist „Unbreakable".

Tokio Hotel

sind eineiige Zwillinge, zwei Jungen, die 1989 geboren sind. Seit sie Kinder sind, machen sie Musik. Im „Kinder-Star-Search" wurde die Popband aus Magdeburg entdeckt.

Ihre Single, „Durch den Monsun", landete auf Platz eins der Charts in Deutschland. Viele Kritiker sagen, dass sie sehr jung sind, aber sie haben schon viele junge meistens weibliche Fans.

Die Toten Hosen

sind eine Punk Rockband. Campino (Andreas Frege) schreibt die Liedtexte und seit 1999 spielt Vom (Stephen George Ritchie) Schlagzeug. Die anderen Mitglieder spielen Gitarre. Die Toten Hosen gehören zu den bekanntesten deutschen Rockbands. Bis heute verkauften sie mehr als 10 Millionen Platten. Sie sind auch in Osteuropa, Südamerika, Asien, Australien und den USA aufgetreten. Sie arbeiten auch mit Tierschutzorganisationen und Greenpeace zusammen. 2004 bekamen sie ihre eigene Show auf MTV und 2005 traten sie auf dem Live 8-Festival auf. Das Platinalbum „Zurück zum Glück" war sofort auf Platz eins der Charts.

Wolfgang Amadeus Mozart

lebte nur von 1756 bis 1791. Er war ein Wunderkind. Sein Vater unterrichtete ihn als Kind und er gab mit seiner Schwester Konzerte in München, Wien, Paris und London, als er sehr klein war. „Eine kleine Nachtmusik" und die Oper „Die Zauberflöte" sind wunderschön und in der ganzen Welt bekannt. Die Reisen in den Kutschen über schlechte Straßen und das kalte Wetter waren sicher nicht gut für Mozarts Gesundheit. Vielleicht ist er deshalb früh gestorben? Man kann sein Geburtshaus in Salzburg besuchen, wenn man in Österreich ist.

Johann Sebastian Bach

lebte von 1685 bis 1750. Er kam aus einer Musikerfamilie. Seit 1723 wohnte er in Leipzig und war am Ende seines Lebens blind.

Bach hatte insgesamt 20 Kinder, und hatte oft nicht viel Geld. Er schrieb viel Kirchenmusik (Kantaten und Orgelmusik), um Geld zu verdienen. Auch die Brandenburgischen Konzerte sind sehr bekannt. Er war 1749 blind, weil er sehr oft nur Kerzenlicht hatte, um seine Musik zu schreiben.

War er der Superstar von 1740?

b Bitte beantworte die folgenden Fragen.

(1) Welche Rockbands hatten Hits auf Platz eins der Charts und wie heißen die Singles?

(2) Welcher Musiker und welche Gruppe machten schon als Kinder Musik?

(3) Welche Rockgruppe und welcher Musiker sind viel gereist?

(4) Nenne ein Instrument einer Rockgruppe und ein typisches Instrument der klassischen Musik.

(5) Warum musste Bach so viel Musik schreiben?

(6) Welche Sinfonie von Beethoven kennen viele Menschen?

(7) Wo ist Mozart geboren?

(8) Welche zwei Musiker haben in Österreich gearbeitet?

(9) Wer ist der älteste und wer ist der jüngste Musiker?

(10) Bitte suche mindestens fünf Imperfektformen in den Texten und schreib sie auf.

(11) Was für Musik hörst du gern? Wer ist dein Lieblingssänger/ Musiker oder deine Lieblingsgruppe? Warum?

2 Bitte hör der Radiodiskussion zu. Was ist richtig und was ist falsch? Bitte korrigiere die falschen Aussagen.

(1) Marius hat CDs von Bach.

(2) Lisas Eltern hören gern Opern.

(3) Lisa findet Opern cool.

(4) Lisa findet die Liedtexte von Tokio Hotel langweilig.

(5) Die Berliner Philharmoniker sind ein Orchester.

(6) Karten für klassische Konzerte sind billig.

(7) Marius findet es gut, dass man Klassik und Rock kombiniert.

3 Wer ist dein Superstar?

Beispiel A Was für Musik hörst du?

B *Ich höre gern ____*
Und du?

A Ich höre oft ____

B *Warum gefällt dir diese Musik?*

A Die Musik hat viel Rhythmus. Und warum hörst du ____ ?

B *Die Liedtexte sind cool.*

A Was magst du nicht und warum?

B *____ mag ich nicht. Die Instrumente gefallen mir nicht.*

A Hast du ____ schon live gesehen?

B *Nein, aber ich habe seine/ihre neue Single.*

4 Schreib etwas über eine Gruppe, einen Popstar, den du besonders magst und warum.

Vielleicht kannst du später in der Klasse kurz darüber sprechen.

Top-Tipp

Die Liedtexte sind langweilig/cool.
Das ist super Musik.
Dieser Künstler ist talentiert.
Das ist ein Publikumsliebling.
Der Auftritt war einfach toll.
Klassische Musik ist nichts für mich.
Die Musik hat viel/keinen Rhythmus.
Ich habe seine/ihre neue Single.
Sie haben ihre eigene Fernsehshow.
Ich habe ihn/sie live gesehen.
Die Instrumente gefallen mir (nicht).

5 Die virtuelle Welt

1 📖 Lies den Text und beantworte die Fragen in ganzen Sätzen. Beginne jeden Satz mit *Man...*.

Beispiel (1) *Man schrieb Ansichtskarten.*

(1) Was machte man früher, wenn man im Urlaub war?

(2) Was erzählte man seinen Freunden vielleicht?

(3) Was kann man heute machen, wenn man im Urlaub ist?

(4) Was muss man bei der Urlaubskarten-App nicht mehr machen?

(5) Mit der Urlaub-App kommt ein neues Problem. Gib Details an.

Grammatik

B7

Indefinitpronomen mit substantivierten Adjektiven (*indefinite pronouns with adjectival nouns*)

The indefinite pronouns are **etwas** (some), **nichts** (nothing), **viel** (a lot), **wenig** (little) and **alles** (everything). Up to now you will have used these words as qualifiers or quantifiers giving more information about verbs:

Ich habe viel/nichts gemacht.

They can also be used with adjectives. In this situation the adjectives are converted to nouns and become adjectival nouns. An *adjectival noun* begins with a capital letter but has adjective endings.

*Ich habe etwas Schön**es** (something nice) gemacht.*

*Wir haben nichts Lecker**es** (nothing tasty) gegessen.*

*Er hat viel Süß**es** (a lot of sweet things) gekauft.*

*Du hast wenig Interessant**es** (little of interest) gesagt.*

Alles Gute (all good wishes) zum Geburtstag!

(1) **How do you say the following?**
   a nothing new
   b many modern things

(2) **The text in Übung 1 includes three examples of indefinite pronouns with adjectival nouns. Find them and translate them.**

Viele Grüße aus dem Urlaub

Früher schrieb man Ansichtskarten aus dem Urlaub mit einem Foto des Urlaubsortes, manchmal auch mit vielen kleinen Fotos. Man schrieb an seine Freunde und erzählte viel Schönes über den Urlaub: wie wunderbar das Wetter war und was man zum Beispiel in den Alpen machen konnte. Dann kaufte man eine Briefmarke und schickte die Karte ab. Irgendwann kam sie dann bei den Freunden an, aber nicht immer, weil die Post die Karte vielleicht verlor.

Heute gibt es etwas Neues – eine Urlaubskarten-App! Man macht ein Selfie auf dem Smartphone, gibt die Adresse der Freunde und etwas Interessantes als Text ein und bevor man selbst aus dem Urlaub zurück ist, haben die Freunde eine schöne Karte mit einem persönlichen Foto – „das bin ich in den Alpen". Man hat weder die Karte noch die Briefmarke gekauft und auch nichts mit der Hand geschrieben. Das hat alles die App gemacht.

Man fragt sich aber, wo diese Information gespeichert ist? Wer weiß, dass man im Urlaub ist? Ist das alles überhaupt sicher?

2 🎧 Sicher im Internet?

a Hör zu und entscheide, welche Aussagen richtig sind.

(1) Annika ist gerade in einem Chatroom.
(2) Annika hat auf Facebook nur ihren Vornamen und ihr Geburtsdatum angegeben.
(3) Annika möchte mit ihren Freunden ein Computerspiel-Event besuchen.
(4) Die meisten von Annikas Freunden sind noch nicht auf Facebook.
(5) Annika meint, dass Facebook für junge Menschen etwas Wichtiges ist.
(6) Annika benutzt ihr Smartphone als Kamera.
(7) Annika chattet nur mit jungen Leuten in ihrem Alter.
(8) Annikas Mutter findet skypen gefährlich.

Top-Tipp

In der Technologie und Computersprache gibt es immer mehr englische Terminologie, die auch im Deutschen benutzt wird. Die Wörter werden einfach in die deutsche Sprache integriert, zum Beispiel *chatten*.

b Hör nochmal zu und finde in dem Dialog 10 Wörter der Computersprache, die aus dem Englischen kommen.

3 Was machst du im Internet?

a 📖 Welche Frage passt zu welcher Antwort?

(1) Benutzt du Facebook oder andere soziale Netzwerke?
(2) Wie oft rufst du Kommentare oder Nachrichten ab?
(3) Wie viele Informationen kann man auf Facebook über dich finden?
(4) Lädst du auch Fotos hoch?
(5) Benutzt du immer dasselbe Passwort?
(6) Wie viele Freunde hast du auf Facebook und siehst du sie auch persönlich?
(7) Benutzt du Facebook für Verabredungen?
(8) Schreibst du auch E-mails?
(9) Hattest du schon einmal Probleme mit sozialen Netzwerken? Vielleicht hat jemand etwas über dich geschrieben, was nicht stimmte?
(10) Was findest du sonst noch im Internet/am Computer interessant?

a Ja, oft: Fotos von meinen Freunden oder von meinen Haustieren.
b Ab und zu, aber ich chatte lieber.
c Ich rufe alle zwei oder drei Stunden Nachrichten ab.
d Ich weiß nicht. Mehr als 50 vielleicht, aber ich sehe die meisten selten.
e Ja, einmal habe ich mich darüber geärgert, als eine Freundin etwas Böses über mich gesagt hat.
f Ja, ich gehe jeden Tag auf Facebook.
g Nein, es ist wichtig, dass man sein Passwort ändert.
h Ich habe nur einen Vornamen angegeben.
i Ich poste Kommentare über alles Mögliche.
j Ja, und auch damit ich sehen kann, was meine Freunde im Ausland tun.

b 💬 Arbeite mit einem Partner/einer Partnerin und macht Dialoge. Benutzt die Fragen (1)–(10) und eure eigenen Antworten.

4 Meine Internetnutzung. Benutz jetzt die Ideen von der Diskussion in Übung 3.

Schreib in ungefähr 50 Wörtern, entweder
• einen Abschnitt über deine eigenen Aktivitäten im Internet oder mit dem Smartphone
oder
• einen Abschnitt über die Aktivitäten deines Partners/deiner Partnerin im Internet oder mit dem Smartphone

Thema 14 Die Umwelt

1 Und wie ist das Wetter?

☑ Talk about the weather
☑ Understand weather reports

1a 📖 Was passt zusammen?

(1) Es ist windig.
(2) Es schneit.
(3) Es ist sonnig.
(4) Es ist neblig.
(5) Es regnet.
(6) Es ist kalt.
(7) Es ist gewittrig.
(8) Es ist wolkig.
(9) Es ist heiß.

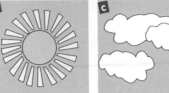

b 🎧 Wettervorhersage. Hör bitte zu. Wie ist das Wetter? Setze die Bilder **a**–**k** in die richtige Reihenfolge.

2 Wie ist das Wetter heute?

a 💬 Partnerarbeit. Bitte macht Sätze über die Vorhersage für heute.

Beispiel **A** Wie ist das Wetter heute in Berlin?
B *Es gibt* ———— .

b 🏔 Wie ist das Wetter heute? Schreib einen Satz mit zwei Details für jede Stadt. Beginn den Satz mit der Stadt, aber pass auf die Wortstellung auf!

Beispiel *In Berlin gibt es heute Gewitter und es ist 8 Grad.*

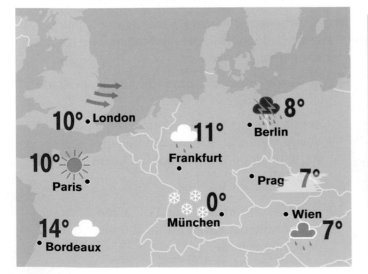

Top-Tipp

Heute ist es...   *...sonnig*   *...windig*   *...wolkig*

Es regnet.   *Es schneit.*   *Es ist gewittrig.*

3 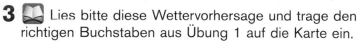 Lies bitte diese Wettervorhersage und trage den richtigen Buchstaben aus Übung 1 auf die Karte ein.

> An der Küste wird es sehr wolkig und es gibt teilweise Regenschauer. Im Osten scheint die Sonne, aber es bleibt weiterhin kalt. Temperaturen um 10 Grad. Im Westen weht ein frischer Wind aus Frankreich, aber der Tag bleibt schön. Im Süden schneit es im Hochland und im Flachland wird es sehr nass. In der Mitte bleibt es trocken aber bewölkt.

4 Und gestern? Wie war das Wetter gestern?

a Partnerarbeit. Bitte macht Sätze.

Dresden **6°**

Lübeck **11°**

Magdeburg **6°**

Rostock **8°**

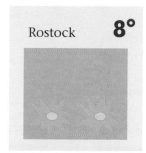

Sylt **7°**

Stuttgart **15°**

Beispiel A Wie war das Wetter gestern in Dresden?
            B *Gestern war es kalt und es hat...*

b Schreib für jede Stadt einen Satz über das Wetter von gestern.

5 Hör bitte zu. Wie ist das Wetter oder wie war das Wetter? Füll die Tabelle aus.

6 Und morgen? Wie wird das Wetter sein...?

Grammatik G1

Mehr über unpersönliche Verben *(more about impersonal verbs)*

Some weather expressions use impersonal verbs. This means that they can only be used in the **es** form.

Infinitive	Present tense	English
schneien	*es schneit*	it's snowing
regnen	*es regnet*	it's raining
frieren	*es friert*	it's freezing

German has verbs to express thunder and lightning where English uses nouns:

donnern	*es donnert*	there is thunder
blitzen	*es blitzt*	there is lightning

 14/1

	Heute?	Gestern?	Wo?	Wetter?
(1)	X		In den Bergen	Es regnet und...
(2)				

2 Luft, Wasser, Müll

Wir verschmutzen die Umwelt. Was würdest du tun?

☑ **Discuss major environmental problems**
☑ **Use the conditional**

1 📖 Bitte lies die Sprechblasen und wähle drei Probleme. Was könntest du ändern?

Schreib für jedes Problem, was du ändern würdest.

Beispiel *Wir sollten nicht zu viel Energie verbrauchen.*

> *Giftige Abfälle wie Tabletten und Chemikalien gefährden das Grundwasser.*

> *Viele Flüsse sind durch die Industrie verschmutzt.*

> *Wir verbrauchen zu viel Energie z. B. Öl und Gas.*

> *Wir produzieren zu viel Müll.*

> *Wir fahren zu viel mit dem Auto.*

> *Die Industrieabgase sind gefährlich.*

> *Der saure Regen tötet die Bäume.*

> *Öltanker sind gefährlich für Strände und die Tiere im Meer.*

> *Ich bin gegen Atomenergie. Wasserkraft und Wind- und Solarenergie sind viel besser.*

Grammatik

Konditionalsätze mit Konjunktiv

(conditional sentences with the subjunctive)

The easiest way to express what you *would* do (the conditional) is to combine the imperfect subjunctive form of *werden* with an infinitive:

ich	*würde*	**wir**	*würden*
du	*würdest*	**ihr**	*würdet*
er/sie/es/ man	*würde*	**Sie/sie**	*würden*

As with all other phrases that contain two verbs, the infinitive goes to the end of the sentence:

> *Ich **würde** mehr Rad **fahren**.*
> I would cycle more.

There are special conditional forms, too, which you do not need to learn for most verbs. However, there are a few verbs for which the imperfect subjunctive form is always used instead of *würde* + infinitive.

> *Ich **wäre** vorsichtig.*
> I **would be** careful.

> *Ich **hätte** kein Auto.*
> I **would** not **have** a car.

> *Ich **könnte** mit dem Bus fahren.*
> I **would be able** to go by bus.

> *Ich **möchte** Windenergie benutzen.*
> I **would like** to use wind energy.

You might be asked questions in the conditional in the Speaking exam. You should reply using the same structure.

> *Was könnten Sie/könntest du tun, um Ihre/deine Umwelt zu verbessern?*
> What could you do to improve your environment?

> *Ich könnte öfter zu Fuß gehen.*
> I could walk more often.

You can develop your conditional sentences by adding a clause beginning with *wenn* (if):

> *Wenn ich mehr Zeit hätte, würde ich immer mit dem Rad fahren.*

> If I had more time, I would always go by bike.

F7

14/2, 14/3

2 🎧 Heute in den Nachrichten. Was ist passiert? Welches Wort passt am Ende jedes Satzes?

(1) Wegen einer Ölpest vor dem Libanon gibt es viel...
(2) Wahrscheinlich sind die Kosten sehr...
(3) Es gab einen Unfall in einem...
(4) Jetzt gibt es viel Öl an der...
(5) Viele Helfer kommen aus einem anderen...
(6) Die Stoffe im Meer und am Strand sind...
(7) Die Folgen sind schlimm für die Fische, Schildkröten und...

a Küste   **e** Umweltverschmutzung

b Vögel   **f** giftig

c hoch   **g** Kraftwerk

d Land

Top-Tipp
Probleme

giftiger Müll

Wasserverschmutzung durch Öl

Luftverschmutzung durch Autoabgase

Luftverschmutzung durch Industrie

Wasserverschmutzung durch Industrie

Atomenergie   Treibhauseffekt

3 💬 Diskutiert in der Gruppe.

Gebt eure eigenen Meinungen zu den Umweltproblemen von heute an.
- Was ist deiner Meinung nach das größe Umweltproblem in der Welt?
  - in deiner Region?
- Was könnte man machen, um die Situation zu verbessern?
- Was würdest du in deinem Leben ändern?
- Was sollte man in Zukunft nicht mehr machen?
- Was würde passieren, wenn man nichts macht?

Top-Tipp
Was würdest du machen?

weniger Auto fahren

das Licht ausmachen

weniger Müll produzieren

mit dem Bus fahren

Solarenergie benutzen

kein Auto kaufen

demonstrieren

Strom sparen

Regenwasser sammeln

mehr Rad fahren

4 📱 Lies den Text über Elektroautos. Schreib einen Artikel für eine Schülerzeitung (etwa 150 Wörter). Beantworte diese Fragen:
- Bist du für oder gegen Elektroautos? Warum?
- Welche anderen Verkehrsmittel sollte man in Zukunft benutzen?
- Was für Umweltprobleme gibt es in deiner Stadt?
- Welche Energieformen sind deiner Meinung nach am umweltfreundlichsten?

Elektroautos – umweltfreundlich oder nicht?

Ein normales Auto verbraucht Erdöl und produziert gefährliche Abgase. Sind Elektroautos eine umweltfreundlichere Alternative? Sicher wäre die Luft in der Stadtmitte sauberer, wenn mehr Fahrer Elektroautos hätten. Da diese Autos keine Abgase haben, wäre das ein Vorteil für Fußgänger. Es gibt aber auch Nachteile. Wenn alle Autos in Deutschland Elektroautos wären, würde man viel mehr Strom brauchen. Und wo kommt der Strom her? Im Moment meistens aus Kohle- und Gaskraftwerken. Aber könnte man in Zukunft neue Energiequellen für Elektroautos benutzen?

3 Und was können wir tun?

Abfall im Überblick

Viele Dinge, die wir nach Gebrauch schnell wegwerfen wollen, lassen sich leicht wiederverwerten, das heißt **recyceln**. Es können sogar wieder neue Produkte entstehen:

- aus der Zeitschrift wird ein neuer Schreibblock
- aus der Getränkedose eine neue Dose
- aus den Küchenabfällen wird wertvoller Kompost

Mülltrennung

Der gelbe Sack oder die gelbe Tonne — für Verpackungen mit dem „Grünen Punkt". In den gelben Sack kommen Verpackungen aus Metall und Kunststoff, z. B. Dosen, Joghurt- und Margarinebecher, Tragetaschen, Milch- und Saftkartons, Kaffeeverpackungen.

Die blaue Tonne — fürs Papier.
In die blaue Tonne kommen Papier wie z. B. Umschläge, Zeitungen und Zeitschriften und auch Papier- und Pappverpackungen mit dem „Grünen Punkt".

Die graue Tonne.
Was gehört in die graue Tonne? Restabfall, wie z. B. Asche, Einwegwindeln, Kerzenreste, Leder, Tapeten, Zigarettenkippen.

Die braune Tonne — Biogut
Alle Küchenabfälle (z. B. Essensreste) und Gartenabfälle kommen in die Bioabfalltonne.

Alles, was **Glas** ist (wie etwa Flaschen), kommt in die grüne Tonne oder in die **Glascontainer (Iglus)**. **Achtung!** nach Farben sortieren (weiß, braun, grün).

1 📖 Lies bitte diesen Artikel über Mülltrennung.

In welche Tonne kommen diese Sachen?

Trage den richtigen Buchstaben in die richtige Kolonne ein.

Die gelbe Tonne	Die blaue Tonne	Die braune Tonne	Die graue Tonne	Die grüne Tonne

2 Lies bitte diese Tipps.

Allgemeine Hinweise und Tipps zum Umweltschutz

Oder: *wie man umweltfreundlich wirkt...*

1. Damit man Wasser spart, soll man lieber duschen statt baden.

2. Im Winter keine Fenster offen lassen. Um Energie zu sparen, soll man lieber häufig kurz und kräftig lüften.

3. Die Heizung soll man auch noch um einen oder zwei Grad herunter drehen.

4. Damit der Müllberg nicht größer wird, soll man zum Einkaufen lieber einen Korb oder eine Jutetasche mitnehmen. Plastiktüten soll man nicht benutzen.

5. Man soll Pfandflaschen oder Einwegflaschen aus Glas benutzen, weil man sie bis zu 60-mal recyceln kann. Plastikflaschen vergrößern den Abfallberg.

6. Essen im Freien? Alles schmeckt besser mit richtigem Porzellangeschirr sowie Messer und Gabel aus Metall. Plastikbestecke und -teller sind umweltfeindlich.

7. Man soll das Auto zu Hause lassen, damit unsere Städte sauber und ruhig sind. Lieber mit dem Rad oder zu Fuß in die Schule kommen.

Welche Bilder sind das? Schreib für jeden Tipp die richtigen Bilder auf.

Beispiel 1 *c*

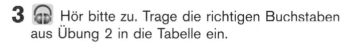

3 Hör bitte zu. Trage die richtigen Buchstaben aus Übung 2 in die Tabelle ein.

Was tut man für die Umwelt?

(1)

(2)

4 Sieh dieses Bild an. Bereite eine Präsentation zum Umweltschutz vor. Beantworte diese Fragen:

- Wo ist diese Frau? Was macht sie dort?
- Wie sieht sie aus? Was trägt sie in der Hand?

- Meinst du, dass sie sich für die Umwelt interessiert oder nicht? Warum?
- Würdest du auch das machen, was diese Frau macht?
- Was machst du sonst, um die Umwelt zu schützen?

4 Das geht uns alle an

1 📖 Lies den Text. Verstehst du alle grünen Wörter im Text? Wenn nicht, benutze ein Wörterbuch. Welches englische Wort im Kasten passt am besten? Mach eine Liste und vergiss den Artikel nicht.

Beispiel *das Weltall* – universe

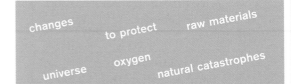

changes
to protect
raw materials
universe
oxygen
natural catastrophes

Unser blauer Planet

Das Weltall ist riesig. Unser blauer Planet, der die Erde heißt, ist kleiner als einige andere Planeten. Wir sind Teil eines Sonnensystems und auf unserer Erde kann man leben. Astronauten können die Erde als Ganzes und als etwas Besonderes sehen. Es gibt Sauerstoff, Trinkwasser und viele Rohstoffe. Das Klima ist gut für Pflanzen und Tiere, aber für wie lange? Es gab schon Naturkatastrophen, die das Leben auf der Erde völlig veränderten. Im Moment sind es die Menschen selbst, die für Veränderungen verantwortlich sind. Was können wir tun, um unsere Erde am besten zu schützen?

Grammatik

B8, B9

Komparativ und Superlativ
(*comparative and superlative*)

You have already learnt to use comparative adjectives to compare two things (*Thema* 9.2). Remember to add **-er** to the adjective, plus the normal adjective ending, and use **als** (than) to compare things:

> *Die Erde ist **kleiner** als Saturn.* Earth is smaller than Saturn.

Some adjectives, e.g. groß, add an umlaut:

> *Saturn ist **größer** als die Erde.* Saturn is bigger than Earth.

To form superlative adjectives, add **-(e)st** plus the normal adjective endings:

> *Der **größte** Planet ist Jupiter.* The biggest planet is Jupiter.

Irregular comparative adjectives:

gut – besser – beste   hoch – höher – höchste
good – better – best   high – higher – highest

Adjective	Comparative	Superlative
groß	*größer*	*der/die/das größte*

> *Das ist das **größere/das größte** Haus.*
> That is the bigger/the biggest house.
> *Das ist **das kleinere/das kleinste** Haus.*
> That is the smaller/smallest house.

Here comparative and superlative are used as adjectives and have adjectival endings.

Comparative and superlative adverbs follow a similar pattern. Use **am** (most) and add **-sten** to the end for the superlative form.

> *Der Zug fährt **schneller** als der Bus.*
> The train travels faster than the bus.
> *Das Flugzeug ist **am schnellsten**.*
> The plane travels fastest.
> *Diese Blumen sehen **schöner/am schönsten** aus.*
> These flowers look nicer/nicest.
> *Man fährt **besser/am besten** mit dem Bus.*
> It is better/best to go by bus.

(1) Re-read *Unser blauer Planet* and find:
  a one comparative adjective
  b one superlative adverb

(2) Make the adverbial form of the comparative and superlative of the following words:
  a wenig   **c** schwer
  b billig   **d** gefährlich

2 🎧 Die Zukunft der Erde

a Bevor du das Gespräch über die Zukunft der Erde hörst, arbeite mit einem Partner/einer Partnerin und suche die englischen Bedeutungen der folgenden Wörter. Geh ins Internet oder benutze ein Wörterbuch.

(1) gefährdet
(2) verantwortlich
(3) überschwemmen
(4) der Meeresspiegel
(5) das ökologische Gleichgewicht
(6) schmelzen
(7) die Durchschnittstemperatur
(8) der Regenwald
(9) abholzen
(10) die Bevölkerung

> **Top-Tipp**
>
> German words are often made up of a combination of words, like *Regenwald* and *Gleichgewicht* (*gleich* = equal, *das Gewicht* = weight — so 'equal weight' = balance). These types of nouns are called compound nouns. You may be able to work out their meaning by looking at both parts separately first. The gender is always the one of the last noun added: *der Wald*, so *der Regenwald*.

b Hör jetzt Annika und Jens zu und entscheide, welche Aussage stimmt. Hör erst Teil 1 an und dann Teil 2 des Dialogs.

Teil 1

(1) **a** Annika denkt, dass wir in Zukunft Probleme auf der Erde haben werden.
b Jens hat sich schon lange große Sorgen um die Erde gemacht.
c Annikas Vater hat kein Interesse an der Umwelt.

(2) **a** Annika würde gern zum Mars fliegen.
b Raketen können nicht auf dem Mars landen.
c Es wird länger dauern, bevor Menschen die Erde verlassen können.

(3) **a** Das Ozonloch ist das größte Umweltproblem.
b Im Moment sind viele Länder und einige Tiere gefährdet.
c Tsunamis sind ein Problem für den großen Panda.

Teil 2

(4) **a** Die Durchschnittstemperatur der Erde bleibt im Moment gleich.
b Der Lebensraum für die Tiere ist jetzt anders als früher.
c Es gibt in den Wäldern kein Wasser mehr.

(5) **a** Die 7 Milliarden Menschen kümmern sich nicht um die Natur.
b Annikas Großmutter glaubt, dass zu viele Menschen auf der Erde wohnen.
c In Zukunft werden sich die Menschen mehr um die Natur kümmern.

(6) **a** Alle Menschen haben genug Rohstoffe zum Leben.
b Annika und Jens wollen sich um die Umwelt kümmern.
c In der Zukunft wird es eine Bevölkerungsexplosion geben.

3 🗻 💬

Ein Weltklimatag. Jedes Jahr gibt es jetzt eine Weltklimakonferenz. Was würdest du für einen Weltklimatag organisieren? Diskutiert in einer kleinen Gruppe, was für euch die Hauptprobleme sind und macht dann ein Poster, das ihr auch illustrieren könnt.

Haltet dann einen kurzen Vortrag in der Klasse.

Macht verschiedene Sätze im Präsens, Perfekt oder Futur für das Poster.

Beispiel   *Wir müssen die Erde schützen.*
             Wir haben die Erde nicht geschützt.
             Wir werden die Erde schützen.

🎧 Paper 1: listening

In part 3 of the exam there are two types of question. This is an example of the first type with multiple-choice answers. The second type requires answers written in German.

Sie hören zweimal ein Interview mit Michael über seine Freizeit. Hören Sie gut zu und beantworten Sie die Fragen.

Sie haben für jede Frage vier Antworten zur Auswahl. Suchen Sie die Antwort heraus, die am besten passt und kreuzen Sie das richtige Kästchen an. Es gibt eine Pause im Interview. Bevor Sie das Interview hören, lesen Sie bitte die Fragen und Antworten durch.

1 Gestern Abend… [1]

A		war Michael nach der Schule sehr müde
B		hat Michael eine Seifenoper gesehen
C		hat Michael gar nicht ferngesehen
D		hat Michael zwei bis drei Stunden ferngesehen

2 Der Fernseher in Michaels Haus… [1]

A		funktioniert nicht
B		ist sehr altmodisch
C		ist neu
D		wird repariert

3 Michael hat gestern… [1]

A		Hausaufgaben für Geschichte gemacht
B		drei Bücher gelesen
C		neue Bücher gekauft
D		einen Roman gelesen

[*Pause*]

4 Diese Geschichte gefällt Michael,… [1]

A		weil er den Film schon gesehen hat
B		weil er Polizist werden will
C		weil der Hauptcharakter 15 Jahre alt ist
D		weil er ins Ausland fahren will

5 Da die Karten so teuer sind, geht Michael… [1]

A		nur ins Kino, wenn ein guter Film läuft
B		nur zu bestimmten Zeiten ins Kino
C		nie ins Kino
D		mit seinen Eltern ins Kino

6 Michael glaubt, dass es nächstes Wochenende… [1]

A		regnen wird
B		Temperaturen von dreißig Grad geben wird
C		besseres Wetter geben wird
D		donnern wird

[**Total: 6**]

Points to remember

- This is the most challenging part of the paper. Many of the words that appear in the possible answers are words that you hear in the recording. For example, in question 4, *Film*, *Polizist* and *Ausland* are used by Michael in the interview. So you have to read the rest of each sentence ending closely. Do they match what he has said about liking the book?
- In the sentence endings you might find synonyms of words you hear in the recording. For example, in question 2 *funktioniert nicht* means the same as *ist kaputt*.

📖 Paper 2: reading

Part 3 of the reading exam also has two sections. In the first section you have to decide whether statements are true or false and then correct the false ones. This is what you will practise below.

> If the statement is false, tick the *Nein* box, but you also have to correct the statement.
>
> You will be told how many statements are true and how many are false.

> **Lesen Sie den folgenden Text und die Aussagen. Wenn die Aussage richtig ist, kreuzen Sie das Kästchen JA an. Sie brauchen dann nichts zu schreiben. Wenn die Aussage falsch ist, kreuzen Sie das Kästchen NEIN an und korrigieren Sie die Aussage. Vermeiden Sie dabei das Wort *nicht*.**
>
> **Achtung:** Zwei Aussagen sind **richtig** und drei Aussagen sind **falsch**.

> If the statement is correct, you just tick the *Ja* box.
>
> Avoid simply making the statement negative by inserting a word like *nicht*.
>
> Five marks are given for getting the true/false correct and three marks are for the corrected statements.

[Total: 8]

Singen und gewinnen!

Alle Schüler in ihrer Klasse waren froh, als sie die SMS-Nachricht von Jasmin bekamen. Das achtzehnjährige Mädchen war im Fernsehstudio, um an einem Wettbewerb für eine Castingshow teilzunehmen.

Jasmin teilte ihren Freunden im Klassenzimmer mit, dass sie am Samstagabend im Fernsehen singen würde. Alle Schüler und Lehrer wussten, wie schön Jasmin singt. Sie hatte schon in mehreren Konzerten in der Schule und im Stadtzentrum gesungen. Sie will unbedingt Fernsehstar werden!

In der Woche vor der Fernsehsendung kam Jasmin nicht zur Schule. Sie musste ein neues Lied lernen und jeden Tag im Studio mit den Musikern üben. Am Donnerstag hatte sie Husten und Halsweh. Das machte sie ein bisschen nervös, aber bis Samstag ging es ihr viel besser.

Samstag, 21 Uhr. Der Musiklehrer, Herr Richter, hatte die ganze Klasse zu sich nach Hause eingeladen. Alle saßen vor dem Fernseher. Jeder hatte sein Handy dabei. Als dritte Sängerin trat Jasmin live auf. Nachdem alle Teilnehmer gesungen hatten, riefen die Schüler an, um für Jasmin zu stimmen. Am Ende der Sendung war es klar – Jasmin hat zwar noch nicht gewonnen, aber sie wird nächste Woche wieder singen!

Heute ist Montag. Am Vormittag kam Jasmin kurz zur Schule und erzählte von ihrer Erfahrung. „Die Teilnehmer sind sehr sympathisch, obwohl alle natürlich gewinnen wollen", berichtete sie. Herr Richter und ihre Klassenkameraden wünschen ihr viel Glück für nächste Woche.

	JA	NEIN	
Beispiel: Jasmin ist 17.		X	Jasmin ist 18.
1 Jasmin will berühmt werden.			
2 Am Samstag war Jasmin krank.			
3 Die Klasse sah die Fernsehsendung in der Schule an.			
4 Jasmin sang ganz am Anfang der Sendung.			
5 Die anderen Sänger sind freundlich.			

📢 Paper 3: speaking

Part 3 of the exam is a general conversation covering two or three topics. It lasts for around 5 minutes and is worth 30 marks. A further 10 marks are awarded for pronunciation, intonation and fluency in the test overall.

Points to remember

- Try to develop every answer as much as possible by making your opinions clear and giving reasons.
- Use a range of tenses. If you are asked a question in the present tense, you can reply in the same tense, but then add something relating to this topic by starting *Letzte Woche…* or *Nächste Woche…*.
- Accuracy is important, but it is also important to sound natural. Aim to talk fluently.

Read this transcript of a conversation about the environment. Does the student answer all the questions as fully as possible using a range of tenses and structures? How could you improve it?

| **Lehrerin** | Wie ist das Wetter heute? |
| **Schülerin** | *Schlecht. Es regnet.* |

You don't have to use whole sentences, but this could have included more detail.

| **Lehrerin** | Beschreiben Sie das Klima in Ihrem Land. |
| **Schülerin** | *Es regnet oft.* |

The only new word here is *oft*. Mention different seasons and other frequency adverbs (*manchmal, nie*).

| **Lehrerin** | Wohnen Sie gern hier? Warum? |
| **Schülerin** | *Ja, ich wohne gern hier.* |

The follow-up question ('Why?') has been ignored. Give reasons.

| **Lehrerin** | Welche Umweltprobleme gibt es in dieser Gegend? |
| **Schülerin** | *Es gibt zu viele Autos in der Stadtmitte. Es gibt Luftverschmutzung.* |

Repetition of the same simple structure *es gibt*. What about linking statements?

| **Lehrerin** | Was kann man machen, um umweltfreundlich zu sein? |
| **Schülerin** | *Man kann Rad fahren oder zu Fuß gehen.* |

Good use of modal verb. What other examples could be included?

| **Lehrerin** | Was haben Sie schon zu Hause oder in der Schule für die Umwelt gemacht? |
| **Schülerin** | *Ich trenne den Müll.* |

The question is in the past tense, but the answer isn't.

| **Lehrerin** | Was werden Sie in Zukunft tun, um umweltfreundlicher zu werden? |
| **Schülerin** | *Kein Auto, Windenergie, Glas recyceln.* |

This needs a future tense rather than this simple list, which doesn't really answer the question.

🎧 Now listen to a different student answering the same questions.

1 Count how many times you hear the following:
  (a) a past tense
  (b) a future tense
  (c) a modal verb
  (d) a subordinate clause (beginning with *weil, dass, wenn, obwohl…*)
  (e) comparatives and superlatives

2 How else does this student make the answers sound interesting?

3 Discuss with a partner what mark you think this student would achieve.

Paper 4: writing

In part 2 of the paper you have a choice of three questions. One of them is a narrative and this is the question type you will focus on in the activity below.

Schreiben Sie 130–140 Wörter **auf Deutsch**.

„Eines Tages wachte ich früh auf, um mit meinem Hund auf dem Land spazieren zu gehen. Als wir im schönen Wald ankamen, sah ich sehr viel dreckigen Müll auf dem Boden und im Fluss...“

- Beschreiben Sie, wie Sie reagierten, als Sie den Müll sahen.
- Erzählen Sie, was Sie gemacht haben, um Ihre Umwelt wieder schön zu machen.
- Sagen Sie, was danach passiert ist.

Tips for success

- Marks are awarded as follows: communication (10), verbs (8) and other linguistic features (12).
- For the highest marks in the verb category, aim to include 18 different examples of verbs.
- Verbs need to be used accurately to be counted, i.e. they must be in the correct tense and must agree with the subject.

This is an accurate paragraph addressing the first bullet point. All of the verb forms have been highlighted, but only some have a tick. Why do you think this is?

Ich war [✓] sehr erschrocken, weil dieser Wald normalerweise so schön ist [✓]. Dort gibt [✓] es riesige dunkelgrüne Bäume und es ist sehr ruhig. Meine Freunde und ich spielen [✓] oft in den Ferien da. Aber jetzt war es nicht schön. Es gab [✓] überall alte Flaschen und Verpackungen. Es war auch gefährlich, weil einige Flaschen kaputt waren [✓]. Ich habe [✓] im Fluss viel Papier gesehen [✓], zum Beispiel alte Zeitungen und Zeitschriften. Wer könnte [✓] so etwas machen [✓]?
[72 words]

Finish this piece of writing by addressing the other two bullet points. Then swap your work with a partner and mark it, using the mark scheme. Explain to your partner how you feel they could improve their work.

Points to remember

- Aim to use 18 different examples of verbs. Verbs used again in different tenses or with different subjects also count. In this example, you need to include eight more in the rest of the piece. You may need to repeat a verb in the same form as it has appeared before and this is fine, but it won't attract another mark.
- Don't forget: 12 marks are allocated for 'other linguistic features'. These include adjectives (also comparatives and superlatives), subordinate clauses, linking words, a variety of prepositions and negatives such as *nie*, *weder...noch*, *kein(e)*.

Cinema and theatre

der **Abenteuerfilm (-e)** adventure film
anfangen to begin, start
anschauen to watch, look at
berühmt famous
buchen to book
drehen to shoot (a film)
der **Eingang ("-e)** entrance
der **Eintritt (-e)** admission, entry, entrance fee
der **Eintrittspreis (-e)** admission/entrance fee
der/die **Filmschauspieler (-)/in (-nen)** screen actor
der **Gruselfilm (-e)** horror film
die **Karte (-n)** ticket
der **Krimi (-s)** thriller
die **Leinwand ("-e)** screen
das **Musical (-s)** musical
das **Parkett** stalls (theatre)
die **Pause (-n)** interval
der **Platz ("-e)** seat
der **Preis (-e)** price, prize
die **Preisliste (-n)** list of prices
der/die **Prominente (-n)** celebrity
der/die **Schauspieler (-)/in (-nen)** actor
der **Sitz (-e)** seat
die **Spezialeffekte** special effects
die **Vorführung (-en)** screening (of a film)
die **Vorpremiere (-n)** preview
die **Vorstellung (-en)** performance, showing
vorzeigen to show
zeigen to show

Television and radio

die **(aktuellen) Nachrichten** current affairs, news
beschreiben to describe
die **Debatte (-n)** debate
die **Dokumentation (-en) (Doku)** documentary
fernsehen to watch television
der **Fernseher (-)** television (set)
die **Fernsehsendung (-en)** television programme
herumzappen to channel hop
hören to hear, listen to
komisch funny
die **Komödie (-n)** comedy
das **Lied (-er)** song
lustig funny, amusing
die **Mattscheibe (-n)** small screen (i.e. television)
mit Untertiteln subtitled
die **Mode** fashion
der/die **Moderator (-en)/in (-nen)** presenter
die **Nachrichtensendung (-en)** news broadcast
das **Programm (-e)** programme, channel
die **Quizsendung (-en)** quiz show
rührend moving
der/die **Sänger (-)/in (-nen)** singer
der **Schirm (-e)** television screen
die **Seifenoper (-n)** soap opera
der **Sender (-)** broadcaster
die **Sendung (-en)** programme, broadcast
die **Serie (-n)** series

der **(Sport)bericht (-e)** (sports) report
synchronisiert dubbed
die **Tagesschau** television news
die **Talkshow (-s)** talkshow
das **Theaterstück (-e)** play
traurig sad
der **Trickfilm (-e)** cartoon
der **Werbespot (-s)** advertisement, advert
zuhören to listen

Reading

das **Bilderbuch ("-er)** picture book
das **Comic-Heft (-e)** comic book
die **Dichtung** poetry
das **Exemplar (-e)** copy (of a book)
das **Fanmagazin (-e)** fanzine
das **Flugblatt ("-er)** broadsheet newspaper
die **Fortsetzung (-en)** episode
das **Gedicht (-e)** poem
die **Gestalt (-en)** character (in a story)
die **Handlung** plot
das **Jahresalbum (Jahresalben)** annual
der/die **Journalist (-en)/in (-nen)** journalist
das **Kapitel (-)** chapter
lesen to read
die **Monatsschrift (-en)** monthly periodical
die **Presse** press
der **Roman (-e)** novel
romantisch romantic
das **Schauspiel (-e)** play
die **Schlagzeile (-n)** headline
die **Sensationspresse** tabloid press
das **Tageblatt ("-er)** daily newspaper
der **Verlag (-e)** publishing house
der/die **Verleger (-)/in (-nen)** publisher
die **Wochenbeilage (-n)** weekend supplement
die **Wochenzeitung (-en)** weekly newspaper
die **Zeitschrift (-en)** magazine
die **Zeitung (-en)** newspaper

Weather

bedeckt overcast
bewölkt cloudy
der **Donner** thunder
donnern to thunder
das **Eis** ice
das **Gewitter (-)** thunderstorm
der **Grad (-e)** degree
der **Hagel** hail
hageln to hail
heiß hot
der **Himmel (-)** sky
die **Hitze** heat
die **Jahreszeit (-en)** season
kalt cold
die **Kälte** cold
der **Mantel (")** coat
nass wet
der **Nebel** fog
nebelig foggy

der **Nord** north
der **Ost** east
der **Regen** rain
der **Regenmantel (")** raincoat
der **Regenschauer (-)** shower
der **Regenschirm (-e)** umbrella
regnen to rain
regnerisch rainy
schlecht bad
der **Schnee** snow
schneien to snow
stark strong
der **Stern (-e)** star
die **Sonne** sun
sonnig sunny
der **Sturm ("-e)** storm
der **Süd** south
die **Temperatur (-en)** temperature
die **Vorhersage (-n)** forecast
wechseln to change
der **West** west
das **Wetter** weather
der **Wetterbericht (-e)** weather report
die **Wettervorhersage (-n)** weather forecast
windig windy
die **Wolke (-n)** cloud
wolkig cloudy

Endangered species

der **Adler (-)** eagle
die **Art (-en)** species
bedroht threatened
der **Eisbär (-en)** polar bear
gefährdet endangered
der **Lebensraum** habitat
die **Meeresschildkröte (-n)** turtle
das **Opfer (-)** victim
retten to save
schützen to protect
die **Tierart (-en)** animal species
töten to kill
vom Aussterben bedroht endangered (species, plants etc.)

Natural and manmade disasters

der **Abfall ("-e)** waste
die **Abgase** exhaust gases
abholzen to deforest
abladen to dump
Angst haben to be afraid
ausbeuten to exploit
brennen to burn
die **Desertifikation** desertification
der **Dünger (-)** fertiliser
die **Dürre (-n)** drought
das **Erdbeben (-)** earthquake
erschöpfen to exhaust
der **Gletscher (-)** glacier
die **Hitzewelle (-n)** heatwave
die **Lärmbelästigung** noise pollution

die **Naturkatastrophe (-n)** natural catastrophe
der **Ölteppich (-e)** oil slick
der **Orkan (-e)** hurricane
der **Regenwald ("-er)** rainforest
der **Sauerregen** acid rain
schädlich harmful
schmutzig dirty
überschwemmen to flood
die **Überschwemmung (-en)** flood
der **Verkehr** traffic
der **Verkehrsstau (-e)** traffic jam
verschmutzt polluted
die **Verwüstung** devastation
der **(Wald)brand ("-e)** (forest) fire
zerstören to destroy

Positive steps and energy-related issues

anbauen to cultivate
die **(Atom)kraft** (nuclear) energy
das **Benzin** petrol
die **Bevölkerung** population
der **Biokraftstoff (-e)** biofuel
die **Energie** energy
die **Energieeinsparung** energy conservation
die **Energiesparlampe (-n)** energy-saving bulb
das **Erdöl** crude oil, petroleum
erneuerbar sustainable
der **fossile Brennstoff** fossil fuel
gentechnisch verändert genetically modified
die **Gezeitenkraft** tidal energy
die **Grünen** Green Party
das **Holz ("-er)** wood, timber
die **Kernkraft** nuclear energy
die **Kohle (-n)** coal
die **Mülltrennung** waste separation
ökologisch ecological
organisch organic
riesig huge, enormous
der **Rohstoff (-e)** raw material
sauber clean
das **Solarkraftwerk (-e)** solar power plant
die **Sonnenkraft/Solarenergie** solar power
trennen to sort
die **Umwelt** environment
umweltbewusst environmentally aware
der **Umweltschutz** environmental protection
der/die **Verbraucher (-)/in (-nen)** consumer
die **Wasserkraft** hydroelectric power
die **Welle (-n)** wave
wiederverwertbar recyclable
die **Wiederverwertung** recycling
die **Windkraft/Windenergie** wind energy

Climate change

die **Atmosphäre** atmosphere
die **Erde** Earth, world
erwärmen to heat up
die **Erwärmung** warming

die **Katastrophe (-n)** catastrophe
das **Klima** climate
kümmern um (sich) to be concerned about
die **Küste (-n)** coast
das **Meer (-e)** sea
der **Ozean (-e)** ocean
der **Sauerstoff** oxygen
schmelzen to melt
die **See (-n)** sea
steigen to go up (temperature)
der **Treibhauseffekt** greenhouse effect
das **Treibhausgas (-e)** greenhouse gas
die **Veränderung (-en)** change
die **Welt** world
das **Weltall** universe

Computers

der **Anhang ("-e)** attachment
der **Anschluss ("-e)** connection
die **Anschlussgebühr (-en)** connection charge
die **App (-s)** app (*informal*)
der **Bildschirm (-e)** screen, monitor
die **Datei (-en)** file
das **Dokument (-e)** document
drahtlos wireless
der **Drucker (-)** printer
der **DVD-Spieler (-)** DVD player
die **E-mail (-s)** e-mail
die **Firewall (s)** firewall
das **Handy (-s)** mobile phone
der/das **Laptop (-s)** laptop
die **Maus (Mäuse)** mouse
das **Mobilfunknetz (-e)** mobile network
der **Mobilfunknetzanbieter (-)** network provider
die **Musik** music
Nachrichten abrufen to check messages
das **Onlinebuch ("-er)** eBook
der **Ordner (-)** folder
das **Passwort ("-er)** password
die **Platte (-n)** disk
das **Profil (-e)** profile
das **Programm (-e)** program
das **Satellitenfernsehen** satellite television
das **Selfie (-s)** selfie
das **Smartphone (-s)** smartphone
die **SMS (-)** text message
die **Software** software
das **soziale Netz (-e)** social network
die **Spielekonsole (-n)** games console
die **Suchmaschine (-n)** search engine
die **Tastatur (-en)** keyboard
verbunden connected
die **Webseite (-n)** web page, website

Using ICT

abschalten to switch off
anschalten to switch on
ausschalten to disconnect
ausschneiden to cut (text)
beiheften to attach

chatten to chat (online)
einfügen to paste (text)
helfen to help
herunterladen to download
hochladen to upload
klicken to click
kopieren to copy
plaudern to chat
programmieren to program
schicken to send
speichern to save
surfen to surf (browse) the internet

Useful verbs

abschicken to send/post
abschmelzen to melt (away)
ändern to change
aufmachen to open
ausdrücken to express
ausgeben to spend (money)
bedeuten to mean
bedienen to serve
bestrafen to punish
Einkäufe machen to go shopping
einsteigen to get in
erklären to explain
erwarten to expect
Feierabend machen to end work for the day
gefährden to endanger
glauben to believe
hoffen to hope
kontrollieren to check
kriegen to get (*informal*)
leben to live
nach oben gehen to go upstairs
nach unten gehen to go downstairs
raten to guess
reparieren to repair
rufen to call, shout
schmecken to taste
schneiden to cut
skateboarden, Skateboard fahren to skateboard
simsen to text
treffen to meet
verbringen to spend (time)
verliebt sein to be in love
verlieren to lose
verschwinden to disappear
verseuchen to contaminate
versuchen to try
wegwerfen to throw away
wiederverwenden to reuse
wissen to know
wohnen to live
wollen to want
wünschen to wish
zelten to camp
ziehen to pull
zuhören to listen

Grammatik

A Nouns

A noun is a:
- person (the teacher)
- name (Connie)
- concept (happiness)
- animal (the guinea pig)
- thing (the whiteboard)

In German all nouns start with a capital letter.

A1 Nouns and gender

All German nouns have a gender: they are masculine (*der*), feminine (*die*) or neuter (*das*).

	m	**f**	**n**
the	*der Mund*	*die Hand*	*das Haus*
a	*ein Mund*	*eine Hand*	*ein Haus*

You must learn the gender of each noun.

A2 Singular and plural forms

When you learn a new noun, learn the singular and plural forms together. German nouns form their plurals in many different ways.

Masculine nouns tend to add an **-e** (where appropriate, there is also an umlaut):
> *der Tisch – die Tische*
> *der Baum – die Bäume*

There is no plural ending for masculine nouns ending in **-el**, **-en** or **-er**:
> *der Lehrer – die Lehrer*
> *der Schlüssel – die Schlüssel*

Feminine nouns tend to add an **-n** or **-en**:
> *die Frau – die Frauen*
> *die Blume – die Blumen*

Neuter nouns tend to add **-e** or **-er** (where appropriate, there is also an umlaut):
> *das Spiel – die Spiele*
> *das Buch – die Bücher*

The ending **-s** is used only to form plurals of nouns taken from another language:
> *das Auto – die Autos*
> *das Kino – die Kinos*
> *das Restaurant – die Restaurants*

A3 Definite article

The word 'the' is known as the **definite article** and can be translated in various ways depending on the **gender** (m, f, n), the **number** (s or pl) and the **case** (see section A6 for explanation of German cases).

	m	**f**	**n**	**pl**
Nom	*der Vater*	*die Mutter*	*das Kind*	*die Hunde*
Acc	*den Vater*	*die Mutter*	*das Kind*	*die Hunde*
Gen	*des Vaters*	*der Mutter*	*des Kindes*	*der Hunde*
Dat	*dem Vater*	*der Mutter*	*dem Kind*	*den Hunden*

In the masculine and neuter genitive singular, nouns that do not already end in *-s* add *-es* if they are one syllable long (*des Kindes*) or *-s* if they are two or more syllables long (*des Vaters*).

In the dative plural, nouns that are not borrowed from other languages and do not already end in *-n* add *-n*. Note that such nouns add *-en* if adding just *-n* makes a word that cannot be pronounced easily (*den Hunden*). *Das Auto* is a borrowed word, so it is *den Autos* in the dative plural.

A4 Indefinite article

The words 'a' and 'an' are known as **indefinite articles** and can be translated in various ways depending on the **gender** (m, f, n) and the **case** (see section A6 for explanation of German cases). In English the plural indefinite article is 'some', but in German there is no plural indefinite article, so 'some children' is simply translated as *Kinder*.

	m	**f**	**n**	**pl**
Nom	*ein Vater*	*eine Mutter*	*ein Kind*	*Hunde*
Acc	*einen Vater*	*eine Mutter*	*ein Kind*	*Hunde*
Gen	*eines Vaters*	*einer Mutter*	*eines Kind(e)s*	*Hunde*
Dat	*einem Vater*	*einer Mutter*	*einem Kind*	*Hunden*

In the masculine and neuter genitive singular, and in the dative plural, the same rules apply as for the definite article.

A5 Negative article

To say 'not a', 'not any' or 'no' in German, use the **negative article**, *kein*. As with positive articles, this varies depending on gender, number and case. In all its forms it is the same as the indefinite article, with a **k-** at the beginning.

	m	**f**	**n**	**pl**
Nom	*kein Vater*	*keine Mutter*	*kein Kind*	*keine Hunde*
Acc	*keinen Vater*	*keine Mutter*	*kein Kind*	*keine Hunde*
Gen	*keines Vaters*	*keiner Mutter*	*keines Kindes*	*keiner Hunde*
Dat	*keinem Vater*	*keiner Mutter*	*keinem Kind*	*keinen Hunden*

A6 German case system

All German nouns must be in a certain case, depending on the part the noun plays in the sentence.

Nominative

The nominative case is used for the subject of the sentence. The subject is the person or thing doing the action (the verb). This case is also always used after *sein* (to be).

> *Der Mann fährt nach Berlin.*
> The man travels to Berlin.

> *Meine Schwester wohnt in Salzburg.*
> My sister lives in Salzburg.

Dieses Meerschweinchen ist süß.
This guinea pig is cute.

Diese Schuhe kosten €80.
These shoes cost €80.

Accusative

The accusative case is used:

- for the direct object of the sentence. The direct object is the person or thing to which the action is being done:

  Ich kaufe einen Bleistift.
  I buy a pencil.

  Er hat keine Schwester.
  He has not got a sister.

  Peter trägt das Hemd.
  Peter is wearing the shirt.

  Elizabeth macht ihre Hausaufgaben.
  Elizabeth is doing her homework.

- after certain prepositions (also see sections E1 and E3):

  Ich gehe durch den Park.
  I go through the park.

  Das Postamt liegt um die Ecke.
  The post office is around the corner.

Genitive

The genitive case is used:

- to indicate possession. This means the person or thing owning something is in the genitive:

  Die Katze meines Onkels ist 2 Jahre alt.
  My uncle's cat is 2 years old.

  Die Wohnung meiner Freundin ist sehr schön.
  My girlfriend's flat is very nice.

  Ich finde die Farbe des Wagens ganz schön.
  I find the colour of the car really attractive.

- after certain prepositions (also see section E4):

  Mario wohnt außerhalb der kleinen Stadt.
  Mario lives outside of the small town.

  Karolina hört während der Arbeit gerne Musik.
  Karolina likes listening to music while she works.

Dative

The dative case is used:

- for the indirect object of the sentence. The indirect object is the person or thing to whom/which or for whom/which something is being done (whatever the verb):

  Ich gebe meinem Bruder das Buch.
  I give the book to my brother.

  Er schreibt seiner Mutter einen Brief.
  He writes a letter to his mother.

  Habib zeigt dem Kind das Bild.
  Habib shows the picture to the child.

  Wir schicken unseren Freunden eine Postkarte.
  We send a postcard to our friends.

- after certain prepositions (also see sections E2 and E3):

  Ich wohne bei meiner Schwester.
  I live at my sister's house.

  Er kommt aus dem Zimmer.
  He comes out of the room.

- with certain verbs:

  gehören (to belong to)

  Das Buch gehört der Schule.
  The book belongs to the school.

  helfen (to help)

  Wir helfen den Kindern.
  We help the children.

  passen (to fit, to suit)

  Die Jeans passt meinem Freund gut.
  The jeans fit/suit my friend.

In the dative plural *-n* is added to the noun if it does not already end in one.

  mit den Freunden   with the friends

A7 Weak nouns

Weak nouns are masculine nouns that end in *-n* or *-en* in all cases of the singular, except for the nominative singular, and throughout the plural. Many weak masculine nouns end in *-e* in the nominative singular, such as *der Junge*. They are frequently people or nationalities such as *der Beamte* (the official) or *der Ire* (the Irishman).

	m	pl
Nom	*der Junge*	*die Jungen*
Acc	*den Jungen*	*die Jungen*
Gen	*des Jungen*	*der Jungen*
Dat	*dem Jungen*	*den Jungen*

A8 Adjectives used as nouns

When adjectives are used as nouns, they have endings that are determined by the gender, number and case, and also by whether the word is being used with the definite or indefinite article (for masculine and neuter nouns in the nominative case). The adjective takes the same ending as if it were placed before a noun and it has a capital letter.

  Ich sehe den Alten in der Stadtmitte.
  I see the old man in the town centre.

  Ich habe eine Verwandte in Cochem.
  I have a (female) relation in Cochem.

  Das Kleine schläft sehr schlecht.
  The little one (baby) sleeps very badly.

  Der Deutsche/Ein Deutscher segelt in die Karibik.
  The/A German is sailing to the Caribbean.

  Krankenschwestern helfen Kranken/den Kranken.
  Nurses help sick people (indefinite article)/the sick (definite article).

A9 Masculine and feminine job titles

All job titles have a masculine and a feminine form. The feminine form is usually the masculine form with *-in* added, such as *der Lehrer – die Lehrerin*. The nearest 'a' or 'o', if there is one, often becomes 'ä' or 'ö' to help pronunciation, as in *der Zahnarzt – die Zahnärztin*.

Masculine job titles ending in *-mann* change to *-frau* in the feminine form, as in *der Kaufmann – die Kauffrau*.

When people describe their own or someone else's job, the indefinite article is not needed in German.

Ich bin Busfahrer.
I am a bus driver.

Deine Freundin ist Fischhändlerin.
Your friend is a fishmonger.

B Adjectives

Adjectives are words that describe nouns.

B1 Adjectives before and after nouns

If you place adjectives after the noun, they do not change:

Mein Garten ist schön.
My garden is beautiful.

Die Hose ist blau.
The trousers are blue.

Das Haus ist groß.
The house is large.

If you place an adjective before a noun, you have to add an ending.

B2 Adjectives after definite articles

Below are the endings for adjectives that come after the definite article:

	m	f	n	pl
Nom	*der schöne Garten*	*die blaue Hose*	*das große Haus*	*die alten Schuhe*
Acc	*den schönen Garten*	*die blaue Hose*	*das große Haus*	*die alten Schuhe*
Gen	*des schönen Gartens*	*der blauen Hose*	*des großen Hauses*	*der alten Schuhe*
Dat	*dem schönen Garten*	*der blauen Hose*	*dem großen Haus*	*den alten Schuhen*

Die schwarze Jacke kostet viel Geld.
The black jacket costs a lot of money.

Ich kaufe den schwarzen Pulli.
I am buying the black jumper.

Die Farbe des eleganten Hemdes ist schön.
The colour of the elegant shirt is attractive.

Der Junge mit den neuen Handschuhen kommt aus der Schweiz.
The boy with the new gloves comes from Switzerland.

B3 Adjectives after indefinite articles

Below are the endings for adjectives that come after the indefinite and negative articles:

	m	f	n	pl
Nom	*ein schöner Garten*	*eine blaue Hose*	*ein großes Haus*	*keine alten Schuhe*
Acc	*einen schönen Garten*	*eine blaue Hose*	*ein großes Haus*	*keine alten Schuhe*
Gen	*eines schönen Gartens*	*einer blauen Hose*	*eines großen Hauses*	*keiner alten Schuhe*
Dat	*einem schönen Garten*	*einer blauen Hose*	*einem großen Haus*	*keinen alten Schuhen*

Es ist eine interessante Zeitung.
It is an interesting newspaper.

Ich schreibe einen freundlichen Brief.
I am writing a friendly letter.

Während einer langen Autofahrt schläft der Kleine oft ein.
During a long car journey the little boy often falls asleep.

Sandra schwimmt gern mit einer guten Freundin.
Sandra likes to swim with a good friend.

Karolina wählt kein ungesundes Essen.
Karolina does not choose any unhealthy food.

B4 Demonstrative adjectives: *dieser* and *jener*

Dieser corresponds to the English 'this', or 'these' in the plural. *Jener* is 'that', or 'those' in the plural.

	m	f	n	pl
Nom	*dieser jener*	*diese jene*	*dieses jenes*	*diese jene*
Acc	*diesen jenen*	*diese jene*	*dieses jenes*	*diese jene*
Gen	*dieses jenes*	*dieser jener*	*dieses jenes*	*dieser jener*
Dat	*diesem jenem*	*dieser jener*	*diesem jenem*	*diesen jenen*

Dieser Pullover ist schön.
This sweater is nice.

Diese Bluse ist zu klein, aber jene Bluse kostet viel.
This blouse is too small but that blouse costs a lot.

Dieses Kleid ist billig.
This dress is cheap.

Diese dicke Frau isst viel fettes Essen, aber jene schlanke Frau ist sehr aktiv.
This fat woman eats a lot of fatty food, but that slim woman is very active.

The endings of *dieser* and *jener* are the same as for the definite article, including for adjective endings. *Jener* tends to be used only in formal speech, to contrast with *dieser*.

Note that *dieser* and *jener* can also be used as demonstrative pronouns. Again, they have the same endings as the definite article:

Welchen Pullover möchtest du kaufen?
Which jumper would you like to buy?

Ich möchte diesen kaufen.
I would like to buy this one.

B5 Possessive adjectives

Possessive adjectives are words like 'my', 'your', 'his', 'her' etc. Their gender and number must agree with the noun they refer to.

	m	f	n	pl
my	mein	meine	mein	meine
your (informal)	dein	deine	dein	deine
his	sein	seine	sein	seine
her	ihr	ihre	ihr	ihre
its	sein	seine	sein	seine
our	unser	unsere	unser	unsere
your (informal)	euer	eure	euer	eure
their	ihr	ihre	ihr	ihre
your (polite)	Ihr	Ihre	Ihr	Ihre

Possessive adjectives also need case endings. These are the same endings as for the indefinite article, including for adjectives.

Ist das dein Vater?
Is that your father?

Ich möchte nicht ohne meine Kinder in Urlaub gehen.
I don't want to go on holiday without my children.

Paul geht mit seiner Mutter ins Kino.
Paul goes to the cinema with his mother.

Die Brüder kaufen ihr Auto von ihrem Onkel.
The brothers buy their car from their uncle.

Können Sie Ihre Frage bitte wiederholen?
Can you repeat your question, please?

B6 Interrogative adjectives

Welcher means 'which' in English.

m	f	n	pl
welcher	welche	welches	welche

Welches Hemd ist zu groß?
Which shirt is too big?

Welchen Film sieht er heute Abend an?
Which film is he watching tonight?

Welcher needs to agree with the noun in number, gender and case. The endings are the same as for the definite article, including for adjectives.

Wie viel, meaning 'how much?', is formed in a similar way.

Wie viele Freunde kommen zur Party?
How many friends are coming to the party?

B7 Adjectival endings after *etwas*, *nichts*, *viel*, *wenig*, *alles*

After these words, adjectives are often used as neuter nouns and take a capital letter and endings. Here are some common examples:

Er liest etwas Interessantes.
He is reading something interesting.

Es gibt hier nichts Schönes.
There is nothing beautiful here.

Hana und Beate essen wenig Süßes.
Hana and Beate do not eat much sweet food.

B8 Comparative adjectives

To compare two things you use the comparative, which is formed by adding *-er* to the adjective:

schnell	fast	schneller	faster
früh	early	früher	earlier
schlecht	bad	schlechter	worse

A preceding vowel (a, o, u) may take an umlaut in the comparative of some common single-syllable adjectives:

warm	warm	wärmer	warmer
groß	big	größer	bigger
gesund	healthy	gesünder	healthier

In English, with longer adjectives, we often say 'more' (e.g. more interesting). In German this does not happen. You still add *-er*:

oft	often	öfter	more often
interessant	interesting	interessanter	more interesting

But note some exceptions:

viel	lots	mehr	more
gut	good	besser	better
hoch	tall/high	höher	taller/higher

Comparative adjectives can also go in front of the noun and add endings in the same way as other adjectives (see sections B2 and B3):

Mein Vater hat ein schnelleres Auto gekauft.
My father has bought a faster car.

B9 Superlative adjectives

The superlative (highest, quickest etc.) is formed by adding *-ste* to the nominative form of the adjective. It agrees with the noun it describes:

schnell	fast	der/die/das schnellste	fastest
freundlich	friendly	der/die/das freundlichste	most friendly

Alle Autos hier sind billig, aber dieses Auto ist das billigste.
All cars here are cheap, but this car is the cheapest

You can also place the superlative in front of the noun. In this case you must add the correct adjective ending:

Ich habe den billigsten Pulli gekauft.
I bought the cheapest sweater.

Note these common exceptions:

gut	good	*der/die/das beste*	best
hoch	tall/high	*der/die/das höchste*	tallest/highest
viel	lots	*der/die/das meiste*	most

B10 Quantifiers and qualifiers

Quantifiers explain how much or how many, whereas qualifiers explain what something is like. Quantifiers and qualifiers go in front of adjectives, but as they tend to be adverbs, they do not have endings, regardless of whether the adjective has an ending. These are common examples:

sehr	very
ziemlich	quite
viel	very, much
wenig	little
ein bisschen	a little

*Mein Bruder hat einen **ziemlich** kleinen Hund.*
My brother has a rather small dog.

*Die Musik ist **ein bisschen** laut.*
The music is a bit loud.

C Adverbs

Adverbs describe verbs, adjectives or other adverbs and generally do not take endings. Some quantifiers and qualifiers (see section B10) are adverbs.

C1 Adjectives used as adverbs

While English usually has one word for the adjective (e.g. 'slow') and another for its equivalent adverb (e.g. 'slowly'), German adjectives can also act as adverbs. When adjectives are used as adverbs, they do not have adjective endings.

*Das Auto ist **langsam**.*
The car is slow.

*Ich fahre **langsam**.*
I travel slowly.

*Der Bäcker ist **böse**.*
The baker is angry.

*Der Bäcker öffnet **böse** die Tür.*
The baker opens the door angrily.

C2 *Gern*

Use *gern* (or *nicht gern*) to indicate whether you do or do not like doing something:

*Ich sehe **gern** fern.*
I like watching television.

*Er arbeitet **gern** im Büro.*
He likes working in the office.

*Ich gehe nicht **gern** ins Kino.*
I don't like going to the cinema.

The comparative and superlative forms of *gern* are *lieber* and *am liebsten*:

*Ich esse **gern** Fisch, aber ich esse **lieber** Hähnchen.*
I like to eat fish, but I prefer to eat chicken.

*Sie lernen **gern** Spanisch, aber sie lernen **am liebsten** Deutsch.*
They like to learn Spanish but they like learning German best.

C3 Interrogative adverbs

These words seek further information than a simple yes/no question can obtain:

***Was** möchtest du morgen früh machen?*
What do you want to do tomorrow morning?

***Wie** bist du nach Luxemburg gefahren?*
How did you travel to Luxembourg?

***Wann** kommt der Zug aus Brüssel an?*
When does the train from Brussels arrive?

For further information see section H (Sentence construction).

C4 Adverbs and adverbial phrases of time

These words and phrases are important to determine the time frame of the sentence (past, present, future):

gestern	yesterday
morgen	tomorrow
vor 2 Jahren	2 years ago
heute	today
am Abend	in the evening
letzte Woche	last week
in 3 Jahren	in 3 years

***Gestern** bin ich nach Straßburg gefahren.*
Yesterday I went to Strasbourg.

*Wir sehen **am Abend** fern.*
We watch television in the evening.

*Wir gehen **in 3 Jahren** auf die Uni.*
We are going to university in 3 years.

C5 Adverbs and adverbial phrases for degrees of certainty

Apart from expressing time, adverbs (and adverbial phrases) can express degrees of certainty or uncertainty.

*Wir trinken **jeden Tag** zwei Liter Wasser.*
We drink two litres of water every day.

*Sie bekommen **vielleicht** einen wichtigen Brief von meinen Eltern.*
You will perhaps receive an important letter from my parents.

*Ich fahre **meistens** mit dem Bus.*
I travel mostly by bus.

*Er nimmt **wahrscheinlich** die Straßenbahn zur Stadtmitte.*
He is probably taking the tram to the town centre.

C6 Comparative and superlative adverbs

Comparative and superlative adjectives can be used adverbially:

*Er spricht **besser** Deutsch.*
He speaks German better.

*Wir spielen **am liebsten** Golf.*
We like playing golf best.

*Sie spricht **leiser** am Telefon.*
She speaks more quietly on the telephone.

Gern is an exception, as seen in section C2.

These adverbs have irregular forms, too:

bald – eher – am ehesten	soon
gut – besser – am besten	good
nah – näher – das nächste	near
viel – mehr – das meiste	much, many

D Pronouns

A pronoun is a word that replaces a noun: a person, animal, thing or idea.

D1 Personal pronouns D/1

German pronouns change according to their case.

	Nom	Acc	Dat
I	*ich*	*mich*	*mir*
you (informal)	*du*	*dich*	*dir*
he, it	*er*	*ihn*	*ihm*
she, it	*sie*	*sie*	*ihr*
it	*es*	*es*	*ihm*
we	*wir*	*uns*	*uns*
you (informal)	*ihr*	*euch*	*euch*
they	*sie*	*sie*	*ihnen*
you (polite)	*Sie*	*Sie*	*Ihnen*

Subject pronouns are used instead of the subject of the verb, when you already know what that subject is. They are therefore always in the **nominative** case. In the following example the subject of the first sentence (*der Mann*) is replaced by the subject pronoun *er* in the second sentence.

Wo wohnt der Mann?
Where does the man live?

Er wohnt in Zürich.
He lives in Zurich.

Personal pronouns are used in the **accusative** case in two situations:

- instead of the direct object of the verb when you already know who or what is being referred to

Wie findest du deine neue Nachbarin?
How do you like your new neighbour?

*Ich finde **sie** sympathisch.*
I think she is nice.

- following prepositions that take the accusative

Das Buch ist für Peter.
The book is for Peter.

*Es ist ein Geschenk für **ihn**.*
It is a present for him.

Personal pronouns are used in the **dative** case in these situations:

- to replace the indirect object of the verb when you already know who or what is being indirectly referred to

*Johann hilft **seinen Freunden** im Garten.*
Johann is helping his friends in the garden.

*Er baut **ihnen** ein Gewächshaus.*
He is building a greenhouse for them.

- following prepositions that take the dative

*Frederick verbringt das Wochenende mit **seinem Onkel**.*
Frederick is spending the weekend with his uncle.

*Er angelt mit **ihm**.*
He is going fishing with him.

D2 Modes of address

Use *du* to address one person you know well, such as a close family member or friend.

Use *Sie* to address one person or more whom you do not know well or with whom you are on polite rather than friendly terms. *Sie* can be used professionally or to an adult whom you have only just met.

Use *ihr* to address more than one person you know well. This could be several family members or classmates.

*Vati, willst **du** am Wochenende Tennis spielen?*
Dad, do you want to play tennis this weekend?

*Herr Meyer, haben **Sie** meine Hausaufgaben bekommen?*
Mr Meyer, have you received my homework?

*Peter und Simone, geht **ihr** heute Abend ins Kino?*
Peter and Simone, are you going to the cinema this evening?

D3 Reflexive pronouns

Reflexive pronouns are used with reflexive verbs. A reflexive verb is one where the person doing the action does it to himself/herself. Most reflexive verbs have pronouns in the accusative case, as in this example. *Sich waschen* means 'to wash (oneself)':

Ich	*wasche **mich***	*wir*	*waschen **uns***
du	*wäschst **dich***	*ihr*	*wascht **euch***
er/sie/es/man	*wäscht **sich***	*Sie/sie*	*waschen **sich***

Some verbs are used reflexively in the dative case. The dative pronouns differ from the accusative pronouns only in the *ich* and *du* forms.

*Ich putze **mir** die Zähne.*
I clean my teeth.

*Du wäschst **dir** die Haare.*
You wash your hair.

D4 Relative pronouns

Relative pronouns ('that', 'who', 'which' etc.):

- introduce relative clauses
- send the verb to the end of the clause
- agree in number and gender with the noun to which they refer
- are preceded by a comma

The grammatical case of the relative pronoun depends on its role within the relative clause. It takes its number and gender from the noun it refers to. We can join the following two sentences with a relative pronoun:

Der Mann heißt Walter. Er spielt gut Tennis.
The man is called Walter. He plays tennis well.

*Der Mann, **der** gut Tennis spielt, heißt Walter.*
The man who plays tennis well is called Walter.

or *Der Mann, **der** Walter heißt, spielt gut Tennis.*
The man who is called Walter plays tennis well.

The relative clauses *der gut Tennis spielt* and *der Walter heißt* cannot stand on their own. They simply tell us more about the man.

The relative pronouns are as follows:

	m	f	n	pl
Nom	der	die	das	die
Acc	den	die	das	die
Gen	dessen	deren	dessen	deren
Dat	dem	der	dem	denen

The relative pronoun can be missed out in English but not in German.

The book (**that**) I bought was boring.
*Das Buch, **das** ich gekauft habe, war langweilig.*

The television (**that**) I bought is too small.
*Der Fernseher, **den** ich gekauft habe, ist zu klein.*

Was is also used as a relative pronoun, but unlike the above, it does not change. It is used after indefinite pronouns such as *alles, viel, nichts* and all superlatives.

*Das ist das Beste, **was** ich gesehen habe.*
It is the best that I have seen.

D5 Possessive pronouns

The forms for these are the same as for *dieser/jener* (see section B4).

*Dein Kuli ist schwarz. **Unserer** ist blau.*
Your biro is black. Ours is blue.

*Du hast deine Jacke. Hast du **ihre** gesehen?*
You have your jacket. Have you seen hers?

*Dein Buch ist langweilig. **Meines** ist interessanter.*
Your book is boring. Mine is more interesting.

D6 Indefinite pronouns

These pronouns are used for more general or vague subjects, rather than specific pronouns such as 'I' or 'he', for example:

jemand	someone
etwas	something
man	one, you (meaning people generally)
nichts	nothing

***Jemand** hat meinen Bleistift genommen.*
Someone has taken my pencil.

Man soll in der Schule ein weißes Hemd tragen.
You are supposed to wear a white shirt at school.

***Nichts** ist unmöglich.*
Nothing is impossible.

D7 Emphatic pronouns

Selbst or *selber* mean 'myself', 'yourself', 'himself' etc. These words are added to give emphasis. No agreement is needed. They can be used with reflexive verbs and in any person.

*Die Arbeit ist leicht. Ich mache sie **selber**.*
The work is easy. I am doing it myself.

*Ich habe das Mittagessen **selbst** vorbereitet.*
I prepared lunch myself.

E Prepositions

Prepositions are words such as 'in', 'under', 'until', 'without'. They are usually placed before a noun or pronoun and show the relationship between that noun or pronoun and the rest of the sentence.

E1 Single-case prepositions + accusative

These prepositions are always followed by the accusative case:

für	for
um	around
durch	through
gegen	against
entlang	along (stands after the noun)
bis	until
ohne	without
wider	against

*Das Geschenk ist für **meine Freundin**.*
The present is for my girlfriend.

To help you remember the above list of prepositions, remember the nonsense word **fudgebow** (f = *für*, u = *um* etc.). All of them are placed before the noun, except *entlang*, which is placed after.

*Ich gehe **den Fluss** entlang.*
I walk along the river.

E2 Single-case prepositions + dative

These prepositions are always followed by the dative case:

ab	from
aus	from, out of
außer	except for
bei	at
gegenüber	opposite
mit	with
nach	after, to
seit	since
von	from
zu	to

Nach der Schule gehe ich schwimmen.
After school I go swimming.

Er kommt aus dem Geschäft.
He comes out of the shop.

Shortened forms:

zu dem – zum	*zu der – zur*
bei dem – beim	*von dem – vom*

E3 Dual-case prepositions + either accusative or dative

Some prepositions can be followed by either the accusative or the dative. The accusative is used to show movement towards a place; the dative is used to show rest or position at a place.

an	at, on (vertical things)
auf	on (horizontal things)
hinter	behind
in	in, into
neben	next to
über	over, above, across
unter	under, among
vor	in front of
zwischen	between

Accusative: *Ich gehe in das Haus.*
I go into the house.

Dative: *Wir wohnen in dem Doppelhaus.*
We live in the semidetached house.

Accusative: *Er hängt das Bild an die Wand.*
He hangs the picture on the wall.

Dative: *Das Bild hängt an der Wand.*
The picture hangs on the wall.

Shortened forms:

in das – ins	*in dem – im*
an das – ans	*an dem – am*

E4 Prepositions + genitive

Some prepositions take the genitive case. These often have 'of' in their English translation, such as 'because of', and include:

außerhalb	outside
statt	instead of
trotz	in spite of
während	during
wegen	because of

Er wohnt außerhalb der Stadt.
He lives outside of the town.

Trotz seines ausgezeichneten Aufsatzes hat er nicht den Preis gewonnen.
Despite his excellent essay, he did not win the prize.

F Verb tenses

Verbs are 'doing' words: they describe actions. The form of the verb depends on:

- the person or thing doing the action; this is the subject of the verb and could be a noun or a pronoun. You must use the correct verb ending for each different noun/pronoun.
- when the action happens; this is known as the **tense**

F1 Present tense

Use this tense to talk about things that are happening now or about what happens every day or regularly.

Weak or regular verbs

All weak or regular verbs behave like *wohnen* (to live). First find the infinitive (e.g. *wohnen*) and take off the *-en* to give the stem **wohn-**. Then add the endings highlighted below:

wohnen

ich	wohne	wir	wohnen
du	wohn**st**	ihr	wohnt
er/sie/es/man	wohnt	Sie/sie	wohnen

Strong or irregular verbs

A few verbs are **strong** or **irregular verbs.** They are irregular in more forms than the *du* and *er/sie/es/man* forms, e.g. *sein* (to be). This is an important verb and you must learn it.

sein

ich	bin	wir	sind
du	bist	ihr	seid
er/sie/es/man	ist	Sie/sie	sind

Mixed verbs

Some verbs are known as **mixed** verbs. These verbs change the stem, usually in the *du* and *er/sie/es/man* forms only. Look at *haben* (to have) below:

haben

ich	habe	wir	haben
du	**hast**	ihr	habt
er/sie/es/man	**hat**	Sie/sie	haben

Modal verbs

There is a small group of six verbs known as **modals.** You usually use modal verbs together with another verb that is in the infinitive and which goes at the end of the sentence. The six modals are:

dürfen (may, to be allowed to)

ich	darf	wir	dürfen
du	darfst	ihr	dürft
er/sie/es/man	darf	Sie/sie	dürfen

können (can/to be able to)

ich	kann	wir	können
du	kannst	ihr	könnt
er/sie/es/man	kann	Sie/sie	können

mögen (to like to)

ich	mag	wir	mögen
du	magst	ihr	mögt
er/sie/es/man	mag	Sie/sie	mögen

müssen (must/to have to)

ich	muss	wir	müssen
du	musst	ihr	müsst
er/sie/es/man	muss	Sie/sie	müssen

sollen (should/ought to)

ich	soll	wir	sollen
du	sollst	ihr	sollt
er/sie/es/man	soll	Sie/sie	sollen

wollen (want to)

ich	will	wir	wollen
du	willst	ihr	wollt
er/sie/es/man	will	Sie/sie	wollen

*Ich **muss** mit dem Zug nach Berlin fahren.*
I have to travel to Berlin by train.

*Er **will** ein neues Auto kaufen.*
He wants to buy a new car.

*Du **kannst** hier Fußball spielen.*
You can play football here.

Separable verbs

Separable verbs come in two parts: the prefix and the verb. In the present tense you separate the prefix from the verb and put the prefix at the end of the sentence. The verb is the second element (see section H1).

Look at these sentences:

***ab**waschen – Ich wasche jeden Tag **ab**.*
I wash up every day.

***auf**räumen – Sie räumt ihr Zimmer nie **auf**.*
She never tidies her room.

***ein**kaufen – Mein Vater kauft gern **ein**.*
My father likes to go shopping.

***fern**sehen – Jeden Abend sehen wir 2 Stunden **fern**.*
We watch television for 2 hours every evening.

In a dictionary (or glossary) the prefix is always listed first, so you would look for *abwaschen* under 'a'.

F2 Imperative

In German you use the imperative form of the verb when you want to give instructions or orders. It is formed from the present tense. The imperative of the polite form *Sie* is the same as the present tense but you place the *Sie* after the verb. For example:

***Gehen Sie** geradeaus.*
Go straight on.

***Nehmen Sie** die zweite Straße links.*
Take the second road on the left.

To make the imperative of the *du* form, take off the *-(e)st* of the present tense:

gehen: du gehst
***Geh** geradeaus.*

nehmen: du nimmst
***Nimm** die erste Straße rechts.*

An important exception is *sein*. For example:

***Sei** ruhig!*   Be quiet!

The imperative *ihr* form is the *ihr* form of the verb without the pronoun. For example:

***Steht auf!**   Stand up.*

With reflexive verbs you must remember to include the appropriate reflexive pronoun in the imperative:

sich setzen: ihr setzt euch → Setzt euch!

Sometimes the infinitive is used to give commands, such as those on official signs:

*Bitte **ziehen**.*   Please pull. [on a door]

*Auf spielende Kinder **achten**!* Watch out for children playing. [on a road sign]

F3 Perfect tense

The perfect tense is used to talk about what happened in the past and is now finished. It is made up of two parts:

1 the **auxiliary**, i.e. the correct form of either *haben* or *sein*
2 the **past participle**, which goes at the end of the sentence

Regular past participles

To form the past participle of a **regular** verb:

- Take the infinitive, e.g. *kaufen*.
- Remove the *-en* at the end and add *-t*.
- Add *ge-* to the beginning of the word.

For example, the past participle of *kaufen* is *gekauft*. The past participle **always** stays the same.

Verbs with a stem ending in *-t*, such as *arbeiten*, add an extra *-e* in the past participle so that they can be pronounced more easily: *gearbeitet*.

Irregular past participles

Irregular past participles still have *ge-* at the beginning but end in *-en* rather than *-t*:

infinitive = *geben*   past participle = *gegeben*

Sometimes the vowel changes as well:

infinitive = *trinken*   past participle = *getrunken*

Refer to the verb table (pages 164–165) to find the correct forms of irregular past participles.

Verbs with inseparable prefixes or that end in *-ieren*

Verbs that begin with inseparable prefixes (e.g. *be-, emp-, ent-, er-, ver-, zer-*) or that end in *-ieren* do not add *ge-* to form the past participle. The past participles of these verbs just take the ending *-t* (regular verbs) or *-en* (irregular verbs):

telefonieren – *telefoniert*

besuchen – *besucht*

empfehlen – *empfohlen*

Auxiliary: *haben* or *sein*

Most verbs form the perfect tense with *haben*:

*Ich **habe** ein T-Shirt **gekauft**.*
I have bought a T-shirt.

*Du **hast** zu viel Schokolade **gegessen**.*
You have eaten too much chocolate.

*Er **hat** einen Schlüssel **gefunden**.*
He found a key.

However, the following verbs form the perfect tense with *sein*:

- verbs of movement, e.g. *gehen, fliegen, fahren*
- verbs indicating a change of state e.g. *aufwachen* (to wake up), *einschlafen* (to go to sleep), *werden* (to become)
- *bleiben* (to stay)

*Ich **bin** nach Hause **gegangen**.*
I went home.

*Wir **sind** nach Amerika **geflogen**.*
We flew to America.

*Er **ist** mit dem Auto **gefahren**.*
He travelled by car.

***Bist** du zu Hause **geblieben**?*
Did you stay at home?

Separable verbs in the perfect tense

With separable verbs the *ge-* goes after the separable prefix:

*Ich bin um 8 Uhr **aufgewacht**.*
I woke up at 8 o'clock.

*Wir haben den Tisch **abgeräumt**.*
We cleared the table.

Inseparable verbs in the perfect tense

Some verbs have a prefix that is inseparable. The prefix therefore remains on the front of the past participle and *ge-* is not added. Examples of inseparable prefixes include *be-, emp-, ent-, er-, ver-* and *zer-*.

*An meinem Geburtstag **habe** ich Geld **bekommen**.*
On my birthday I received money.

*Der Lehrer **hat** die Hausaufgaben **vergessen**.*
The teacher forgot the homework.

F4 Imperfect tense

The imperfect tense is used to describe past events or situations that are now finished. Except for some common verbs, it is not usually used in speech.

Regular (weak) verbs in the imperfect tense

Take the infinitive of the verb (e.g. *machen*), remove the *-en* (*mach-*) and add the endings shown in bold below:

ich	machte	wir	machten
du	machtest	ihr	machtet
er/sie/es/man	machte	Sie/sie	machten

Note that *ich arbeite* becomes *ich arbeitete*.

Irregular (strong) verbs in the imperfect tense

These verbs have set stems to which the following endings are added:

geben

ich	gab	wir	gaben
du	gabst	ihr	gabt
er/sie/es/man	gab	Sie/sie	gaben

Mixed verbs

These are weak or regular verbs that have a different stem in the imperfect tense from the one used in the present tense. These different stems can be found by looking in the imperfect column in the verb table on pages 164–165.

When you have found the irregular imperfect stem, add the regular endings. For example:

denken

ich	dachte	wir	dachten
du	dachtest	ihr	dachtet
er/sie/es/man	dachte	Sie/sie	dachten

Common irregular verbs used in the imperfect in speech

sein (to be)

ich	war	wir	waren
du	warst	ihr	wart
er/sie/es/man	war	Sie/sie	waren

haben (to have)

ich	hatte	wir	hatten
du	hattest	ihr	hattet
er/sie/es/man	hatte	Sie/sie	hatten

Modal verbs in the imperfect tense

Modal verbs are frequently used in the imperfect in spoken German. For example:

können

ich	konnte	wir	konnten
du	konntest	ihr	konntet
er/sie/es/man	konnte	Sie/sie	konnten

Note that the imperfect tense of *können* means 'could' as in 'was able to' (i.e. in the past). To say 'could' as in 'would be able to', use the imperfect subjunctive of *können* (see F7).

F5 Pluperfect tense

The pluperfect expresses something that had happened before another event in the past that is being talked about. To form the pluperfect tense, use the imperfect tense of *haben* or *sein* together with the relevant past participle.

The rules about whether to use *haben* or *sein* are the same as in the perfect tense (see section F3).

ich	hatte gegessen	wir	hatten gegessen
du	hattest gegessen	ihr	hattet gegessen
er/sie/es/man	hatte gegessen	Sie/sie	hatten gegessen

ich	war gekommen	wir	waren gekommen
du	warst gekommen	ihr	wart gekommen
er/sie/es/man	war gekommen	Sie/sie	waren gekommen

Ich hatte meine Hausaufgaben schon gemacht, als mein Freund ankam.

I had already done my homework when my friend arrived.

F6 Future tense

In German, as in English, the present tense is often used to express future ideas if a future time phrase is included:

Ich fahre nächste Woche nach Berlin.
I'm going to Berlin next week.

To form the future tense, use the correct form of the present tense of *werden* plus the infinitive of the relevant verb. The infinitive goes at the end of the sentence. Here is the present tense of *werden*:

ich	werde	wir	werden
du	wirst	ihr	werdet
er/sie/es/man	wird	Sie/sie	werden

*Ich **werde** in einem Büro **arbeiten.***
I shall/will work in an office.

*Er **wird** nächste Woche nach Berlin **fahren.***
He will go to Berlin next week.

If the future tense is being used in a subordinate clause, the *werden* part is last:

*Er denkt, dass ich morgen Fußball **spielen werde.***
He thinks that I will play football tomorrow.

F7 Conditional

The conditional expresses the idea of 'would'. It is used to talk about actions that depend on certain conditions being fulfilled. The easiest way to express what you 'would do' is to use the conditional. It is formed by combining the appropriate form of *würde* with the relevant infinitive (which goes at the end of the sentence):

*ich **würde** mehr Rad **fahren***   I would cycle more

*du **würdest** in der Schweiz **wohnen***

*er/sie/man **würde** an der Uni **studieren***

*wir **würden** mehr Rad **fahren***

*ihr **würdet** in der Schweiz **wohnen***

*sie **würden** an der Uni **studieren***

*Sie **würden** an der Uni **studieren***

Würden is the **imperfect subjunctive** form of the verb *werden*. For some common verbs, you do not need to use *würden* as they have their own imperfect subjunctive forms. These have the same endings as *würden* (shown above), but the stem for each verb is irregular:

*Ich **wäre** reich.*
I would be rich.

*Ich **hätte** ein großes Haus.*
I would have a large house.

*Ich **könnte** mit dem Rad fahren.*
I could (= would be able to) travel by bike.

*Ich **möchte** im Ausland arbeiten.*
I would like to work abroad.

*Ich **sollte** früh ins Bett gehen.*
I should go to bed early

Note that the imperfect subjunctive form *könnte* means 'could' as in 'would be able to', whereas the imperfect tense form *konnte* means 'could' as in 'was able to'.

The conditional is often used with the subordinating conjunction *wenn* (if) (see also section H4).

*Wenn ich viel Geld **hätte**, **würde** ich eine Weltreise **machen**.*
If I had lots of money, I would go on a world tour.

*Ich **würde** in Frankreich **wohnen**, **wenn** ich Französisch sprechen **könnte**.*
I would live in France if I could speak French.

G Verb usage

G1 Impersonal verbs

These verbs do not refer to any person or thing in particular. They are often used in set phrases or idioms, for example:

- weather expressions (*es regnet, es schneit, es friert* etc.)
- *gefallen, schmecken: Ich kaufe oft Brot. Es schmeckt mir gut.*
- *es gibt* + accusative: *Es gibt einen Dom in Köln.*
- *es ist mir kalt/warm/schwindlig/übel*
- *es tut mir Leid*
- *es freut mich*
- *es geht (nicht), es geht (mir/ihr etc.) gut/schlecht/besser:*
- *Es geht mir gut, aber es geht meiner Schwester schlecht.*

G2 Infinitive constructions

The infinitive can be used in the following ways:

- to form the future or conditional:
  *Ich werde mit dem Bus **fahren**.*
  I will travel by bus.
  *Wir würden uns in Spanien **sonnen**.*
  We would sunbathe in Spain.

- after modal verbs:
  *Sie muss gesündere Gerichte **essen**.*
  She must eat healthier dishes.
  *Er will auf dem Land **wohnen**.*
  He wants to live in the countryside.

- with *gehen*:
  *Ich gehe **schwimmen**.*
  I go swimming.
- with *zu*:
  *Es ist nicht erlaubt, Kaugummi in die Schule **zu bringen**.*
  It is forbidden to bring chewing gum into school.
- *um...zu* and *ohne...zu* (see below):
  *Wir duschen, **um** Wasser **zu sparen**.*
  We have a shower in order to save water.
- with *lassen*:
  *Er **lässt** sich die Haare **schneiden**.*
  He has his hair cut.
- with *Könntest du/Könnten Sie*:
  *Könnten Sie mir das Buch **reichen**, bitte?*
  Please could you pass me the book?

Um...zu and ohne...zu

To say 'in order to...' you use the construction *um...zu* plus the infinitive at the end of the clause. There is a comma before *um*.

*Jan fährt nach Zürich, **um** seine Großmutter **zu** besuchen.*
Jan is travelling to Zürich in order to visit his grandmother.

Ohne...zu means 'without...'. There is a comma before *ohne* and the infinitive goes at the end of the clause:

*Meine Mutter hat den Urlaub gebucht, **ohne** meinen Vater **zu fragen**.*
My mother has booked the holiday without asking my father.

G3 *Seit* and *schon*

Seit means 'for' or 'since'. If the situation that is being talked about is still going on, the present tense is used in German (whereas the past tense is used in English). If *seit* is followed by a noun, the dative case must be used. *Schon* means 'already'.

*Ich wohne hier **seit** 2004.*
I have lived here since 2004.

*Ich lerne Deutsch **seit** 3 Jahren.*
I have been learning German for 3 years.

*Ich wohne **schon seit** meiner Geburt in Mannheim.*
I have lived in Mannheim since my birth.

*Wir fuhren **schon** seit 10 Jahren nach Frankreich, als ich endlich Paris besuchte.*
We had been going to France for 10 years before I finally visited Paris.

G4 Negative constructions

Nicht

Nicht means 'not' and tends to go directly after the verb in the present tense.

*Mein Bruder ist **nicht** freundlich.*
My brother is not friendly.

*Ich gehe **nicht** ins Kino.*
I'm not going to the cinema.

Nie

Nie means 'never'.

*Wir kochen **nie** fettiges Essen.*
We never cook greasy food.

Kein

Kein means 'no', 'not a' or 'not any'. It agrees with the noun that comes after it. (See section A5 for information about agreement.)

*Ich bin Vegetarierin und ich esse **kein** Fleisch.*
I am a vegetarian and I do not eat meat.

*Er hat **kein** Geld.*
He has not got any money.

Nichts

Nichts means 'nothing' or 'not anything'. If you add *gar* or *überhaupt* in front of *nichts*, it means 'nothing at all'.

*Er hat **gar nichts** gemacht.*
He did nothing at all.

Niemand

Niemand means 'no one' and, as it is a pronoun, takes endings in the accusative and dative cases:

Niemand erklärt mir die Situation.
No one explains the situation to me.

*Ich habe **niemanden** im Supermarkt getroffen.*
I did not meet anyone in the supermarket.

G5 Passive voice and how to avoid it

The passive voice is used when the subject of the verb is not carrying out the action but is on the receiving end of it. The subject carrying out the action is often missing completely, but when it is included, it is introduced by *von* + dative. To form the passive voice, use *werden* as the auxiliary plus the past participle of the verb:

*Die Bücher **werden gekauft**.*
The books are bought.

*Die Frau **wird** von dem Jungen **gesehen**.*
The woman is seen by the boy.

*Viele Politiker **werden** im Fernsehen **interviewt**.*
Many sports people are interviewed on television.

The passive voice is less common in German than in English. A common way of avoiding the passive is the use of *man*:

Man sieht die Frau.
The woman is seen. (literally 'one sees the woman')

Man interviewt viele Politiker.
Many politicians are interviewed. (literally 'one interviews many politicians')

H Sentence construction

H1 Main clauses

In German the verb must always be the **second idea** in the clause or sentence:

*Wir **fahren** am Mittwoch in die Stadt.*
We travel into the town on Wednesday.

Sometimes you might want to stress a particular piece of information by putting it at the beginning of the sentence, but the verb must always be the second idea (not necessarily the second word, but the second idea):

*Am Mittwoch **fahren** wir in die Stadt.*
On Wednesday we travel into the town.

This leads to inversion of the subject (*wir*) and verb (*fahren*).

H2 Time, manner, place

When you mention **when** (time), **how** (manner) and **where** (place) you do something in a sentence, the order they take is:

time - manner - place

Wir fahren am Mittwoch mit dem Bus in die Stadt.

We travel on Wednesday by bus into the town.

Even if there are only two types of this information in the sentence, the word order still follows this pattern:

Wir fahren am Mittwoch in die Stadt.

We travel on Wednesday into the town.

Wir fahren mit dem Bus in die Stadt.

We travel by bus into the town.

H3 Coordinating conjunctions

You can join sentences together by using linking words (conjunctions). The coordinating conjunctions *aber, sondern, und* and *oder* do not change the word order.

Ich spiele Fußball. Ich sehe fern.
I play football. I watch television.

*Ich spiele Fußball **und** ich sehe fern.*
I play football and I watch television.

Er hat eine Schwester. Er hat keinen Bruder.
He has a sister. He has not got a brother.

*Er hat eine Schwester, **aber** er hat keinen Bruder.*
He has a sister but he has not got a brother.

H4 Subordinating conjunctions

Subordinating conjunctions (e.g. *dass*) introduce subordinate clauses. A subordinate clause does not make sense on its own and so cannot stand alone: it needs a main clause. Subordinating conjunctions send the verb to the end of the sentence they introduce. Common subordinating conjunctions include:

als	when (in past actions)
bevor	before
damit	so that
dass	that
nachdem	after
obwohl	although
seitdem	since
so dass	so that
während	while
weil	because
wenn	when, if

*Er weiß, **dass** Drogen illegal sind.*
He knows that drugs are illegal.

*Er bleibt zu Hause, **weil** er krank ist.*
He is staying at home because he is ill.

*Ich fahre morgen an die Küste, **wenn** das Wetter schön ist.*
I am going to the coast tomorrow if the weather is fine.

*Sie spart ihr Taschengeld, **damit** sie ein neues Fahrrad kaufen kann.*
She is saving her pocket money so that she can buy a new bicycle.

*Wir haben sofort unsere Hausaufgaben gemacht, **als** wir zu Hause angekommen sind.*
We did our homework straightaway when we got home.

*Wir sind spazieren gegangen, **obwohl** es geregnet hat.*
We went for a walk although it was raining.

You can place the subordinate clause before the main clause. In this case the subordinate clause is the first idea, so the verb in the main clause is the second idea.

***Wenn** das Wetter schön ist, **fahre** ich morgen an die Küste.*
If the weather is fine, I am going to the coast tomorrow.

H5 Forming questions

Inversion

You can turn a statement into a question by using inversion. This means rearranging the statement to put the verb first and the subject second.

Du gehst am Samstag ins Kino.
You are going to the cinema on Saturday.

***Gehst du** am Samstag ins Kino?*
Are you going to the cinema on Saturday?

Er hat viele Hausaufgaben.
He has got a lot of homework.

***Hat er** viele Hausaufgaben?*
Has he got a lot of homework? (*or* Does he have...?)

Adding *ja, nicht, oder*

Adding these words can help to make your German sound more natural:

*Du möchtest ins Theater gehen, **oder**?*
Do you want to go to the theatre, or something else...?

Question words

You can also ask a question by starting the sentence with a question word (interrogative adverb). Most question words in German begin with 'w':

Wann?	When?
Warum?	Why?

Was?	What?
Wer?	Who?
Wie?	How?
Wo?	Where?

All these question words can be followed immediately by a verb. The form of these question words never changes:

> *Wo wohnst du?*
> Where do you live?

> *Warum macht ihr das?*
> Why are you doing that?

> *Wann beginnt der Film?*
> When does the film begin?

Some questions words, such as *welcher* and *wie viel* (interrogative adjectives), tend to be followed immediately by a noun. They agree in number, gender and case with the noun that comes after (see section B6).

> **Welches Kleid** *kaufst du?*
> Which dress are you buying?

> **Wie viel Taschengeld** *bekommst du?*
> How much pocket money do you get?

> **Wie viele Freunde** *treffen wir heute Abend?*
> How many friends are we meeting this evening?

I Numbers and dates

I1 Cardinal numbers

0	*null*	20	*zwanzig*
1	*eins*	21	*einundzwanzig*
2	*zwei*	22	*zweiundzwanzig*
3	*drei*	23	*dreiundzwanzig*
4	*vier*	24	*vierundzwanzig*
5	*fünf*	25	*fünfundzwanzig*
6	*sechs*	30	*dreißig*
7	*sieben*	40	*vierzig*
8	*acht*	50	*fünfzig*
9	*neun*	60	*sechzig*
10	*zehn*	70	*siebzig*
11	*elf*	80	*achtzig*
12	*zwölf*	90	*neunzig*
13	*dreizehn*	100	*(ein)hundert*
14	*vierzehn*	200	*zweihundert*
15	*fünfzehn*	300	*dreihundert*
16	*sechzehn*	1000	*(ein)tausend*
17	*siebzehn*	2000	*zweitausend*
18	*achtzehn*	3500	*dreitausendfünfhundert*
19	*neunzehn*		

Zwo can replace *zwei* in Switzerland and on the telephone.

This is how to express dates:
- 1791 = *siebzehnhunderteinundneunzig*
- 1995 = *neunzehnhundertfünfundneunzig*
- 2008 = *zweitausendacht*
- 2022 = *zweitausendzweiundzwanzig*

I2 Ordinal numbers

Up to 19th

To make ordinal numbers (first, second, third, fourth etc.) up to 19th, you simply add **-te** to the cardinal number, e.g. *fünfte, elfte, siebzehnte*. There are a few exceptions, such as:

erste	first
dritte	third
siebte	seventh
achte	eighth

Ordinal numbers are adjectives that may be used with an article, most often the definite article. In this situation, they have definite article adjective endings (see section B2):

> *Er ist der **elfte** Schüler, der zu spät kommt.*
> He is the eleventh pupil to arrive late.

From 20th upwards

To make ordinal numbers from 20th upwards, you must add **-ste** to the cardinal number:

zwanzigste	20th
einunddreißigste	31st
hundertste	100th

When giving dates, if you need to use *am*, you must add **-n** to the ordinal number since *am* takes the dative case:

> *Ich habe **am vierundzwanzigsten** Juni Geburtstag.*
> My birthday is on 24 June.

> *Heute ist Dienstag, **der fünfte** Dezember.*
> Today is Tuesday 5 December.

> *Nehmen Sie **die dritte** Straße links.*
> Take the third street on the left.

Ordinal numbers can be written as digits, in which case a full stop is added. This is common in dates:

> *Ich habe am **24.** Juni Geburtstag.*

J Verb table

* denotes verbs that take *sein* in the perfect and pluperfect tenses

Infinitive	Present	Imperfect	Perfect	English
beginnen	*beginnt*	*begann*	*begonnen*	to begin
bieten	*bietet*	*bot*	*geboten*	to offer
bleiben	*bleibt*	*blieb*	*geblieben* *	to stay
brechen	*bricht*	*brach*	*gebrochen*	to break
bringen	*bringt*	*brachte*	*gebracht*	to bring
denken	*denkt*	*dachte*	*gedacht*	to think
dürfen	*darf*	*durfte*	*gedurft*	to be allowed to
essen	*isst*	*aß*	*gegessen*	to eat
fahren	*fährt*	*fuhr*	*gefahren* *	to go, travel
fallen	*fällt*	*fiel*	*gefallen* *	to fall
fangen	*fängt*	*fing*	*gefangen*	to catch
finden	*findet*	*fand*	*gefunden*	to find
fliegen	*fliegt*	*flog*	*geflogen* *	to fly
geben	*gibt*	*gab*	*gegeben*	to give
gehen	*geht*	*ging*	*gegangen* *	to go
genießen	*genießt*	*genoss*	*genossen*	to enjoy
gewinnen	*gewinnt*	*gewann*	*gewonnen*	to win
haben	*hat*	*hatte*	*gehabt*	to have
halten	*hält*	*hielt*	*gehalten*	to stop, to hold
hängen	*hängt*	*hing*	*gehangen*	to hang
helfen	*hilft*	*half*	*geholfen*	to help
kennen	*kennt*	*kannte*	*gekannt*	to know
kommen	*kommt*	*kam*	*gekommen* *	to come
können	*kann*	*konnte*	*gekonnt*	to be able to
lassen	*lässt*	*ließ*	*gelassen*	to leave, to allow
laufen	*läuft*	*lief*	*gelaufen* *	to run
leiden	*leidet*	*litt*	*gelitten*	to suffer
lesen	*liest*	*las*	*gelesen*	to read
liegen	*liegt*	*lag*	*gelegen*	to lie
mögen	*mag*	*mochte*	*gemocht*	to like
müssen	*muss*	*musste*	*gemusst*	to have to
nehmen	*nimmt*	*nahm*	*genommen*	to take
reiten	*reitet*	*ritt*	*geritten*	to ride
rennen	*rennt*	*rannte*	*gerannt* *	to run
rufen	*ruft*	*rief*	*gerufen*	to call
scheinen	*scheint*	*schien*	*geschienen*	to shine
schlafen	*schläft*	*schlief*	*geschlafen*	to sleep
schließen	*schließt*	*schloss*	*geschlossen*	to shut
schneiden	*schneidet*	*schnitt*	*geschnitten*	to cut

Infinitive	Present	Imperfect	Perfect	English
schreiben	schreibt	schrieb	geschrieben	to write
schwimmen	schwimmt	schwamm	geschwommen *	to swim
sehen	sieht	sah	gesehen	to see
sein	ist	war	gewesen *	to be
singen	singt	sang	gesungen	to sing
sitzen	sitzt	saß	gesessen	to sit
sollen	soll	sollte	gesollt	ought to
sprechen	spricht	sprach	gesprochen	to speak
stehen	steht	stand	gestanden	to stand
stehlen	stiehlt	stahl	gestohlen	to steal
steigen	steigt	stieg	gestiegen *	to climb
sterben	stirbt	starb	gestorben *	to die
tragen	trägt	trug	getragen	to carry, to wear
treffen	trifft	traf	getroffen	to meet
trinken	trinkt	trank	getrunken	to drink
tun	tut	tat	getan	to do
vergessen	vergisst	vergaß	vergessen	to forget
verlieren	verliert	verlor	verloren	to forget
waschen	wäscht	wusch	gewaschen	to wash
werden	wird	wurde	geworden *	to become
werfen	wirft	warf	geworfen	to throw
wissen	weiß	wusste	gewusst	to know
ziehen	zieht	zog	gezogen	to pull

Wortschatz

(f) = feminine
(m) = masculine
(pl) = plural
(prep) = preposition
(sep) = separable verb

A

abbiegen to turn (off) (sep)
der **Abend (-e)** evening
das **Abendessen (-)** evening meal, dinner
abends in the evening
der **Abenteuerfilm (-e)** adventure film
aber but
abfahren to leave/depart (sep)
die **Abfahrt** departure
der **Abfahrtslauf** downhill skiing
der **Abfall (¨-e)** rubbish, waste
der **Abfallberg (-e)** mountain of rubbish
abfliegen to depart (by plane) (sep)
der **Abflug (¨-e)** departure (by plane)
die **Abgase** exhaust gases
die **Abgrenzung (-en)** limitation
abholzen to deforest
das **Abifach (¨-er)** A-level subject
das **Abitur** equivalent to GCE A-levels
der **Abiturient (-en)** A-level candidate
die **Abiturprüfung (-en)** A-level exam
abladen to dump
abnehmen to lose weight (sep)
die **Abreise (-n)** departure
abreisen to depart (sep)
abschalten to switch off (sep)
abschicken to send, to post (sep)
die **Abschlussprüfung** final exam
abschmelzen to melt (away) (sep)
die **Absicht** intention
abspülen to wash up (sep)
die **Abteilung (-en)** department
abwaschen to wash up (sep)
abwechslungsreich varied
die **Achtung** attention
der **Adler (-)** eagle
das **Afrika** Africa
ähnlich similar
aktiv active
die **Aktivität (-en)** activity
der **Alkohol** alcohol

allein alone
allerdings though, mind you
allerlei all sorts of things
allgemein general
allzu too
die **Alpen** the Alps
als when; than (comparative)
also so, therefore, well
alt (älter) old (older)
das **Altenheim (-e)** old people's home
das **Alter (-)** age
das **Altglas** recyclable glass
altmodisch old-fashioned
das **Altpapier** recyclable paper
der **Amerikaner (-)** American (m)
die **Amerikanerin (-nen)** American (f)
die **Ampel (-n)** traffic light
sich **amüsieren** to amuse oneself, to have fun
an on
die **Ananas (-)** pineapple
anbauen to cultivate (sep)
anbieten to offer (sep)
anbraten to fry a little (sep)
andere other
ändern to change, to alter
anders different
anfangen to start, begin (sep)
anfangs at the beginning
der **Anführer (-)** ringleader
angeln to go fishing
angenehm pleasant, nice, kind
der/die **Angestellte (-n)** employee
der **Angriff (-e)** attack
Angst haben to be afraid
der **Anhang (¨-e)** attachment
ankommen to arrive (sep)
ankreuzen to mark with a cross/tick (sep)
die **Ankunft (¨-e)** arrival
der **Anleger (-)** pier
anprobieren to try on (sep)
anrichten to prepare; to lay out (sep)
der **Anruf (-e)** phone call
anrufen to phone (sep)
anschalten to switch on (sep)
anschauen to watch, look at (sep)
anschließend afterwards
der **Anschluss (¨-e)** connection
die **Anschlussgebühr** connection charge
ansehen to look at (sep)
die **Ansichtskarte (–n)** picture postcard
anstatt instead of
anstrengend exhausting

die **Antwort (-en)** answer
die **Anzeige (-n)** advertisement
sich **anziehen** to get dressed (sep)
der **Apfel (¨)** apple
der **Apfelkuchen (-)** apple cake
der **Apfelsaft** apple juice
die **Apfelsine (-n)** orange
die **Apotheke (-n)** chemist's shop (dispensing)
der **Apotheker (-)** pharmacist (m)
die **Apothekerin (-nen)** pharmacist (f)
die **App (-s)** app (informal)
am **Apparat** on the telephone ('speaking')
die **Aprikose (-n)** apricot
das **Aquarium (Aquarien)** aquarium
die **Arbeit (-en)** work
arbeiten to work
der **Arbeitnehmer (-)** employee, worker (m)
die **Arbeitnehmerin (-nen)** employee, worker (f)
der **Arbeitgeber (-)** employer (m)
die **Arbeitgeberin (-nen)** employer (f)
die **Arbeitserfahrung** work experience
die **Arbeitsgemeinschaft** after-school club
der **Arbeitskollege (-n)** work colleague (m)
die **Arbeitskollegin (-nen)** work colleague (f)
arbeitslos unemployed
der/die **Arbeitslose (-n)** unemployed person
die **Arbeitslosigkeit** unemployment
der **Arbeitsplatz (¨-e)** place of work
das **Arbeitspraktikum** work placement/experience
die **Arbeitsstelle (-n)** work position
der **Arbeitstag (-e)** working day
ärgerlich angry
sich **ärgern über** to be angry about
arm poor
der **Arm (¨-e)** arm
die **Armbanduhr (-en)** watch
die **Art** species, kind
der **Arzt (¨-e)** doctor (m)
die **Ärztin (-nen)** doctor (f)
Asien Asia
atmen to breathe
die **Atmosphäre** atmosphere
die **Atomenergie** nuclear energy
die **Atomkraft** nuclear energy
auch also, too
auf on
auf dem Lande in the country

Auf Wiederhören Goodbye (when speaking on phone)
aufbleiben to stay up late (*sep*)
der **Aufenthalt (-e)** stay
die **Aufgabe (-n)** task
aufheben to keep (*sep*)
die **Aufheiterung (-en)** cheering up, bright spell
aufhören to stop, finish (*sep*)
aufmachen to open (*sep*)
aufnehmen to record (music) (*sep*)
aufräumen to tidy up (*sep*)
aufregend exciting
der **Aufschnitt** assorted sliced cold meats
aufschreiben to write down (*sep*)
aufstehen to get up (*sep*)
aufteilen to share out (*sep*)
auftreten to arise (problem) (*sep*)
der **Auftritt (-e)** appearance (theatre)
aufwachen to wake up (*sep*)
aufwärmen to heat up (*sep*)
der **Aufzug ("-e)** lift
das **Auge (-n)** eye
die **Augentropfen** eye drops
die **Aula** school hall
ausbeuten to exploit (*sep*)
ausbilden to train (*sep*)
die **Ausbildung (-en)** education, training
der **Ausdruck ("-e)** expression
ausdrücken to express (*sep*)
die **Ausfahrt (-en)** exit
der **Ausflug ("-e)** excursion
die **Ausflugsmöglichkeit (-en)** excursion options
ausfüllen to complete, fill in (*sep*)
der **Ausgang ("-e)** way out, exit
ausgeben to spend (money) (*sep*)
ausgebucht booked up, fully booked
ausgehen to go out (*sep*)
ausgezeichnet excellent
die **Auskunft ("-e)** information
auslachen to laugh at someone (*sep*)
das **Ausland** countries abroad
im Ausland abroad
ausmachen to arrange; to switch/turn off (*sep*)
auspacken to unpack (*sep*)
sich **ausruhen** to rest, relax (*sep*)
die **Aussage (-n)** statement
ausschalten to switch off; to disconnect (*sep*)

ausschlafen to have a lie in (*sep*)
ausschneiden to cut (text) (*sep*)
aussehen to look like (*sep*)
außer except
außerdem apart from that
außerhalb outside
die **Aussicht (-en)** view
die **Ausstattung** furnishings
aussteigen to get off (*sep*)
der **Austausch** exchange
austragen to deliver (newspapers etc.) (*sep*)
die **Auswahl** selection, choice
auswählen to choose (*sep*)
der **Ausweis (-e)** identity card
sich **ausziehen** to get undressed; to move out (*sep*)
der/die **Auszubildende** trainee
das **Auto (-s)** car
die **Autoabgase** exhaust fumes
die **Autobahn (-en)** motorway
der **Automechaniker (-)** car mechanic (*m*)
die **Automechanikerin (-nen)** car mechanic (*f*)
die **Autowerkstatt ("-en)** repair garage

B

backen to bake
der **Bäcker (-)** baker (*m*)
die **Bäckerin (-nen)** baker (*f*)
die **Bäckerei (-en)** bakery
das **Bad ("-er)** bathroom, bath
baden to have a bath; to swim (in the sea)
das **Badezimmer (-)** bathroom
die **Bahn (-en)** train, railway
die **Bahnfahrt (-en)** train journey
der **Bahnhof ("-e)** (railway) station
der **Bahnsteig (-e)** platform
bald soon, shortly
der **Balkon (-s)** balcony
der **Ballaststoff (-e)** dietary fibre
die **Bankkauffrau (-en)** qualified bank clerk (*f*)
der **Bankkaufmann ("-er)** qualified bank clerk (*m*)
bar with cash
das **Bargeld** cash
der **Bart ("-e)** beard
basteln to do handicrafts
der **Bauarbeiter (-)** building worker (*m*)
die **Bauarbeiterin (-nen)** building worker (*f*)
der **Bauch (Bäuche)** tummy

die **Bauchschmerzen** tummy ache
bauen to build
der **Bauer (-)** farmer (*m*)
die **Bäuerin (-nen)** farmer (*f*)
das **Bauernhaus ("-er)** farmhouse
der **Bauernhof ("-e)** farm
der **Baum ("-e)** tree
die **Baumwolle** cotton
das **Bayern** Bavaria
beabsichtigen to intend
der **Beamer (-)** data projector
beantworten to answer
der **Becher (-)** mug
bedanken to thank
bedeckt overcast
bedeuten to mean
bedienen to serve
die **Bedienung** service
bedroht threatened
sich **befinden** to be situated, located
begabt gifted
begründen to give reasons for
begrüßen to greet
behalten to keep
behandeln to treat
beide both
beiheften to attach (*sep*)
das **Bein (-e)** leg
das **Beispiel (-e)** example
der **Beitrag ("-e)** contribution
bekannt well-known
der/die **Bekannte (-n)** acquaintance
bekommen to receive, to get
belastbar resilient
Belgien Belgium
der **Belgier (-)** Belgian (*m*)
die **Belgierin (-nen)** Belgian (*f*)
benutzen to use
das **Benzin** petrol
bequem comfortable
beraten to advise
der **Bereich (-e)** region, area, sphere
der **Berg (-e)** mountain
der **Bericht (-e)** report
der **Beruf (-e)** job, profession
die **Berufsausbildung (-en)** professional training
der **Berufsberater (-)** careers adviser (*m*)
die **Berufsberaterin (-nen)** careers adviser (*f*)
das **Berufspraktikum** work experience
die **Berufsschule** vocational school, technical college
berühmt famous
die **Beschäftigung (-en)** occupation
Bescheid sagen to inform

die **Bescherung** giving out of Christmas presents

beschließen to decide

beschreiben to describe

die **Beschreibung (-en)** description

sich **beschweren über** to complain about

beseitigen to remove

besetzt occupied, taken, full

besichtigen to visit (a sight)

besitzen to own

besondere special

besonders especially

besorgen to get something

besprechen to discuss

besser better

besser gehen to be better

das **Besteck** cutlery

bestehen to pass (exams)

bestehlen to steal something from somebody

bestellen to order

die **Bestellung (-en)** order

bestimmen to determine

bestimmt definitely

bestrafen to punish

der **Besuch (-e)** visit

besuchen to visit

betreffen to concern

das **Betriebspraktikum** work placement

das **Bett (-en)** bed

im **Bett bleiben** to stay in bed

ins **Bett gehen** to go to bed

das **Bett machen** to make the bed

die **Bettdecke (-n)** blanket, duvet

die **Bevölkerung** population

bevor before

bevorzugen to prefer

bewegen to move (body)

die **Bewegung (-en)** movement

sich **bewerben um** to apply for

der **Bewerber (-)** applicant

die **Bewerbung** application

der **Bewerbungsbrief (-e)** letter of application

das **Bewerbungsformular (-)** application form

bewölkt cloudy

bezahlen to pay

die **Bibliothek (-en)** library

das **Bier (-e)** beer

bieten to offer

das **Bild (-er)** picture

das **Bilderbuch (-̈er)** picture book

der **Bildschirm (-e)** screen, monitor

billig cheap

die **Bioabfalltonne (-en)** bin for vegetable rubbish

der **Biokraftstoff (-e)** biofuel

die **Biologie** biology

die **Birne (-n)** pear

bis until

bis morgen see you tomorrow

bisher up to now

ein **bisschen** a little

bitten to ask (a favour)

blau blue

bleiben to stay

Bleiben Sie bitte am Apparat Please stay on the line

bleifrei lead free, unleaded

der **Bleistift (-e)** pencil

der **Blick (-e)** view

blitzen to flash (lightning)

die **Blockflöte (-n)** recorder

blöd stupid

bloß mere

die **Blume (-n)** flower

das **Blumenbeet (-e)** flowerbed

der **Blumenkohl (-)** cauliflower

die **Bluse (-n)** blouse, shirt

das **Blut** blood

die **Blutwurst (-̈e)** black pudding

der **Boden (-̈)** ground; floor

der **Bodensee** Lake Constance

der **Bonbon (-s)** sweet

das **Boot (-e)** boat

böse angry

die **Bratkartoffeln** fried potatoes

die **Bratwurst (-̈e)** fried sausage

brauchen to need

braun brown

brav well-behaved

breit wide

brennen to burn

das **Brettspiel (-e)** board game

der **Brief (-e)** letter

der **Brieffreund (-e)** pen friend (m)

die **Brieffreundin (-nen)** pen friend (f)

der **Briefkasten (-̈)** letter box

die **Briefmarke (-en)** postage stamp

der **Briefträger (-)** postman

die **Briefträgerin (-nen)** postwoman

die **Brille (-n)** glasses, spectacles

bringen to bring, to take

der **Brite (-n)** British person (m)

die **Britin (-nen)** British person (f)

das **Brot (-e)** bread

das **Brötchen (-)** bread roll

die **Brücke (-n)** bridge

der **Bruder (-̈)** brother

der **Brunnen (-)** well, fountain

die **Brust (-̈e)** breast, chest

das **Buch (-̈er)** book

buchen to book

der **Buchgutschein (-e)** book token

der **Buchhalter (-)** accountant (m)

die **Buchhalterin (-nen)** accountant (f)

die **Buchhandlung (-en)** bookshop

der **Buchladen (-̈)** bookshop

der **Buchstabe (-n)** letter of the alphabet

buchstabieren to spell

bügeln to iron

die **Bühne (-n)** stage

das **Bundesland (-̈er)** federal state in Germany

die **Bundesregierung** federal government in Germany

die **Bundesrepublik** federal republic

die **Bundesstraße (-n)** A-road

der **Bundestag** German parliament

die **Bundeswehr** federal army in Germany

bunt colourful

die **Burg (-en)** castle

der **Bürgerkrieg (-e)** civil war

das **Büro (-s)** office, study

der **Busbahnhof (-̈e)** bus station

der **Busfahrer (-)** bus driver (m)

die **Busfahrerin (-nen)** bus driver (f)

die **Bushaltestelle (-n)** bus stop

die **Busverbindung (-en)** bus connections

das **Butterbrot (-e)** sandwich

C

das **Call-Center (-)** call centre

der **Campingplatz (-̈e)** campsite

der **Champignon (-s)** mushroom

die **Champignonsuppe (-n)** mushroom soup

die **Charaktereigenschaft (-en)** character trait

chatten to chat (online)

der **Chef (-s)** boss, manager (m)

die **Chefin (-nen)** boss, manager (f)

die **Chemie** chemistry

die **Chemikalie (-n)** chemical

die **Chip (-s)** crisp

das **Comic-Heft (-e)** comic book

der **Computer (-)** computer

der **Cousin (-s)** cousin (m)

die **Cousine (-n)** cousin (f)

D

damit   so that
danach   afterwards
der **Däne (-n)**   Dane (*m*)
die **Dänin (-nen)**   Dane (*f*)
die **Dänemark**   Denmark
danken   to thank
dann   then
dass   that
die **Datei (-en)**   file
dauern   to last
der **Daumen (-)**   thumb
dazugeben   to add (*sep*)
die **Debatte (-n)**   debate
decken   to set/lay (the table), to cover
   den Tisch decken   to lay (the table)
denken   to think
das **Denkmal (¨-er)**   monument
die **Desertifikation**   desertification
deshalb/deswegen   that is why
das **Deutsch**   German
die **Deutsche Post**   German postal service
der **Deutsche (-)**   German (*m*)
die **Deutsche (-n)**   German (*f*)
Deutschland   Germany
die **Dichtung**   poetry
dick   fat
der **Dieb (-e)**   thief (*m*)
die **Diebin (-nen)**   thief (*f*)
das **Ding (-e)**   thing, item
das **Diplom**   diploma
der **Direktor (-en)**   principal, head teacher (*m*)
die **Direktorin (-nen)**   principal, head teacher (*f*)
doch   but still, anyway
das **Dokument (-e)**   document
die **Dokumentation (-en) (Doku)**   documentary
der **Dolmetscher (-)**   interpreter (*m*)
die **Dolmetscherin (-nen)**   interpreter (*f*)
der **Dom (-e)**   cathedral
der **Donner**   thunder
donnern   to thunder
das **Doppelbett (-en)**   double bed
das **Doppelhaus (¨-er)**   semidetached house
die **Doppelstunde (-n)**   double lesson
das **Doppelzimmer (-)**   double room
das **Dorf (¨-er)**   village
die **Dose (-n)**   tin, can
der **Dosenöffner (-)**   tin opener

drahtlos   wireless
draußen   outside
drehen   to turn; to shoot (a film)
das **Drittel (-)**   third
die **Droge (-n)**   drug
der **Drogenhandel**   drug trade
der **Drogenkonsum**   drug-taking
das **Drogenopfer**   drug victim
die **Drogerie (-n)**   chemist's (non-dispensing)
drucken   to print
drücken   to push
der **Drucker (-)**   printer
dumm   stupid
der **Dünger (-)**   fertiliser
dunkel   dark
der **Durchfall**   diarrhoea
durchführen   to implement, to enforce (*sep*)
dürfen   to be allowed to
die **Dürre (-n)**   drought
der **Durst**   thirst
die **Dusche (-n)**   shower
(sich) **duschen**   to shower
das **Dutzend (-e)**   dozen
der **DVD-Spieler (-)**   DVD player

E

die **E-mail (-s)**   e-mail
echt   genuine
die **Ecke (-n)**   corner
egal (Das ist egal)   that does not matter
ehrgeizig   ambitious
ehrlich   honest, decent, fair
das **Ei (-er)**   egg
eigen   own
die **Eigenschaft (-en)**   attribute
eigentlich   really, actually
ein bisschen   a bit
die **Einbahnstraße (-n)**   one-way street
der **Einblick (-e)**   insight
eineiig   identical (twins)
einfach   easy, simple; single
das **Einfamilienhaus (¨-er)**   detached house
einfügen   to paste (text) (*sep*)
der **Eingang (¨-e)**   entrance
die **Einheit**   unity
sich **einigen**   to agree
Einkäufe machen   to go shopping
einkaufen   to go shopping (*sep*)
einkaufen gehen   to go shopping
die **Einkaufsliste (-n)**   shopping list
das **Einkaufszentrum**

(Einkaufszentren)   shopping centre, mall
einladen   to invite (*sep*)
die **Einladung (-en)**   invitation
einmalig   unique, fantastic
einpacken   to wrap, pack (*sep*)
die **Einrichtung**   furnishings; arrangement
einsam   lonely
einschlafen   to go to sleep (*sep*)
einschließlich   including, inclusive
einsteigen   to get in (*sep*)
der **Eintopf (¨-e)**   stew
der **Eintritt (-e)**   admission, entry, entrance fee
der **Eintrittspreis (-e)**   admission/entrance fee
die **Einwegflasche (-n)**   non-deposit bottle
der **Einwohner (-)**   inhabitant (*m*)
die **Einwohnerin (-nen)**   inhabitant (*f*)
die **Einzelfahrkarte (-n)**   single ticket
die **Einzelkarte (-n)**   single ticket
das **Einzelkind (-er)**   only child
das **Einzelzimmer (-)**   single room
das **Eis (-)**   ice, ice cream
die **Eisbahn (¨-en)**   ice rink
der **Eisbär (-en)**   polar bear
die **Eisdiele (-n)**   ice-cream parlour
die **Eisenbahn**   railway
die **Eisenbahnlinie (-n)**   railway line
die **Eishalle (-n)**   indoor ice-skating rink
eiskalt   very cold
ekelhaft   disgusting
der **Elektriker (-)**   electrician (*m*)
die **Elektrikerin (-nen)**   electrician (*f*)
die **Eltern**   parents
der **Elternabend (-e)**   parents' evening
der **Empfang (¨-e)**   reception
enden   to end, finish
endlich   at last
die **Energie**   energy
die **Energieeinsparung**   energy conservation
die **Energiesparlampe (-n)**   energy-saving bulb
eng   tight, narrow
engagiert   active
der **Engel (-)**   angel
England   England
der **Engländer (-)**   Englishman
die **Engländerin (-nen)**   Englishwoman
das **Englisch**   English
entdecken   to discover

die **Ente (-n)** duck
enthalten to contain
entlang along
entscheiden to decide
sich **entschuldigen** to apologise
Entschuldigung! I am sorry; excuse me
(sich) **entspannen** to relax
entspannend relaxing
die **Entspannung** relaxation
entsprechen to correspond to
entstehen to arise, to develop
entweder...oder either...or
entwickeln to develop
die **Entwicklung (-en)** development
(sich) **erbrechen** to vomit
die **Erbse (-n)** pea
das **Erdbeben (-)** earthquake
die **Erdbeere (-n)** strawberry
die **Erde** Earth, the Earth
das **Erdgeschoss (-e)** ground floor
die **Erdkunde** geography
das **Erdöl** crude oil, petroleum
das **Ereignis (-se)** event
erfahren to learn, to hear about, to experience
die **Erfahrung (-en)** experience
erfinden to make up, invent
das **Ergebnis (-se)** result
erhältlich obtainable
sich **erholen** to recover
sich **erinnern** to remember
erkältet sein to have a cold
erklären to explain
erlauben to allow
erledigen to take care of, to carry out
die **Erleichterung** relief
erlernen to learn, to hear about
die **Ermäßigung (-en)** reduction
ermüdend tiring
die **Ernährung** diet, nutrition
erneuerbar sustainable
ernst serious
erreichbar reachable, obtainable
erreichen to reach
erschöpfen to exhaust
erschöpft exhausted
erschrecken to frighten
Erste Hilfe leisten to give first aid
erstklassig first class
der/die **Erwachsene (-n)** adult
erwähnen to mention
erwärmen to heat up
die **Erwärmung** warming
erwarten to expect
erzählen to tell
die **Erziehung** upbringing, education

Es tut mir leid I'm sorry
die **Essecke (-n)** dining corner
essen to eat
das **Essen** food
das **Esszimmer (-)** dining room
die **Etage (-n)** floor, storey
etwa approximately
etwas something
Europa Europe
der **Eurotunnel** Channel Tunnel
eventuell perhaps
das **Exemplar (-e)** copy (of a book)

F

fabelhaft splendid
die **Fabrik (-en)** factory
das **Fach (¨-er)** subject
die **Fachzeitschrift (-en)** specialist journal
die **Fähre (-n)** ferry
fahren to go, to travel, to drive
der **Fahrer (-)** driver (m)
die **Fahrerin (-nen)** driver (f)
die **Fahrkarte (-n)** ticket
der **Fahrkartenautomat (-en)** ticket machine
der **Fahrkartenschalter (-)** ticket office
das **Fahrrad (¨-er)** bicycle
die **Fahrradvermietung (-en)** bicycle hire
der **Fahrstuhl (¨-e)** lift
die **Fahrt (-en)** journey
der **Fall (¨-e)** case
fallen to fall
falls in case
falsch incorrect, false
die **Familie (-n)** family
der **Familienname (-n)** surname
das **Fanmagazin (-e)** fanzine
die **Farbe (-n)** colour
der **Fasching** carnival
fast nearly, almost
die **Fastenzeit** Lent
die **Fastnacht** carnival
faul lazy
faulenzen to be lazy
der **Fehler (-)** mistake, fault
Feierabend machen to end work for the day
feiern to celebrate
der **Feiertag (-e)** public holiday
das **Feld (-er)** field
das **Fenster (-)** window
die **Ferien** holidays
das **Ferienhaus (¨-er)** holiday house
der **Ferienjob (-s)** holiday job

fernsehen to watch television (sep)
der **Fernseher (-)** television set
die **Fernsehsendung (-en)** television programme
der **Fernsehturm (¨-e)** television tower
fertig ready
das **Fest (-e)** celebration, festival
feststellen to notice (sep)
das **Fett (-e)** fat
fettarm reduced fat
fettig fatty
die **Fettleibigkeit** obesity
die **Feuerwehrfrau (-en)** firefighter (f)
der **Feuerwehrmann (¨-er)** firefighter (m)
das **Feuerwerk** fireworks
das **Fieber** fever, high temperature
der **Filmschauspieler (-)** screen actor (m)
die **Filmschauspielerin (-nen)** screen actor (f)
finden to find
der **Finger (-)** finger
die **Firewall** firewall
die **Firma (Firmen)** company, firm
das **Flachland** lowland, plains
das **Fladenbrot** flatbread
die **Flamme (-n)** flame
die **Flasche (-n)** bottle
der **Flaschenöffner (-)** bottle opener
das **Fleisch** meat
der/die **Fleischer (-)** butcher (m)
die **Fleischerin (-nen)** butcher (f)
die **Fleischwaren** meat products
fleißig hard-working
fliegen to fly
fliehen to flee
fließend fluently
die **Flöte (-n)** flute
der **Flug (¨-e)** flight
das **Flugblatt (¨-er)** broadsheet newspaper
der **Flughafen (¨)** airport
das **Flugzeug (-e)** aeroplane
der **Fluss (¨-e)** river
die **Flüssigkeit (-en)** liquid
die **Folge (-n)** consequence
folgende the following
das **Formular (-e)** form (to fill in)
der **Forscher (-)** researcher (m)
die **Forscherin (-nen)** researcher (f)
der **Fortschritt** progress, improvement
die **Fortsetzung (-en)** episode

der **fossile Brennstoff** fossil fuel
die **Foto-AG** after-school photo club
der **Fotoapparat (-e)** camera
die **Frage (-n)** question
   fragen to ask
das **Fragewort (¨-er)** question word
   Frankreich France
der **Franzose (-n)** Frenchman
die **Französin (-nen)** Frenchwoman
das **Französisch** French
die **Frau (-en)** woman, wife
   frech cheeky
   frei free, vacant, unoccupied
das **Freibad (¨-er)** outdoor
   swimming pool
im **Freien** outdoors
die **Freiheit (-en)** freedom
   freiwillig voluntary
die **Freizeit** free time, spare time
die **Freizeitmöglichkeit**
   (-en) leisure opportunities
die **Fremdsprache (-n)** foreign
   language
   fressen to eat (use for animals
   eating only)
sich **freuen auf** to look forward to
sich **freuen über** to be delighted
   with
der **Freund (-e)** friend (m)
die **Freundin (-nen)** friend (f)
   freundlich friendly, kind, nice
   friedlich peaceful
   frisch fresh, cool
der **Friseur/Frisör (-e)** hairdresser
   (m)
die **Friseuse/Frisöse**
   (-n) hairdresser (f)
   froh happy
   frohe/fröhliche
   Weihnachten Merry Christmas
der **Früchtetee (-s)** fruit tea
   früh early
im **Frühling** in the spring
der **Frühling (-e)** spring
die **Frühlingsrolle (-n)** Chinese
   spring roll
die **Frühschicht (-en)** early shift
das **Frühstück** breakfast
   frühstücken to have breakfast
   Frühstückscerealien
   (pl) breakfast cereals
der **Frühstücksraum (¨-e)**
   breakfast room
   fühlen to feel
   führen to lead
der **Führerschein (-e)** driving licence
   füllen to fill
die **Füllung (-en)** filling
das **Fundbüro (-s)** lost-property office

   fünfzehn Tage a fortnight
   furchtbar terrible
der **Fuß (¨-e)** foot
der **Fußball (¨-e)** football
die **Fußballmannschaft**
   (-en) football team
das **Fußballspiel (-e)** football match
der **Fußboden (¨)** floor
der **Fußgänger (-)** pedestrian (m)
die **Fußgängerin (-nen)**
   pedestrian (f)
die **Fußgängerzone (-n)** pedestrian
   precinct

G

die **Gabel (-n)** fork
   ganz completely
   gar cooked through
   gar kein none at all
der **Garten (¨)** garden
der **Gärtner (-)** gardener (m)
die **Gärtnerin (-nen)** gardener (f)
der **Gast (¨-e)** guest
die **Gastfamilie (-n)** host family
das **Gasthaus (¨-er)** inn
das **Gebäck** biscuits, pastries
das **Gebäude (-)** building
   geben to give
   geboren born
der **Gebrauch** use
   gebrochen broken
die **Gebühr (-en)** charge, fee
das **Geburtsdatum (-daten)** date
   of birth
der **Geburtstag (-e)** birthday
das **Gedicht (-e)** poem
die **Geduld** patience
   geduldig patient
   geeignet suitable
die **Gefahr (-en)** danger
   gefährden to endanger
   gefährdet endangered
   gefährlich dangerous
   gefallen to like, to please
das **Gefängnis (-se)** prison
   gefärbt dyed
der **Gefrierschrank (¨-e)** freezer
   gegen against
die **Gegend** area
der **Gegenstand (¨-e)** item, object
das **Gegenteil (-e)** opposite
   gegenüber opposite (prep)
   gehen to go, to walk
die **Gehirnerschütterung**
   concussion
   gehören to belong to
die **Geige (-n)** violin

   geil cool
   gelaunt, gut/schlecht
   gelaunt good-/bad-tempered
   gelb yellow
das **Geld (-er)** money
der **Geldautomat (-en)** cashpoint
der **Geldbeutel (-)** purse
   gelingen to succeed, to manage
   gemischt mixed
das **Gemüse** vegetable(s)
die **Gemüsesuppe (-n)**
   vegetable soup
   gemütlich cosy
   genau exact(ly)
   genießen to enjoy
   gentechnisch verändert
   genetically modified
   genug enough
   geöffnet open
das **Gepäck** luggage
die **Gepäckaufbewahrung**
   (-en) left-luggage office
   gerade just
   geradeaus straight on
   geräuchert smoked
das **Geräusch (-e)** noise
das **Gericht (-e)** dish
   gering slight
   gern with pleasure
   gern (haben) to like
die **Gesamtschule (-n)**
   comprehensive school
das **Geschäft (-e)** shop, business
die **Geschäftsfrau**
   (-en) businesswoman
der **Geschäftsmann**
   (¨-er) businessman
das **Geschenk (-e)** present, gift
die **Geschichte (-n)** story; history
   geschickt skilful
   geschieden divorced
der **Geschirrspüler (-)** dishwasher
die **Geschirrspülmaschine**
   (-n) dishwasher
   geschlossen closed
der **Geschmack (¨-e)** flavour, taste
die **Geschwindigkeit (-en)** speed
die **Geschwister (pl)** brothers and
   sisters
die **Gesellschaft (-en)** society,
   corporation, company
das **Gesetz (-e)** law
   gesetzlich legally
das **Gesicht (-er)** face
   gespannt excited
das **Gespräch (-e)** conversation
die **Gestalt (-en)** character
   (in a story)
   gestern yesterday

gestorben   dead
gestreift   striped
gestresst   stressed
gesund   healthy
die Gesundheit   health
gesundheitsschädlich
   damaging to health
gesüßt   sweetened
das Getränk (-e)   drink
getrennt   separate(ly)
das Gewitter (-)   thunderstorm
die Gewohnheit (-en)   habit
die Gewürze   spices
die Gezeitenkraft   tidal energy
giftig   poisonous
das Glas ("-er)   glass
glatt   straight
glauben   to think; to believe
gleich   equal, soon, same
gleichen   to be like somebody or
   something
das Gleis (-e)   track, platform
der Gletscher (-)   glacier
das Glück   luck, happiness
glücklich   happy, pleased, glad
der Glühwein   mulled wine
der Goldfisch (-e)   goldfish
der Grad (-e)   degree
grau   grey
greifen   to grab, to take hold of
die Grenze (-n)   border
die Grenzkontrolle (-n)   border
   control
Griechenland   Greece
die Grippe   flu
groß   big, tall
Großbritannien   Great Britain
die Größe (-n)   height, size
die Großeltern   grandparents
die Großmutter (˙)   grandmother
die Großstadt ("-e)   city
der Großvater (˙)   grandfather
großzügig   generous
grün   green
der Grund ("-e)   reason
der Grundkurs (-e)   minor subject
die Grundschule (-n)   primary
   school
der Grundschullehrer (-)   primary
   school teacher (m)
die Grundschullehrerin (-nen)
   primary school teacher (f)
die Grünen   Green Party
die Gruppe (-n)   group
der Gruselfilm (-e)   horror film
der Gruß ("-e)   greeting
gucken   to look
günstig   favourable, convenient
die Gurke (-n)   cucumber

gut   good; well
gut bezahlt   well paid
gut gelaunt   in a good mood
gut schmecken   to taste good
Gute Besserung!   Get well soon!
gute Reise   safe journey
Guten Appetit!   Enjoy your meal!
das Gymnasium (Gymnasien)
   grammar school

H

das Haar (-e)   hair
das Hackbällchen (-)   meatball
der Hafen (˙)   port, harbour
die Hafenrundfahrt (-en)
   harbour trip
der Hagel   hail
hageln   to hail
das Hähnchen (-)   chicken
halb   half
der Halbbruder (˙)   half-brother
die Halbpension   half-board
die Halbschwester (-n)   half-sister
halbtags   half-day (morning or
   afternoon)
die Hälfte (-n)   half
das Hallenbad ("-er)   indoor
   swimming pool
der Hals ("-e)   neck; throat
die Halsschmerzen   sore throat
halten   to stop
die Haltestelle (-n)   bus/tram stop
das Hammelfleisch   mutton
die Hand ("-e)   hand
das Handgepäck   hand luggage
die Handlung (-en)   shop; story plot
der Handschuh (-e)   glove
das Handtuch ("-er)   towel
das Handy (-s)   mobile phone
hängen   to hang
hart   hard
hassen   to hate
hässlich   ugly
häufig   frequent(ly)
das Hauptgericht (-e)   main course
hauptsächlich   mainly
die Hauptschule (-n)   secondary
   school
die Hauptstadt ("-e)   capital city
das Haus ("-er)   house
die Hausaufgabe (-n)   homework
der Hausberg (-e)   the 'local'
   mountain
zu Hause   at home
nach Hause gehen   to go home
die Hausfrau (-en)   housewife
der Haushalt (-e)   household

der Hausmann ("-er)   house
   husband
das Haustier (-e)   pet
das Heft (-e)   exercise book
der Heiligabend   Christmas Eve
der Heimatort (-e)   home town
die Heimatstadt ("-e)   home town
die Heimfahrt (-en)   journey home
heiraten   to marry
heiß   hot
heißen   to be called
die Heizung (-en)   heating
helfen   to help
der Helfer (-)   helper
hell   bright, light place
der Helm (-e)   helmet
das Hemd (-e)   shirt
im Herbst   in the autumn
der Herd (-e)   cooker
herrlich   marvellous
herrschen   to rule, to dominate
herum   (a)round
herumzappen   to channel-hop
   (sep)
herunter   down
herunterladen   to download
   (sep)
das Herz (-en)   heart
die Herzkrankheit (-en)   heart
   disease
heute   today
heute Abend   this evening
heute Morgen   this morning
hier   here
die Hilfe   help
hilfsbereit   ready to help
die Himbeere (-n)   raspberry
der Himmel (-)   sky
hin und zurück   return, there
   and back
hinten   behind
hinter   behind (prep)
hinterher   afterwards
hinzu   besides
die Hitze   heat
hitzefrei   (rest of) day off owing
   to very hot weather
die Hitzewelle (-n)   heatwave
das Hobby (-s)   hobby, pastime
hoch   high, tall
das Hochhaus ("-er)   skyscraper,
   high-rise building
hochladen   to upload (sep)
das Hochland   highland
die Hochschule (-n)   university
die Höchsttemperatur (-en)
   maximum temperature
die Hochzeit (-en)   wedding
der Hof ("-e)   playground

hoffen to hope
hoffentlich hopefully
höflich polite
holen to collect
der **Holländer (-)** Dutchman
die **Holländerin (-nen)** Dutchwoman
der **Holz (¨-er)** wood, timber
der **Honig** honey
hören to hear, to listen to
die **Horrorgeschichte (-n)** horror story
die **Hose (-n)** trousers
hübsch pretty
der **Hügel (-)** hill
hügelig hilly
humorvoll humorous, amusing
der **Hund (-e)** dog
der **Husten** cough
husten to cough
der **Hustensaft (¨-e)** cough mixture
der **Hut (¨-e)** hat
die **Hütte (-n)** hut

I

die **Idee (-n)** idea
im voraus in advance
der **Imbiss (-e)** snack
die **Imbissstube (-n)** snack bar
immer always
immer (noch) always, still
die **Impfung** vaccination
in in
die **Industriestadt (¨-e)** industrial town
die **Informatik** IT, computer science
der **Informatiker (-)** computer specialist, IT expert (m)
die **Informatikerin (-nen)** computer specialist, IT expert (f)
das **Informationsbüro (-s)** information office
der **Ingenieur (-e)** engineer (m)
die **Ingenieurin (-nen)** engineer (f)
die **Innenstadt (¨-e)** town centre
innerhalb within
die **Insel (-n)** island
insgesamt altogether, all in all
das **interaktives Whiteboard (-s)** interactive whiteboard
interessant interesting
das **Interesse (-n)** interest
sich **interessieren für** to be interested in
irgendwo somewhere
isoliert isolated
Italien Italy

der **Italiener (-)** Italian (m)
die **Italienerin (-nen)** Italian (f)
das **Italienisch** Italian

J

die **Jacke (-n)** jacket
das **Jahr (-e)** year
das **Jahresalbum (-alben)** annual
die **Jahreszeit (-en)** season
jederzeit at any time
jemand somebody
jemanden erschießen to shoot somebody
jetzt now
jeweils at a time, each time
jobben to do casual jobs
joggen to jog
der **Journalist (-en)** journalist (m)
die **Journalistin (-nen)** journalist (f)
die **Jugend** youth
die **Jugendgruppe (-n)** youth group
die **Jugendherberge (-n)** youth hostel
der **Jugendklub (-s)** youth club
die **Jugendkriminalität** youth crime
der/die **Jugendliche (-n)** young person
jung (jünger) young (younger)
der **Junge (-n)** boy
Junge Pioniere Young Pioneers (DDR youth organisation)
die **Jura** law (as a subject)
die **Jutetasche (-n)** jute bag

K

der **Käfer (-)** beetle
der **Kaffee** coffee
Kaffee und Kuchen coffee and cake (afternoon snack)
die **Kaffeemaschine (-n)** coffee maker
das **Kalbfleisch** veal
kalt cold
die **Kälte** cold
Kanada Canada
der **Kanadier (-)** Canadian (m)
die **Kanadierin (-nen)** Canadian (f)
das **Kaninchen (-)** rabbit
das **Kännchen (-)** jug, pot
die **Kantine (-n)** canteen
der **Kanzler (-)** Chancellor (m)
die **Kanzlerin (-nen)** Chancellor (f)
das **Kapitel (-)** chapter
kaputt broken
der **Karpfen (-)** carp
der **Karneval (-e)** carnival

das **Karnevalskostüm (-e)** carnival costume
der **Karnevalszug (¨-e)** carnival procession
die **Karotte (-n)** carrot
die **Karriere (-n)** career
die **Karte (-n)** card; ticket; map
die **Kartoffel (-n)** potatoes
die **Kartoffelchips** crisps
das **Karussell (-s)** merry-go-round
der **Käse (-)** cheese
die **Kasse (-n)** till, cash desk, checkout
der **Kassierer (-)** cashier (m)
die **Kassiererin (-nen)** cashier (f)
der **Kasten (¨)** box
die **Katastrophe (-n)** catastrophe
die **Kathedrale (-n)** cathedral
die **Katze (-n)** cat
kaufen to buy
die **Kauffrau (-en)** businesswoman
das **Kaufhaus (¨-er)** department store
der **Kaufmann (¨-er)** businessman
kaum hardly
die **Kegelbahn (-en)** bowling alley
kegeln to play nine-pin bowling
der **Keks (-e)** biscuit
der **Keller (-)** cellar
der **Kellner (-)** waiter
die **Kellnerin (-nen)** waitress
kennen to know (somebody)
kennen to know
kennen lernen to get to know, to meet
die **Kernkraft** nuclear energy
die **Kerze (-n)** candle
das **Kind (-er)** child
das **Kinderfest (-e)** children's festival
der **Kindergarten (¨)** kindergarten, nursery school
die **Kindergärtnerin (-nen)** kindergarten teacher
die **Kinderkrippe (-n)** nursery/crèche
der **Kinderspielplatz (¨-e)** playground
kippen to tilt, to tip, to overturn
die **Kirche (-n)** church
die **Kirchengemeinde (-n)** congregation
die **Kirsche (-n)** cherry
der **Kirschkuchen (-)** cherry cake
die **Klamotten** clothes, gear
klar clear
klasse great, brilliant
die **Klassenarbeit (-en)** exam, test
die **Klassenfahrt (-en)** school trip

das **Klassenzimmer (-)** classroom
klassisch classical
das **Klavier (-e)** piano
der **Klavierunterricht** piano lessons
das **Kleid (-er)** dress
der **Kleiderschrank ("-e)** wardrobe
die **Kleidung (-en)** clothes
das **Kleidungsgeschäft (-e)** clothes shop
klein small, short, little
das **Kleingeld (-)** loose change
die **Kleinstadt ("-e)** small town
der **Klempner (-)** plumber (*m*)
die **Klempnerin (-nen)** plumber (*f*)
klettern to climb
klicken to click
das **Klima** climate
die **Klimaerwärmung** climatic temperature increase
die **Klimatisierung (-en)** air conditioning
die **Klinik (-en)** clinic
das **Klo (-s)** loo (toilet)
klug clever
die **Kneipe (-n)** pub, bar
das **Knie (-)** knee
der **Knoblauch** garlic
der **Knochenbruch (-brüche)** broken bone
der **Koch ("-e)** cook, chef (*m*)
die **Köchin (-nen)** cook, chef (*f*)
kochen to cook
der **Koffer (-)** suitcase
der **Kofferraum (-räume)** boot (of car)
der **Kohl (-e)** cabbage
die **Kohle** coal
das **kohlensäurehaltiges Getränk** fizzy drink
der **Kollege (-n)** colleague (*m*)
die **Kollegin (-nen)** colleague (*f*)
Köln Cologne
komisch strange; funny
kommen to come
die **Kommode (-n)** chest of drawers
die **Komödie (-n)** comedy
komplett complete
kompliziert complicated
der **Komponist (-en)** composer (*m*)
die **Komponistin (-nen)** composer (*f*)
die **Konditorei (-en)** cake shop
der **König (-e)** king
die **Königin (-nen)** queen
die **Konkurrenz** competition
können to be able to
konsumieren to consume
der **Kontakt (-e)** contact
das **Konto (-s)** bank account
die **Kontrolle (-n)** control

der **Kontrolleur (-)** inspector (*m*)
die **Kontrolleurin (-nen)** inspector (*f*)
kontrollieren to control, to check
sich **konzentrieren (auf)** to concentrate (on)
der **Kopf ("-e)** head
der **Kopfhörer (-)** headphones
die **Kopfschmerzen** headache
die **Kopie (-n)** copy
kopieren to copy
der **Korb ("-e)** basket
der **Körper (-)** body
körperlich physical
die **Körperverletzung** physical injury
korrigieren to correct
kosten to cost
das **Kotelett (-s)** chop, cutlet
kräftig strong
das **Kraftwerk (-e)** power station
krank ill, sick
sich **krank fühlen** to feel ill, sick
das **Krankenhaus ("-er)** hospital
der **Krankenpfleger (-)** male nurse
die **Krankenschwester (-n)** female nurse
der **Krankenwagen (-)** ambulance
die **Krankheit (-en)** illness
der **Kräutertee (-s)** herbal tea
die **Krawatte (-n)** tie
die **Kreditkarte (-n)** credit card
der **Kreisverkehr (-)** roundabout
die **Kreuzung (-en)** crossroads
der **Krieg (-e)** war
kriegen to get (informal)
der **Krimi (-s)** thriller
kriminell criminal
die **Küche (-n)** kitchen
der **Kuchen (-)** cake
der **Kugelschreiber (-)** ballpoint pen
die **Kuh ("-e)** cow
kühl cool
der **Kühlschrank ("-e)** fridge
der **Kuli (-s)** ballpoint pen
die **Kultur** culture
sich **kümmern um** to look after; to be concerned about
der **Kunde (-n)** customer, client (*m*)
die **Kundin (-nen)** customer, client (*f*)
die **Kunst ("-e)** art
die **Kunstgalerie (-n)** art gallery
der **Künstler (-)** artist (*m*)
die **Künstlerin (-nen)** artist (*f*)
der **Kunststoff (-e)** plastic
kurz short, brief
die **Kusine (-n)** cousin (*f*)
die **Küste (-n)** coast, seaside

L

das **Labor (-)** laboratory
lachen to laugh
der **Lachs** salmon
der **Laden (')** shop
die **Lage** position
das **Lammfleisch** lamb
das **Land ("-er)** country, countryside, land
landen to land
die **Landschaft (-en)** scenery, landscape, countryside
die **Landstraße (-n)** main arterial road
lang long
die **Länge** length
langsam slow(ly)
sich **langweilen** to be bored
langweilig boring
der/das **Laptop (-s)** laptop
die **Lärmbelästigung** noise pollution
lassen to let; to get something done
das **Latein** Latin
der **Lauch** leeks
laufen to walk; to run
launisch moody
laut loud, noisy
leben to live
das **Leben** life
die **Lebensmittel** provisions, food, groceries
das **Lebensmittelgeschäft (-e)** food shop
der **Lebensraum** habitat
die **Leber** liver
die **Leberwurst ("-e)** liver sausage
lecker delicious, tasty
das **Leder** leather
ledig single, unmarried
leer empty
legen to lay; to put
die **Lehre (-n)** apprenticeship
der **Lehrer (-)** teacher (*m*)
die **Lehrerin (-nen)** teacher (*f*)
das **Lehrerzimmer (-)** staffroom
der **Lehrling (-e)** apprentice
die **Lehrstelle (-n)** trainee position
leicht easy
die **Leichtathletik** athletics
leid (es tut mir leid) I am sorry
leiden to suffer
leidenschaftlich passionate
leider unfortunately
die **Leinwand ("-e)** screen, canvas
leise quiet(ly)
leisten to achieve
der **Leistungskurs (-e)** major subject

lernen to learn
lesen to read
die **Leseratte (-n)** bookworm
letzte(r,s) last
die **Leute** people
das **Licht (-er)** light
lieb kind
Liebe(r)... Dear...
lieben to love
lieber (haben) to prefer
der **Liebesroman (-e)** romantic novel
Lieblings- favourite
das **Lieblingsauto (-s)** favourite car
das **Lieblingsfach (¨-er)** favourite subject
das **Lieblingsgericht (-e)** favourite meal
die **Lieblingssendung (-en)** favourite television programme
das **Lied (-er)** song
liegen to lie
das **Lineal (-e)** ruler
die **Linie (-n)** line
links (on the) left
die **Liste (-n)** list
das **Loch (¨-er)** hole
lockig curly
der **Löffel (-)** spoon
der **Lohn** wage(s), pay
die **Lokalzeitung (-en)** local newspaper
los (hier ist nichts los) nothing happens here
löschen to extinguish, to delete
lösen to solve
der **Löwe (-n)** lion
die **Lücke (-n)** gap
die **Luft** air
lüften to air
der **Luftsteward (-s)** air steward
die **Luftstewardess (-en)** air stewardess
die **Luftverschmutzung** air pollution
Lust/ich habe (keine) Lust... I fancy (don't fancy) doing something
lustig funny, amusing

M

das **Mädchen (-)** girl
das **Mädchengymnasium (-gymnasien)** girls' grammar school
der **Magen** stomach
die **Magenschmerzen** stomach ache
die **Mahlzeit (-en)** meal
malen to paint

malerisch picturesque
der **Malkurs (-e)** painting course
man one (you)
manche(r,s) a good many
manchmal sometimes
der **Mann (¨-er)** man, husband
die **Mannschaft (-en)** team
der **Mantel (¨)** coat
die **Mappe (-n)** briefcase, folder, file
der **Margarinebecher (-)** margarine tub
der **Markt (¨-e)** market
der **Marktplatz (¨-e)** market square
die **Marmelade (-n)** jam
die **Maschine (-n)** plane
mäßig moderate
die **Mathe** maths
der **Matrose (-n)** sailor
die **Mattscheibe** small screen (meaning television)
die **Mauer (-n)** wall
das **Maul (¨-er)** mouth (of an animal)
der **Maurer (-)** bricklayer, mason, builder (m)
die **Maurerin (-nen)** bricklayer, mason, builder (f)
die **Maus (¨-e)** mouse
der **Mechaniker (-)** mechanic (m)
die **Mechanikerin (-nen)** mechanic (f)
die **Medaille (-n)** medal
die **Medien** media
das **Medikament (-e)** medicine
die **Medizin** medicine (academic subject)
das **Meer (-e)** sea, ocean
die **Meeresfrüchte** seafood
die **Meeresschildkröte (-n)** turtle
das **Meerschweinchen (-)** guinea pig
mehrere several
meinen to think
die **Meinung (-en)** opinion
meistens mostly
die **Melone (-n)** melon
die **Menge (-n)** amount
die **Menschenrechte** human rights
das **Menü (-s)** set meal
das **Messer (-)** knife
der **Metzger (-)** butcher (m)
die **Metzgerei (-en)** butcher's shop
die **Metzgerin (-nen)** butcher (f)
die **Miete (-n)** rent
mieten to rent, to hire
die **Mikrowelle (-n)** microwave
die **Milch** milk
mindestens at least
das **Mineralwasser** mineral water
der **Mitarbeiter (-)** colleague (m)
die **Mitarbeiterin (-nen)** colleague (f)

mitbringen to bring with you (sep)
miteinander together
das **Mitglied (-er)** member
mitnehmen to take with you (sep)
der **Mitschüler (-)** fellow pupil
der **Mittag** lunchtime; midday
das **Mittagessen (-)** lunch
mittags at lunchtime
die **Mittagspause (-n)** lunch break
die **Mitte** middle
das **Mittelalter** Middle Ages
mittelgroß of medium height
mitten in the middle of
die **Mitternacht** midnight
die **Mittlere Reife** equivalent of GCSEs
mittlere(r,s) middle
die **Möbel (-)** furniture
das **Möbelstück (-e)** piece of furniture
das **Mobilfunknetz (-s)** mobile network
der **Mobilfunknetzanbieter (-)** network provider
die **Mode** fashion
das **Modell (-e)** model
das **Modellflugzeug (-e)** model aeroplane
der **Moderator (-en)** presenter (m)
die **Moderatorin (-nen)** presenter (f)
modisch fashionable
das **Mofa (-s)** moped
mögen to like
möglich possible
möglicherweise possibly
der **Monat (-e)** month
monatlich monthly
die **Monatskarte (-)** monthly ticket
die **Monatsschrift (-en)** monthly periodical
der **Morgen (-)** morning
morgen tomorrow
morgen früh tomorrow morning
morgens in the morning
motiviert motivated
das **Motor (-en)** engine
das **Motorrad (¨-er)** motorbike
die **Mücke (-n)** midge, mosquito, gnat
müde tired
die **Mühe** trouble
der **Müll** rubbish, refuse
der **Müllberg (-e)** rubbish heap
der **Mülleimer (-)** dustbin
die **Mülltrennung** sorting of rubbish
München Munich
der **Mund (¨-er)** mouth
mündlich oral
die **Münze (-n)** coin

die **Muscheln** mussels
das **Museum (Museen)** museum
das **Musical (-s)** musical
die **Musik** music
der **Musiker (-)** musician
der **Musikladen (ˈ)** music shop
der **Musiksaal (Musiksäle)**
music room
musizieren to play a musical
instrument
müssen must, to have to
die **Mutter (ˈ)** mother
der **Muttertag/Vatertag** Mother's
Day/Father's Day

N

nach oben gehen to go upstairs
nach unten gehen to go
downstairs
der **Nachbar (-n)** neighbour
nachher afterwards
der **Nachmittag (-e)** afternoon
nachmittags in the afternoon
der **Nachname (-n)** surname
die **Nachricht (-en)** news
die **(aktuellen) Nachrichten** current
affairs, news
Nachrichten abrufen to check
messages (*sep*)
die **Nachrichtensendung (-en)**
news broadcast
nachsitzen to have a detention
(*sep*)
die **Nachspeise (-n)** dessert, pudding
nächst next
der **Nächste** next one
nächste(r,s) nearest
die **Nacht (ˈ-e)** night
der **Nachteil (-e)** disadvantage
der **Nachtisch** dessert, pudding
der **Nachtklub (-s)** nightclub
das **Nachtleben** nightlife
nachts at night
nagelneu brand new
die **Nähe (in der Nähe von)** near…
die **Nahrung** food
der **Name (-n)** name
nämlich namely, to be exact
die **Nase (-n)** nose
nass wet
die **Nationalität (-en)** nationality
die **Naturkatastrophe (-n)** natural
catastrophe
natürlich natural(ly), of course
die **Naturwissenschaften** sciences,
science subjects
der **Nebel** fog

neb(e)lig foggy
neben next to, beside, near to
der **Nebenjob (-s)** part-time job
der **Neffe (-n)** nephew
nehmen to take
nennen to name, to give
(an example)
nerven to get on someone's
nerves
nett nice, friendly
neu new
die **Neubausiedlung (-en)** new
housing estate
das **Neujahr** New Year,
New Year's Day
der **Neujahrstag** New Year's Day
neulich recently
Neuseeland New Zealand
die **Nichte (-n)** niece
der **Nichtraucher (-)** non-smoker
nie never
die **Niederlande** the Netherlands
niedrig low
niemand nobody
die **Niere (-n)** kidney
nirgends nowhere
noch still
nochmals another time, again
der **Nord** north
Nordamerika North America
der **Norden** north
nördlich northern
normalerweise normally
der **Notanruf (-e)** emergency call
die **Note (-n)** mark at school;
musical note
der **Notfall (ˈ-e)** emergency
notieren to make a note of
nötig necessary
notwendig necessary
die **Nudeln** pasta, noodles
nun now
nur only
nützen to be of use
nützlich useful

O

ob whether
oben at the top
die **Oberstufe** upper school,
sixth form
das **Obst** fruit
obwohl although
oder or
offen open
öffentlich public; open to
the public

öffnen to open
die **Öffnungszeit (-en)** opening time
oft often
ohne without
das **Ohr (-en)** ear
die **Ohrenschmerzen** earache
der **Ohrring (-e)** earring
ökologisch ecological
das **Öl** oil
der **Ölteppich (-e)** oil slick
die **Olympischen Spiele**
Olympic Games
die **Oma (-s)** grandma
der **Onkel (-s)** uncle
das **Onlinebuch (ˈ-er)** eBook
der **Opa (-s)** grandpa
die **Oper (-n)** opera
das **Opfer (-)** victim
der **Orangensaft** orange juice
ordentlich tidy
der **Ordner (-)** folder
die **Ordnung** tidiness, order
organisch organic
der **Orkan (-e)** hurricane
der **Ort (-e)** place
der **Osten** east
das **Osterei (-er)** Easter egg
die **Osterferien** Easter holidays
der **Osterhase (-n)** Easter bunny
Ostern Easter
Österreich Austria
der **Österreicher (-)** Austrian (*m*)
die **Österreicherin (-nen)** Austrian (*f*)
der **Ozean (-e)** ocean

P

paar (ein paar) a few
die **Packung (-en)** pack, packet
das **Paket (-e)** package
der **Palast (ˈ-e)** palace
die **Panne (-n)** breakdown, puncture
das **Papier** paper
die **Pappe** cardboard
parken to park
im **Parkett** in the stalls
der **Parkplatz (ˈ-e)** car park
der **Partner (-)** partner (*m*)
die **Partnerin (-nen)** partner (*f*)
der **Pass (ˈ-e)** passport
passen to fit, to suit
passend convenient, suitable
passieren to happen
das **Passwort (ˈ-er)** password
die **Pastete (-n)** paté
die **Pauschalreise (-n)** package
holiday
die **Pause (-n)** pause, break

die **Pension (-en)** guest house
per Anhalter fahren to hitchhike
persönlich personal(ly)
der **Pfad (-e)** path
die **Pfandflasche (-n)** returnable bottle
die **Pfanne (-n)** pan
der **Pfannkuchen (-)** pancake
der **Pfeffer** pepper
das **Pferd (-e)** horse
der **Pfirsich (-e)** peach
das **Pflaster (-)** plaster
die **Pflaume (-n)** plum
die **Pflicht (-en)** duty
das **Pflichtfach (¨-er)** compulsory subject
die **Physik** physics
das **Picknick (-s)** picnic
der **Pilot (-en)** pilot (*m*)
die **Pilotin (-nen)** pilot (*f*)
der **Pilz (-e)** mushroom
die **Piste (-n)** piste
das **Plakat (-e)** poster
die **Platte (-n)** record, disc
der **Platz (¨-e)** square; space; seat
plaudern to chat
plötzlich suddenly
Polen Poland
die **Politik** politics
der **Politiker (-)** politician (*m*)
die **Politikerin (-nen)** politician (*f*)
die **Polizei** police
die **Polizeiwache** police station
der **Polizist (-en)** police officer (*m*)
die **Polizistin (-nen)** police officer (*f*)
die **Pommes (frites)** chips, fries
das **Portemonnaie (-s)** purse, wallet
die **Post** post office; letters
das **Postamt (¨-er)** post office
die **Postkarte (-n)** postcard
das **Praktikum (Praktika)** period of practical training
praktisch practical
prallen to hit
die **Präsentation (-en)** presentation
die **Praxis** doctor's surgery
der **Preis (-e)** price; prize
preisgünstig inexpensive
die **Preisliste (-n)** list of prices
preiswert good value, inexpensive, cheap
die **Presse** press
prima great
probieren to try, to have a go
die **Problemseite (-n)** problem page
das **Profil (-e)** profile
das **Programm (-e)** programme, channel

programmieren to program
die **Programmvorschau** preview
der/die **Prominente (-en)** celebrity
provisorisch provisional, temporary
die **Prüfung (-en)** exam
die **Psychologie** psychology
das **Publikum** audience
der **Pulli** jumper
der **Punkt (-e)** spot, point, full stop
pünktlich punctual(ly), on time
die **Pute (-n)** turkey
putzen to clean
die **Putzhilfe** cleaning person

Q

die **Qualifikation (-en)** qualification
qualifiziert qualified
quatschen to chat
die **Querflöte (-n)** flute
die **Quittung (-en)** receipt
die **Quizsendung (-en)** quiz show

R

das **Rad (¨-er)** wheel, bicycle
Rad fahren to ride a bike, go cycling
radeln to cycle
der **Radfahrer (-)** cyclist (*m*)
die **Radfahrerin (-nen)** cyclist (*f*)
das **Radiergummi (-s)** rubber, eraser
die **Radtour (-en)** cycle trip
die **Rakete (-n)** rocket
der **Rasen (-)** lawn
der **Rat** advice
raten to advise; to guess
das **Rathaus (¨-er)** town hall
der **Raub** robbery
der **Rauch** smoke
rauchen to smoke
der **Raum (¨-e)** room, space
der **Rauschgiftmissbrauch** drug abuse
die **Realschule (-n)** secondary school
rechnen to calculate
der **Rechner (-)** calculator
die **Rechnung (-en)** bill
recht (das ist mir recht) right (that is ok with me)
rechts (on the) right
der **Rechtsanwalt (¨-e)** solicitor (*m*)
die **Rechtsanwältin (-nen)** solicitor (*f*)
recyceln to recycle

reden to talk
das **Regal (-e)** shelf
die **Regel (-n)** rule, regulation
regelmäßig regular(ly)
der **Regen** rain
der **Regenmantel (¨)** raincoat
der **Regenschauer (-)** rain shower
der **Regenschirm (-e)** umbrella
der **Regenwald (¨-er)** rainforest
das **Regenwasser** rainwater
regnen to rain
regnerisch rainy
reiben to rub, to grate
reich rich
reichen to be sufficient
die **Reife** maturity
der **Reifen (-)** tyre
die **Reihenfolge** order
der **Reis** rice
die **Reise (-n)** journey
der **Reisebedarf** travel necessities
das **Reisebüro (-s)** travel agent
der **Reisebus (-se)** coach
der **Reiseleiter (-)** tourist guide (*m*)
die **Reiseleiterin (-nen)** tourist guide (*f*)
reisen to travel
der/die **Reisende (-n)** traveller
der **Reisescheck** traveller's cheque
das **Reiseziel (-e)** destination
reißen to tear, to rip
reiten to ride (horses)
der **Reitstall (¨-e)** riding stable
die **Reklame** advertising
relaxen to rest, relax
die **Religion** religious education, religion
rennen to run
reparieren to repair
reservieren to reserve
retten to save
das **Rezept (-e)** recipe; doctor's prescription
die **Rezeption** reception
richtig correct, true, right
riesig huge, enormous
das **Rindfleisch** beef
das **Risiko** risk
der **Rock (¨-e)** skirt
der **Rohstoff (-e)** raw material
der **Rollschuh (-e)** roller skate
die **Rolltreppe (-n)** escalator
der **Roman (-e)** novel
romantisch romantic
die **Römerzeit** Roman era
rot red
der **Rücken** back
die **Rückenschmerzen** backache
die **Rückfahrkarte (-n)** return ticket

der **Rucksack** (¨-e) rucksack
rudern to row
rufen to call, to shout
die **Ruhe** peace, quiet
ruhig quiet, peaceful
rührend moving
der **Rundfunk** radio, radio broadcasting

S

das **Sachbuch** (¨-er) nonfiction book
die **Sache** (-n) object, thing
die **Sackgasse** (-n) cul-de-sac
der **Saft** (¨-e) juice
saftig juicy
sagen to say
die **Sahne** cream
die **Saisonkarte** (-n) season ticket
der **Salat** (-e) lettuce, salad
die **Salbe** (-n) (medicinal) cream
das **Salz** salt
salzig salty
sammeln to collect
die **Sandburg** (-en) sand castle
der **Sänger** (-) singer (m)
die **Sängerin** (-nen) singer (f)
das **Satellitenfernsehen** satellite TV
satt replete, full
der **Satz** (¨-e) sentence
sauber clean
sauber machen to clean
sauer sour, sharp
das **Sauerkraut** pickled cabbage
der **Sauerregen** acid rain
der **Sauerstoff** oxygen
das **Schach** chess
die **Schachtel** (-n) small box, packet
schade what a pity
schaden to damage, to harm
der **Schaden** (¨) damage
schädlich harmful
das **Schaf** (-e) sheep
der **Schalter** (-) ticket window; switch
die **Schalterhalle** (-n) booking/ticket hall
schauen to look
die **Schaufel** (-n) shovel
das **Schaufenster** (-) shop window
der **Schaufensterbummel** (-) window shopping
das **Schauspiel** (-e) play
der **Schauspieler** (-) actor (m)
die **Schauspielerin** (-nen) actor (f)
die **Scheckkarte** (-n) cheque card
die **Scheibe** (-n) slice
der **Schein** (-e) note, bill (money)

scheinen to shine; to seem
schenken to give as a present
die **Schichtarbeit** shift work
schick elegant, smart
schicken to send
schießen to shoot
das **Schiff** (-e) ship
die **Schildkröte** (-n) tortoise
der **Schinken** ham
der **Schirm** (-e) television screen
schlafen to sleep
der **Schlafsack** (¨-e) sleeping bag
das **Schlafzimmer** (-) bedroom
schlagen to hit, knock
der **Schläger** (-) racket
die **Schlagzeile** (-n) headline
das **Schlagzeug** percussion, drums
die **Schlange** (-n) snake; queue
schlank slim
schlapp worn out, listless
schlecht bad; badly
schlecht bezahlt poorly paid
schlecht gelaunt in a bad mood
schließen to close; to lock
das **Schließfach** (¨-er) locker (at the train station)
schlimm bad
der **Schlips** (-e) tie
der **Schlittschuh** (-e) ice skate
das **Schlittschuhlaufen** ice skating
das **Schloss** (¨-er) castle; lock
der **Schluss** end
der **Schlüssel** (-) key
der **Schlussverkauf** (-verkäufe) end-of-season sale
schmecken (gut/schlecht) to taste (good/bad)
schmelzen to melt
die **Schmerztablette** (-n) painkiller
sich **schminken** to put make-up on
der **Schmuck** jewellery, decoration
schmücken to decorate
das **Schmuckgeschäft** (-e) jewellery shop
schmutzig dirty
der **Schnee** snow
schneiden to cut
der **Schneider** (-) tailor
schneien to snow
schnell fast, quickly
das **Schnitzel** (-) veal, pork cutlet
die **Schokolade** chocolate
schon already
schön beautiful, nice, lovely
der **Schotte** (-n) Scot (m)
die **Schottin** (-nen) Scot (f)
Schottland Scotland
der **Schrank** (¨-e) cupboard
schrecklich terrible, dreadful

der **Schreibblock** (¨-e) writing pad
schreiben to write
der **Schreibtisch** (-e) writing desk
das **Schreibwarengeschäft** (-e) stationery shop
schriftlich in writing, written
schüchtern shy
der **Schuh** (-e) shoe
der **Schulanfang** beginning of term
die **Schulausbildung** school education
die **Schulden** debts
die **Schule** (-n) school
die **Schule verlassen** to leave school
der **Schüler** (-) pupil, student (m)
die **Schülerin** (-nen) pupil, student (f)
das **Schulfach** (¨-er) school subject
schulfrei no school
das **Schulgebäude** (-) school building
der **Schulhof** (¨-e) school playground
der **Schultag** (-e) school day
die **Schulter** (-n) shoulder
schulterlang shoulder length
schützen to protect
schwach weak
der **Schwager** brother-in-law
die **Schwägerin** sister-in-law
schwarz black
der **Schwarzwald** Black Forest
Schweden Sweden
das **Schwein** (-e) pig
das **Schweinefleisch** pork
die **Schweiz** Switzerland
der **Schweizer** (-) Swiss (m)
die **Schweizerin** (-nen) Swiss (f)
schwer heavy, hard, difficult
die **Schwester** (-n) sister
schwierig difficult
die **Schwierigkeit** (-en) difficulty
das **Schwimmbad** (¨-er) swimming pool
schwimmen to swim
schwindlig dizzy
der **See** (-n) lake
die **See** (-n) sea
segeln to sail
sehen to see
sehenswert worth seeing
die **Sehenswürdigkeit** (-en) tourist sight, place of interest
sehr very
die **Seide** silk
die **Seife** soap
die **Seifenoper** (-n) soap opera
seit since, for
die **Seite** (-n) side, page

der **Sekretär (-e)** secretary (m)
die **Sekretärin (-nen)** secretary (f)
der **Sekt** champagne
selbst (ich selbst, du selbst...) I myself, you yourself, alone
der **Selbstbedienungsautomat (-en)** self-service machine
selbstsicher self-confident
selbstsüchtig selfish
selbstverständlich of course
das **Selfie (-s)** selfie
der **Sellerie** celery
selten seldom, rare(ly)
das **Semester (-)** semester
der **Sender** television station, broadcaster
die **Sendung (-en)** television programme
der **Senf** mustard
die **Sensationspresse** tabloid press
die **Serie (-n)** series
der **Sessel (-)** armchair, easy chair
sich **setzen** to sit down
die **Seuche (-n)** epidemic
sicher sure, certain, safe
die **Sicherheit** safety
die **Siedlung (-en)** housing estate
Silvester New Year's Eve
Silvester feiern to celebrate New Year
simsen to text
singen to sing
sinken to sink
sinnvoll meaningful, sensible
der **Sitz (-e)** seat
sitzen to sit down
sitzen bleiben to stay down a year
skateboarden, Skateboard fahren to skateboard
der **Ski (-er)** ski
Ski laufen to ski
das **Skilaufen** skiing
der **Skiurlaub** skiing holiday
das **Smartphone (-s)** smartphone
die **SMS (-)** text message
die **Socke (-n)** sock
das **Sofa (-s)** sofa, settee
sofort immediately
die **Software** software
sogar even
der **Sohn (¨-e)** son
die **Solarenergie** solar energy
das **Solarkraftwerk (-e)** solar power plant
solche(r,s) such
der **Soldat (-en)** soldier (m)
die **Soldatin (-nen)** soldier (f)
sollen to be supposed to

im **Sommer** in the summer
der **Sommer (-)** summer
die **Sommerferien** summer holidays
sondern but
die **Sonne** sun
sich **sonnen** to sun yourself, to sunbathe
der **Sonnenbrand (-)** sunburn
die **Sonnenbrille (-n)** sunglasses
die **Sonnencreme (-s)** sun cream
die **Sonnenkraft/**die **Solarenergie** solar power
sonnig sunny
sonst else, otherwise
sorgen to worry
sortieren to sort
sowie as well as
sowieso in any case
sowohl...als auch as well as
das **soziale Netz** social network
die **Sozialkunde** social studies
der **Spanier (-)** Spaniard (m)
die **Spanierin (-nen)** Spaniard (f)
spannend exciting
sparen to save
die **Sparkasse** savings bank
das **Sparkonto (-s)** savings account
sparsam thrifty, economical
der **Spaß** fun
Spaß machen to be fun
Spaß haben to have fun
spät late
die **Spätschicht** late shift
spazieren to walk
spazieren gehen to go for a walk
der **Speck** bacon
speichern to save
die **Speise (-n)** meal, food
die **Speisekarte (-n)** menu
der **Speisesaal (Speisesäle)** dining room
spenden to donate
die **Spezialeffekte** special effects
der **Spiegel (-)** mirror
das **Spiegelei (-er)** fried egg
das **Spiel (-e)** game, match
die **Spielekonsole (-n)** games console
spielen to play
der **Spieler (-)** player (m)
die **Spielerin (-nen)** player (f)
der **Spielfilm (-e)** feature film
der **Spielplatz (¨-e)** playground
das **Spielzeug (-e)** toy
der **Spion (-e)** spy (m)
die **Spionin (-nen)** spy (f)
der **Spitzer (-)** sharpener
der **Sportbericht (-e)** sports report

Sport treiben to do/play sport
die **Sportart (-en)** type of sport
das **Sportgeschäft (-e)** sports shop
der **Sportler (-)** sportsman
die **Sportlerin (-nen)** sportswoman
sportlich sporty
die **Sportstunde (-n)** PE lesson
der **Sportverein (-e)** sports club
das **Sportzentrum (Sportzentren)** sports centre
die **Sprache (-n)** language
die **Sprachkenntnisse** knowledge of a foreign language
sprechen to talk, speak
die **Sprechstunde (-)** consultation/surgery hour(s)
springen to jump
die **Spritze (-n)** injection
der **Sprudel** sparkling mineral water
die **Spülmaschine (-n)** dishwasher
der **Staat (-en)** state
die **Staatsangehörigkeit (-en)** nationality
das **Stadion (Stadien)** stadium
die **Stadt (¨-e)** town
die **Stadtmitte** town centre
der **Stadtplan (¨-e)** street plan/map
der **Stadtrand** outskirts
das **Stadtviertel (-)** district in a town
das **Stadtzentrum (-zentren)** town centre
der **Stammbaum** family tree
stark strong
starten to take off
statt instead of
stattfinden to take place (sep)
der **Stau (-s)** traffic jam
der **Staub** dust
stehen to stand
steigen to climb
der **Stein (-e)** stone
die **Stelle (-n)** job, post, position
stellen to put, to place; to ask (a question)
die **Stellenanzeige (-n)** job advertisement
sterben to die
der **Stern (-e)** star
der **Steward (-s)** flight attendant (m)
die **Stewardess (-en)** flight attendant (f)
der **Stich (-e)** sting, bite
das **Stichwort (¨-er)** cue, notes, main point
der **Stiefbruder (¨-er)** stepbrother
die **Stiefeltern** stepparents
die **Stiefmutter (¨)** stepmother
die **Stiefschwester (-n)** stepsister
der **Stiefvater (¨)** stepfather

der **Stift (-e)** pen
stimmen to be correct
stinken to stink
stinklangweilig extremely boring
der **Stock (¨-e)** floor, storey
der **Stoff (-e)** material, fabric
die **Stofftasche (-n)** cloth bag
die **Strafe (-n)** punishment
straiten to argue
der **Strand (¨-e)** beach
die **Straße (-n)** road, street
die **Straßenbahn (-en)** tram
streichen to paint (a wall etc.)
das **Streichinstrument (-e)** string instrument
der **Streifen (-)** stripe
streiken to strike
streng strict
der **Stress** stress
stressig stressful
der **Strom** electricity
die **Strumpfhose (-n)** tights
das **Stück (-e)** piece
der **Student (-en)** student (m)
die **Studentin (-nen)** student (f)
der **Studienplatz (¨-e)** university place
studieren to study
das **Studium (Studien)** study
der **Stuhl (¨-e)** chair
die **Stunde (-n)** hour; lesson
der **Stundenlohn** hourly pay
der **Stundenplan (¨-e)** timetable
der **Sturm (¨-e)** storm
stürzen to fall (over/down)
suchen to look for
die **Suchmaschine (-n)** search engine
der **Süden** south
die **Suppe (-n)** soup
surfen to surf
süß sweet
die **Süßigkeiten** sweets
die **Süßwaren** confectionery
das **Süßwarengeschäft (-e)** sweet shop
sympathisch pleasant, nice
synchronisiert dubbed

T

der **Tabak** tobacco
die **Tablette (-n)** tablet
die **Tafel (-n)** board
der **Tag (-e)** day
jeden Tag every day
das **Tageblatt (¨-er)** daily newspaper

der **Tagesausflug (¨-e)** day trip
das **Tagesgericht (-e)** today's special
die **Tagesschau** regular German news programme
die **Tageszeitung (-en)** daily newspaper
täglich daily, every day
tagsüber during the day
die **Talkshow (-s)** talkshow
tanken to fill up with petrol
die **Tankstelle (-n)** petrol station
die **Tante (-n)** aunt
tanzen to dance
die **Tapete (-n)** wallpaper
die **Tasche (-n)** bag; pocket
das **Taschengeld** pocket money
die **Taschenlampe (-n)** torch
der **Taschenrechner (-)** pocket calculator
das **Taschentuch (¨-er)** handkerchief
die **Tasse (-n)** cup
die **Tastatur (-en)** keyboard
taub deaf
tauchen to dive
tauschen to swap, to exchange
der **Taxifahrer (-)** taxi driver (m)
die **Taxifahrerin (-nen)** taxi driver (f)
die **Technik** technology
der **Tee** tea
der **Teil (-e)** part
teilen to share, divide
teilnehmen to take part (sep)
die **Teilung** division
teilweise partly
das **Telefonat** telephone call
der **Telefonbeantworter** answering machine
telefonieren to telephone
telefonisch by phone
die **Telefonnummer (-n)** telephone number
der **Teller (-)** plate
die **Temperatur (-en)** temperature
der **Tennisplatz (¨-e)** tennis court
der **Teppich (-e)** carpet
der **Teppichboden (¨)** fitted carpet
der **Termin (-e)** appointment
die **Terrasse (-n)** patio, terrace
teuer expensive
das **Textbuch (¨-er)** textbook
das **Theaterstück (-e)** play
das **Thema (Themen)** topic
der **Thunfisch** tuna
die **Tiefgarage (-n)** underground garage, car park
das **Tier (-e)** animal
die **Tierart (-en)** animal species

der **Tierarzt (¨-e)** vet (m)
die **Tierärztin (-nen)** vet (f)
das **Tierheim (-e)** animal home
die **Tierschutzorganisation (-en)** animal protection organisation
die **Tiersendung (-en)** wildlife programme
tippen to type
der **Tisch (-e)** table
das **Tischtennis** table tennis
die **Tischtennisplatte (-n)** table-tennis table
die **Tochter (¨)** daughter
die **Toilette (-n)** toilet
toll fantastic, mad, crazy, great, super
die **Tomate (-n)** tomato
die **Tonne (-n)** bin
die **Torte (-n)** gateau, flan
tot dead
töten to kill
der **Tourist (-en)** tourist (m)
die **Touristin (-nen)** tourist (f)
das **Touristenbüro (-s)** tourist office
tragen to carry, to wear
die **Tragetasche (-n)** carrier bag
der **Trainingsanzug (¨-e)** tracksuit
die **Traube (-n)** grape
der **Traumberuf (-e)** dream job
das **Traumhaus (¨-er)** dream house
traurig sad
treffen to meet (by prior arrangement)
sich **treffen mit** to meet up with
der **Treibhauseffekt** greenhouse effect
das **Treibhausgas (-e)** greenhouse gas
trennen to separate, sort
die **Treppe (-n)** stairs
der **Trickfilm (-e)** cartoon film
trinken to drink
das **Trinkgeld (-er)** tip (for a service)
trocken dry
die **Trompete (-n)** trumpet
trotzdem nevertheless
tschüs(s) bye
tun to do
die **Tür (-en)** door
der **Türke (-n)** Turk (m)
die **Türkin (-nen)** Turk (f)
die **Türkei** Turkey
turnen to do gymnastics
das **Turnen** gymnastics; PE
die **Turnhalle (-n)** sports hall, gym
die **Tüte (-n)** paper/plastic bag

U

die **U-Bahn** underground, tube
die **U-Bahn-Station** underground stop
übel bad, nauseous
üben to practise
überall everywhere
der **Überblick** overview
sich **übergeben** to be sick, to vomit
überhaupt in general, anyhow
übermorgen the day after tomorrow
übernachten to stay overnight
überqueren to cross over
überraschen to surprise
die **Überraschung (-en)** surprise
überschwemmen to flood
die **Überschwemmung (-en)** flood
übrig left over
übrigens by the way
die **Übung (-en)** exercise
die **Uhr (-en)** clock
die **Uhrzeit** time
sich **umdrehen** to turn round (sep)
die **Umfrage (-n)** survey
die **Umgebung** surroundings
die **Umkleidekabine (-n)** changing cubicle
der **Umkleideraum ("-e)** changing room
die **Umleitung (-en)** traffic diversion
der **Umschlag ("-e)** envelope
umsteigen to change (trains etc.) (sep)
umtauschen to exchange goods, money (sep)
die **Umwelt** environment
umweltbewusst environmentally aware
umweltfeindlich environmentally damaging
umweltfreundlich environmentally friendly
das **Umweltproblem (-e)** environmental problem
der **Umweltschutz** environmental protection
(sich) **umziehen** to change clothes; to move (sep)
unbedingt absolutely, definitely
unbezahlt unpaid
und and
unerwartet unexpected
der **Unfall ("-e)** accident
ungefähr approximately
ungesund unhealthy
unheimlich frightening
unhöflich rude, impolite

die **Universität (-en)** university
die **Universitätsstadt ("-e)** university town
unordentlich untidy
unpünktlich unpunctual
unsportlich unsporty
sich **unterhalten** to chat
die **Unterhaltung** entertainment
die **Unterhaltungsmöglichkeit (-en)** entertainment options
die **Unterkunft** accommodation
unternehmen to do something
der **Unterricht** lessons
unterrichten to teach
der **Unterschied (-e)** difference
unterschreiben to sign
mit **Untertiteln** subtitled
unterwegs on the way, away
unwichtig unimportant
unzufrieden dissatisfied, unhappy
der **Urlaub** holiday(s)
der **Urlauber (-)** holiday-maker
usw. (und so weiter) and so on, etc.

V

der **Valentinstag** Valentine's Day
der **Vater (")** father
der **Vegetarier (-)** vegetarian (m)
die **Vegetarierin (-nen)** vegetarian (f)
vegetarisch vegetarian (adjective)
die **Verabredung (-en)** appointment
die **Veränderung (-en)** change
verbessern to correct, to improve
verbieten to forbid
verbinden to connect; to bandage
verboten forbidden
verbrauchen to use
der **Verbraucher (-)** consumer (m)
die **Verbraucherin (-nen)** consumer (f)
verbringen to spend time
verbunden connected
verdienen to earn, deserve
das **Vereinigte Königreich** United Kingdom
die **Vereinigten Staaten** United States of America
vereint united
vereinzelt occasional
vergangen last, past
vergessen to forget
vergrößern to enlarge
verheiratet married
verkaufen to sell
der **Verkäufer (-)** sales/shop assistant (m)

die **Verkäuferin (-nen)** sales/shop assistant (f)
der **Verkehr** traffic
das **Verkehrsamt ("-er)** tourist information office
verkehrsgünstig conveniently situated
die **Verkehrsmeldung** traffic news
das **Verkehrsmittel (-)** means of transport
der **Verkehrsstau (-s)** traffic jam
sich **verkleiden** to dress up
der **Verlag** publishing house
verlassen to leave (a place)
der **Verleger (-)** publisher (m)
die **Verlegerin (-nen)** publisher (f)
verletzen to injure, to hurt, to wound
die **Verletzung (-en)** injury
verliebt sein to be in love
verlieren to lose
die **Verpackung (-en)** packaging
verpassen to miss (train, bus)
verrückt crazy
verschieden different
verschmutzt polluted
verschwinden to disappear
verseuchen to contaminate
verspätet delayed
die **Verspätung** delay
das **Versteck (-e)** hiding place
verstecken to hide
verstehen to understand
versuchen to try
verteilen to share out, to distribute
verunglücken to have an accident
verurteilen to condemn
der/die **Verwandte (-n)** relation
verwenden to make use of
verwitwet widowed
verwöhnt spoilt
die **Verwüstung** devastation
viel a lot
viele many
vielleicht perhaps
das **Viertel (-)** district; quarter
der **Vogel (")** bird
das **Volk ("-er)** people, nation
völlig completely
die **Vollpension** full board
volltanken to fill up (with fuel) (sep)
vom Aussterben bedroht endangered (species, plants etc)
vor in front of, before
die **Vorführung (-en)** screening (of a film)

vorgestern the day before yesterday

vorhaben to intend to (sep)

der Vorhang (¨-e) curtains

vorher before

die Vorhersage (-n) forecast

der Vormittag (-e) morning (until lunchtime)

der Vorname (-n) first name

vorne in front

der Vorort (-e) suburb

die Vorpremiere (-n) preview

die Vorschau preview

der Vorschlag (¨-e) suggestion

vorschlagen to suggest (sep)

vorsichtig careful

die Vorspeise (-n) starter

die Vorstellung (-en) performance, showing

das Vorstellungsgespräch (-e) job interview

der Vorteil (-e) advantage

vorzeigen to show (sep)

W

wach awake

der Wagen (-) car, van

wählen to choose; to dial a number; to vote

das Wahlfach (¨-er) optional subject

wahnsinnig mad, crazy, incredible

wahr true

während during

wahrscheinlich probably

der Wald (¨-er) wood, forest

der Waldbrand (¨-e) forest fire

der Waliser (-) Welshman

die Waliserin (-nen) Welshwoman

die Wand (¨-e) wall (internal, inside)

wandern to walk, to hike

die Wanderung (-en) walk, hike

wann? when?

das Warenhaus (¨-er) department store

warm warm

die Wartehalle (-n) waiting room

warten to wait

warum? why?

was? what?

waschen to wash

die Waschmaschine (-n) washing machine

das Waschpulver washing powder

das Wasser water

die Wasserkraft hydroelectric power

der Wasserski waterskiing

Wasserski fahren to waterski

---

der Wassersport water sports

die Wasserverschmutzung water pollution

WDR German radio station

die Webseite (-n) web page, website

der Wechsel change

wechselhaft changeable

wechseln to exchange, to change

die Wechselstube (-n) bureau de change

der Wecker (-) alarm clock

der Weg (-e) path

wegen because of

wegwerfen to throw away (sep)

weh (es tut weh) it hurts

wehen to blow

weiblich female

weiche Drogen soft drugs

das Weihnachten Christmas

der Weihnachtsbaum (¨-e) Christmas tree

die Weihnachtsferien Christmas holidays

das Weihnachtsgeschenk (-e) Christmas present

der Weihnachtsmarkt (¨-e) Christmas market

das Weihnachtsplätzchen (-) Christmas biscuits

der Weihnachtsschmuck Christmas decorations

der Weihnachtstag Christmas Day

weil because

der Wein (-e) wine

das Weingebiet (-e) wine-growing areas

weiß white

weit far

Weitere(s) further details

weiterempfehlen to recommend (sep)

weiterfahren to continue, drive on (sep)

weiterhin furthermore

welche(r,s) which

die Welle (-n) wave

der Wellensittich (-e) budgie

die Welt world

das Weltall universe

weltbekannt world-famous

der Weltkrieg (-e) world war

wem? whom?

die Wende German reunification; turning point

wenden to turn

wenig little

wenn if, when

wer? who?

---

die Werbefachfrau advertising specialist (f)

der Werbefachmann advertising specialist (m)

der Werbespot (-s) advert

die Werbung advertising; advert

werden to become

werfen to throw

die Werkstatt (¨-en) repair garage

wertvoll precious

der Westen west

westlich western

das Wetter weather

der Wetterbericht (-e) weather news/report

die Wettervorhersage (-n) weather forecast

wichtig important

Wie komme ich...? How do I get (to...)?

wie viel(e)? how much/how many?

wie? how?

wieder again

wieder verwerten to recycle

wiederholen to repeat

die Wiederholung revision

(Auf) Wiedersehen goodbye

wiederverwenden to reuse (sep)

wiederverwertbar recyclable

die Wiederverwertung recycling

Wien Vienna

wieso? why? how come?

willkommen heißen to welcome

die Windenergie wind power

windig windy

die Windkraft wind energy

das Windsurfbrett (-er) windsurfing board

windsurfen to windsurf

der Winter winter

im Winter in the winter

das Wintersemester (-) winter semester

wirken to have an effect

wirklich really

die Wirklichkeit reality

wissen to know

das Wissen knowledge

die Wissenschaft (-en) science

wo? where?

die Woche (-n) week

die Wochenbeilage (-n) weekend supplement

das Wochenende weekend

die Wochenzeitung (-en) weekly newspaper

woher? where from?

wohin? where to?

wohl   probably, no doubt
der **Wohnblock** (¨-e)/(s)   block of flats
wohnen   to live
das **Wohnhaus** (¨-er)   residential building
der **Wohnort** (-e)   place of residence
die **Wohnung** (-en)   flat
der **Wohnwagen** (-)   caravan
das **Wohnzimmer** (-)   sitting room
die **Wolke** (-n)   cloud
wolkig   cloudy
wollen   to want
das **Wort** (¨-er)   word
das **Wörterbuch** (¨-er)   dictionary
wunderbar   wonderful
wunderschön   beautiful, lovely
der **Wunsch** (¨-e)   wish
wünschen   to wish
der **Würfel** (-)   cube, dice
die **Wurst** (¨-e)   sausage
das **Würstchen** (-)   small sausage

Z

die **Zahl** (-en)   number
zahlen   to pay
zählen   to count
der **Zahn** (¨-e)   tooth
der **Zahnarzt** (¨-e)   dentist (*m*)

die **Zahnärztin** (-nen)   dentist (*f*)
sich **die Zähne putzen**   to clean one's teeth
die **Zahnschmerzen**   toothache
ZDF   German television channel
die **Zehe** (-n)   toe
zeichnen   to draw
zeigen   to show
die **Zeile** (-n)   line, row
die **Zeit** (-en)   time
der **Zeitraum** (**Zeiträume**)   period (of time)
die **Zeitschrift** (-en)   magazine
die **Zeitung** (-en)   newspaper
der **Zeitungskiosk** (-e)   newspaper kiosk/stand
zeitweise   at times
das **Zelt** (-e)   tent
zelten   to camp
zerstören   to destroy
der **Zettel** (-)   note
das **Zeugnis** (-se)   school report
ziehen   to pull
das **Ziel** (-e)   destination
ziemlich   fairly, quite, rather
die **Zigarette** (-n)   cigarette
das **Zimmer** (-)   room
die **Zitrone** (-n)   lemon
der **Zoll**   customs
die **Zollkontrolle** (-n)   customs check
zu Fuß   on foot

der **Zucker**   sugar
zuerst   to start with; first
zufrieden   content
der **Zug** (¨-e)   train
das **Zuhause**   home
zuhören   to listen (*sep*)
die **Zukunft**   future
zuletzt   finally
zunehmen   to put on weight (*sep*)
die **Zunge** (-n)   tongue
zurück   back
zurückkommen   to return, to come back (*sep*)
zurückrufen   to call back (*sep*)
zusammen   together
zusammenarbeiten   to work together (*sep*)
der **Zuschauer** (-)   spectator
die **Zutaten**   ingredients
zuverlässig   reliable
zwar   in fact, actually
die **Zwiebel** (-n)   onion
der **Zwilling** (-e)   twin
der **Zwillingsbruder** (¨)   twin brother
die **Zwillingsschwester** (-n)   twin sister
zwischen   in between; between
zwischendurch   in between times, meantime